WOOD ISLAND
LIGHTHOUSE

Stories from the Edge of the Sea

Richard Parsons

Published by The History Press
Charleston, SC
www.historypress.com

Copyright © 2022 by Richard Parsons
All rights reserved

Front cover, top: The Wood Island Light Station provides the backdrop for this 1912 Knights Templar clambake at Biddeford Pool, Maine. *Detail of a photo by Charles Moody provided courtesy of the McArthur Library, Biddeford, Maine*; *bottom*: The winter sun rises to begin another spectacular day at the Wood Island Light Station. *Courtesy of Shutterbugs4charity.*
Back cover, bottom: Keeper Thomas Henry Orcutt casts an approving look at Sailor, the "lighthouse dog," as he rings the fog bell to greet a passing vessel at Wood Island. *Courtesy of Friends of the Wood Island Lighthouse.*

First published 2022

ISBN 9781540252111

Library of Congress Control Number: 2021950613

Notice: The information in this book is true and complete to the best of our knowledge. It is offered without guarantee on the part of the author or The History Press. The author and The History Press disclaim all liability in connection with the use of this book.

All rights reserved. No part of this book may be reproduced or transmitted in any form whatsoever without prior written permission from the publisher except in the case of brief quotations embodied in critical articles and reviews.

For Shari
My Beacon

And now, as gather the shades of night,
See the flashing gleam of Wood Island Light!
Which points the course that our sloop must steer,
And shines o'er the waters, our way to cheer.

—*Major Alexander W. Pearson, in Joseph Warren Smith,*
Gleanings from the Sea *(1887)*

CONTENTS

Acknowledgements	9
Introduction	11
1. The Unfortunate Benjamin Cole: 1807–08	21
2. The War of 1812 Comes to Wood Island: 1809–32	31
3. Political Partisanship and Acrimony in the Lighthouse Service: 1841–61	39
4. Of Gales, Quakes and a Woodless Wood Island: 1849–1906	49
5. The Heroism of Ebenezer "Eben" Emerson: 1861–65	57
6. Trials and Triumphs of Albert Norwood: 1872–86	62
7. Of Dogs and Men: 1886–1905	71
8. The Murder House on Wood Island: 1896–1921	79
9. The Farmer in the Lighthouse: 1819–1933	89
10. Wrecks and Rescues, Part I: 1898–1909	95
11. A Lighthouse Education: 1872–1963	107
12. The Scrapbook: 1905 and 2019	114
13. Unexpected Encounters: 1925–82	123
14. Wood Island Poets: 1900–2013	129
15. Monsters, Serpents and Things That Go Bump in the Night: 1905–2006	144
16. Keeper Benson's War: 1934–51	150
17. Wrecks and Rescues, Part II: 1917–86	156
18. Animal Kingdom: 1939–86	165

Contents

19. Coast Guard Wives: 1939–86	172
20. Children of the Light: 1939–86	180
21. Living at the Edge of the Sea: 1939–86	188
Epilogue, by Brad Coupe, Past Chairman and Co-Founder of the Friends of the Wood Island Lighthouse	199
Notes	203
Bibliography	219
About the Author	223

ACKNOWLEDGEMENTS

In its edition of June 1992, the *Lighthouse Digest* announced that the Wood Island Light Station had been added to its "Doomsday List." The Coast Guard had removed the lighthouse keepers in 1986 when the station became fully automated, and as a result, the lighthouse and its historic dwelling remained relatively unattended. Gradually, it was beaten down by the elements and defaced by vandals. The Friends of the Wood Island Lighthouse recognized that this treasure was deteriorating and was in danger of being forever lost as a symbol of America's maritime history. The men and women who heroically brought the station back from the brink of ruin are the new lighthouse keepers. They, like the heroes of the past, deserve recognition and thanks for the noble service they have performed to make the cherished historical landmark available to future generations who love the sea and the maritime history of the United States and, of course, value good stories.

Many of those stories have been animated by the photographs, artifacts and testimonies provided by the men and women who lived them and by their descendants and friends. Special appreciation is extended to those who generously sat for interviews: Eloise Frank and son Steve and daughter Michele; Lily and Holly Burnham; Jackie Netherwood Kennedy; Pat "P.J." Winchester; Rick Savageau; Catherine Roche and son Jim; Keeper Clifford Trebilcock; Keeper Andrew Ralph Pruneau; Susan Murray; Keeper Mike McQuade; and Keeper Russ Lowell and his wife, Terry. This author is also grateful to other "friends" of the Wood Island Lighthouse who have graciously shared their memories: members of the family of Keeper Earle

Acknowledgements

Benson; members of the family of Keeper Thomas Orcutt; Barbara Burke, the grandniece of Charles Albert Burke; David Katon and Julie Katon, son and daughter of Keeper David Katon; Del Jakeman; Iona Desmond; and Harold Hanson.

This project would have been overwhelming had it not been for the tireless efforts of two talented editors. Sheri Poftak has spent nearly two decades assembling and organizing many of the archival resources that underlie the stories recounted in this text. In assembling and recommending the spectacular images used to enhance these stories, she served as a valued guide to all things connected to the Wood Island Light Station. Shari Robinson, my partner in life and literature, gently urged improvements in the grammar and the shape and arrangement of the content. In so doing, Shari created a more coherent and engaging whole from the sum of so many disparate parts.

Thanks to Sue Maccalous, Carol Bassett and Debbie Lamb, who agreed to suffer through early drafts of the various chapters and offer insightful suggestions for improvements.

Special thanks also are due to the librarians and archivists who battled through the recent pandemic to assist in research that might otherwise have been brought to an unanticipated halt. When Covid restrictions forced the closing of libraries and archives, Renee DesRoberts, special collections librarian at the McArthur Library in Biddeford, Maine, and Anatole Brown, education and program manager at the Saco Museum, provided much-needed materials virtually. Thank you as well to Leslie Rounds, director of the Dyer Library, who provided the key that opened the vault in the basement of the Dyer Library, granting access to the ancient newspapers that were stored there. Thanks also to the archivists at the Maine Historical Society, National Archives and Records Administration and the Maine Maritime Museum who offered guidance and resources that brought so many indistinct historical mysteries into sharper focus.

And finally, this book would not have been nearly as colorful without the images that were unselfishly provided by Brad Coupe, Jeremy D'Entremont, Elaine Jones, Kathleen Larsen, Richard Levy, Sean Murphy, Shari Robinson and Bob Trapani. A special thank-you is extended to Mark Jones and Shutterbugs4Charity (Shutterbugs4Charity.org) for generously allowing us to use their images and hopefully to assist in their mission to "inspire a better world through the lens." This nonprofit organization is dedicated to using photography to support fundraising efforts directed toward groups serving the homeless, children/teens, mental health, animal welfare and more.

INTRODUCTION

For over two hundred years, the regal old lighthouse had cast its beacon into Saco Bay and the Gulf of Maine, its flashing beam warning mariners to steer clear of the hazards that lay just beneath the surface of the frigid waters and serving as a continuing reminder of the many unlucky vessels that had met their end on those jagged ledges. In the late nineteenth century, it blinked red, viewed as far east as Prout's Neck, providing an inspiration for the painter Winslow Homer, who captured its eerie presence in his *Moonlight, Wood Island Light* (1894). Most recently, the light alternates green and white. Each color flashes every ten seconds in warning while also signaling a welcome to fishermen and pleasure craft sailing into the safety of Biddeford Pool and the entrance to the Saco River. The three-mile river route leads past the University of New England, picturesque homes and summer cottages sprinkled along the water's edge and the several marinas that dot the shoreline before eventually stalling at the impressive falls at the foot of the historic commercial centers of Biddeford and Saco.

Over the years of its physical presence stretching back to 1808, the Wood Island Lighthouse has undergone many changes. It could not be expected that the original structure and mechanisms would survive intact over the course of those two hundred years. Consequently, technical improvements have combined with the ravages of time, occasioning modifications and alterations. And as the nation expanded economically and developed politically, the lighthouse system of governance was transformed as well. During a large segment of the nineteenth century, lighthouse keepers were

Introduction

replaced regularly under patronage arrangements in which presidential administrations rewarded the faithful. With time, however, a Lighthouse Board of experts and engineers replaced the authoritarian self-interest characteristic of the early nineteenth-century Lighthouse Service, and a more equitable civil service superseded the spoils system as a means of selecting lighthouse keepers. A new era in the governance of lighthouses began in 1939 when President Franklin D. Roosevelt signed his Reorganization Order #11, turning control of all lighthouses in the United States over to the U.S. Coast Guard.

But as the twentieth century drew to an end, the once-proud lighthouse sitting on the easternmost point of Wood Island had fallen on hard times. In 1986, the Coast Guard automated the Wood Island Light Station, eliminating the need for a permanent light keeper. Lacking maintenance and oversight, the buildings and grounds fell into terrible disrepair. Vandals, braving the poison ivy and hornets, joined with the elements, and over time, the roof and plaster ceilings had deteriorated to the point of collapse. In June 1992, the *Lighthouse Digest* announcement of "Wood Island Light Station Added to Doomsday List" was followed by a report that Coast Guard officials "do not have the funds to repair, maintain, and save this or any other light stations." Concluding on a note of desperation, the *Digest* wished hopefully that "somewhere there must be someone that has the funds to save this lighthouse which has been neglected by most, but still remembered by many."[1]

The wish was granted in 2003, when a few intrepid and enthusiastic champions stepped forward and met for the first time as an organization and chose to call themselves the Friends of the Wood Island Lighthouse, a chapter of the American Lighthouse Foundation. Over the course of the next fifteen years, the Friends embarked on a renovation project that has restored the keeper's home and the light tower. Today, visitors are able to board the *Lightrunner* and make their way a mile across the harbor to the island's boat ramp. Along the way, gulls and cormorants might direct voyagers' attention to a nearby island and its distinctive sixty-foot tower. This is Stage Island.

Stage Island

Fishermen gave Stage Island its name. George Folsom in his *History of Saco and Biddeford*, first published in 1830, reports that as early as 1672, fishermen had established stages along the New England coast: "About 8 or 9 miles

Introduction

In 1825, John Lowell fell to his death during the construction of the Stage Island Day Mark, pictured here in 1887 with Wood Island in the distance. *Saco Museum, photo by Hartley Dennett.*

to the east of Cape Porpoise is Winter Harbor, a noted place for fishers; here they have many stages."[2] A fishing stage, the precursor to a fishing "camp," generally consisted of a rough, traditional building associated with the cod fishery and likely had its origin in Newfoundland, Canada. Elevated platforms and working tables were set up at the water's edge with the intention of processing the catch by salting and drying.

Today, Stage Island is easily recognizable by its narrow conical-like structure that reaches more than sixty feet above the shoreline. For this reason, local residents sometimes refer to it as Monument Island, but this would be a misnomer. The structure is not a memorial but rather is intended as a "day mark" or navigational aid. Like so many places along the coast of Maine, there is a story.

On Friday, February 23, 1821, the brig *Hesper* under the command of a Captain Stevens went ashore on Wood Island in a snowstorm. The cargo of salt was thrown overboard in order to lighten the ship and was totally lost. A few days later, concerns were expressed by Stevens that the passage into Winter Harbor described in the *American Coast Pilot* was misleading because it omitted mention of nearby Negro Island and the shallow bar that connects it

Introduction

to Wood Island. The editor of that important navigational aid, Edmund M. Blunt, responded defensively, writing, "He who attempts to hide or palliate his want of judgement, attaching blame where it does not exist, creates an alarm which may…do injury which cannot be repaired."[3]

Back and forth went the bitter argument for weeks in the New England press. Finally, in May 1825, the government contracted with three Portland stonemasons to erect a sixty-foot marker on Stage Island to signal the proper channel leading into Winter Harbor. On June 18, 1825, Samuel Knight was working on the tower along with John Lowell. They were approximately fifty-four feet above the ground when the structure suddenly settled. In the resulting collapse, Lowell fell to his death, while Knight suffered serious injuries that would leave him permanently handicapped.

But the story doesn't end there. In spite of the tragedy, the remaining contractors forged ahead and completed the structure, all the while incurring additional costs in the rebuilding. On December 28, 1825, Lowell's widow and the other contractors petitioned the Congress for "compensation for a loss sustained by them in the fall of a monument erected by them, under contract with the Government, on Stage Island, near Winter Harbor." The petition that was referred to the Committee on Commerce was denied.[4]

Twenty years later, on December 30, 1845, the Congress heard another petition, this time from Samuel Knight, Lowell's assistant, who was badly injured from the collapse. In the petition, Knight sought a "pension for injuries received while engaged in the service of the United States, in the erection of a monument on Stage Island, in the State of Maine." Knight's petition went to the Committee on Pensions, which on March 25, 1846, rendered its decision:

> *The petitioner alleges that while at work on a monument, erected on Stage Island, in Maine, in the year 1825, the foundation gave way, and he fell with the monument, and was so injured as to become a cripple for life. The monument was erected by the United States as a landmark, it is believed, for vessels on the coast. No petition ever having been granted in such a case, the committee recommend the adoption of the following resolutions: Resolved: That the prayer of the petition ought **not** to be granted.*[5]

Throughout the nineteenth century, Stage Island continued its close connection to the Wood Island Lighthouse. Gradually, the fishing shacks (stages) began to be replaced by more permanent structures. Lyman Frank

Introduction

Verrill, after leaving his position as light keeper at Wood Island in 1857, built a home on Stage Island and lived there for three years. Some years later, following Keeper Verrill's death, his widow rented the home to Abraham Norwood, one of several sons of Albert Norwood, who kept the Wood Island Light from 1872 to 1886. Tragically, on Saturday, March 29, 1879, the house was destroyed by fire. The *Saco Union and Journal* reported the incident: "The house was an old-fashioned structure, a story and a half high, but covering considerable ground. The family all slept upstairs. Between ten and eleven o'clock at night they were awakened and found the house on fire beneath them, and it is stated made their escape with some difficulty, losing nearly everything.... The house was owned by Mrs. L.F. Verrill."[6]

Today, there are no houses beneath the prominent structure that identifies Stage Island. The Audubon Society, which acquired the entire island in September 1980, protects the island's habitat for visitors and wildlife to enjoy.

Wood Island

Disembarking at the boat landing on Wood Island, a picturesque walk along the nearly half-mile, recently upgraded boardwalk will transport sightseers back in time to 1906. Just beyond a slight rise along the walkway, the light tower first appears, followed by the keeper's residence, the last remaining Dutch Colonial–style light keeper's house in the state of Maine.

Once there, guests are invited to climb the sixty stairs that lead to the lantern room and the top of the tower. Carefully ducking through the iron door that leads to the outdoor catwalk, lighthouse sightseers are able to enjoy a spectacular 360-degree view of Biddeford Pool and the islands of Saco Bay. Later, while touring the keeper's dwelling, their guide retells many of the enchanting stories that bring the old tower's granite walls to life.

Mariners traveling northeast from the New Hampshire border will notice that Wood Island appears in Saco Bay about midway between Maine's southern border and the state's largest city, Portland. The island takes the shape of a half-mile-long fleshy finger pointing westward in the general direction of the Saco River and Biddeford Pool, an anchorage known as Winter Harbor in the 1800s. The island is overgrown with thick, wild vegetation today, but in 1806, when the United States Congress authorized a lighthouse to be built there, it was covered with hardwoods, described by

Introduction

Champlain as "fine oaks and nut-trees." Thick tangles of wild grapes likely covered the island's floor. The perimeter of the thirty-five-acre island is made up of a rugged and treacherous shoreline. Hazardous ledges combine with the rock-strewn coastline to create a constant symphony of crashing waves, making any landing challenging, in many cases nearly impossible.

Samuel de Champlain was not the first European to visit the locality around Wood Island, but in 1605, during his second voyage in the New World, he was probably the first to both notice it and document it for the record. Sailing generally southward from Acadia during that year with Pierre Dugua de Monts, Champlain served as geographer and unofficial cartographer on the voyage. Following an earlier failed attempt at colonization, French explorers searched the coastline of what is now northern New England for a suitable location for another attempt at a viable settlement.

In July, the expedition reached Saco Bay and on the eighth dropped anchor in a sheltered cove behind Stratton Island. While there, Champlain reports that "Sieur de Monts visited an island, which is very beautiful...for it has fine oaks and nut-trees, the soil cleared up, and many vineyards bearing beautiful grapes in their season....We named it Isle of Bacchus." Today, we know this to be Richmond Island, not Wood Island, as is sometimes claimed.[7]

In the days following, the party moved on to explore the banks of the Saco River, which the Natives called Choiiacoet. In his account, Champlain again comments on the productivity of the area: "The Indian corn which we saw was at that time about two feet high, some of it as high as three.... We saw also a great many nuts...and many grape-vines, on which there was a remarkably fine berry....We had heretofore seen grapes only on the Island of Bacchus, distant nearly two leagues from this river." Before leaving on July 12, Champlain concluded, "The place is very pleasant [and] abundant in fish, and is bordered by meadows. At the mouth there is a small island [likely Ram Island] adapted for the construction of a good fortress." He also left a remarkably accurate depth chart of the mouth of the Saco River, which includes sketches of Wood Island and Biddeford Pool.[8]

Unlike some of the islands and territories in northern New England, the name given to Wood Island seems to have been with it from the very beginning of colonial settlement. As early as 1658, a deed chronicles that Robert Jordan conferred on Bryan Pendleton and Roger Spencer "a Necke of Land In Sacoe River, together with ye one halfe of wood Yland, & Gybbons his Yland, which sd Land was formly in the hand of Mr. Robert Jordan."[9]

Introduction

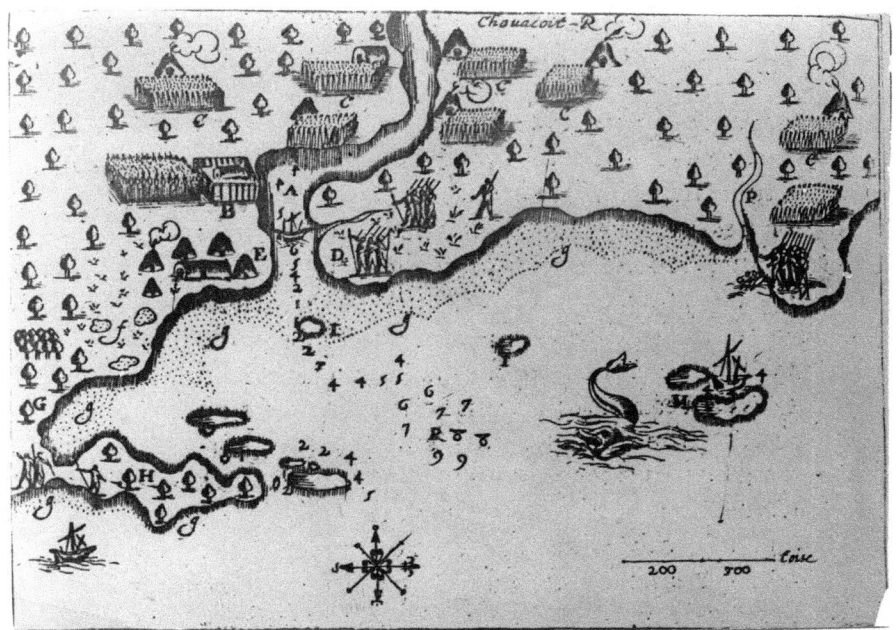

Champlain's 1605 chart of Saco Bay shows the Saco River entering the Gulf of Maine. The islands in the lower left are Wood Island, Negro Island, Stage Island and Basket Island. Ram Island is seen at the mouth of the river. *McArthur Library.*

Spencer would immediately relinquish his claim and, in a deed dated the same day, August 13, 1658, turn his portion of the title over to Bryan Pendleton. And then in 1671, Bryan Pendleton made his adopted son, Pendleton Fletcher, his heir apparent, referring to the island again in the deed as Wood Island. Later, in 1734, in an agreement between Pendleton Fletcher and William Pepperell, the deed refers once more to "an island lying to Eastward of the sd Neck of Land [referring to 'Fletcher's Neck'] containing by Estimation Thirty acres be ye same more or less called Wood Island."[10]

Ownership of Wood Island passed eventually to Bachelor Hussey in 1737 and then on to Hussey's grandson Christopher Hussey. By 1806, ownership of the island was shared in common by six owners: Pendleton Fletcher and Pendleton Fletcher Jr., who owned half a share; Batchelor Bunker, who owned one-fourth; Christopher Hussey, who owned one-eighth; and Elihu Coffin and Thomas Cutts each owning one-sixteenth. It was this group of landowners that was approached by representatives of Albert Gallatin, the secretary of the treasury, with authorization to purchase an appropriate tract of land sufficient

Introduction

Treasury secretary Albert Gallatin's letter of March 27, 1806, informing Benjamin Lincoln that Congress had authorized a lighthouse on either Wood Island or Fletcher's Neck. *National Archives and Records Administration (NARA).*

Introduction

for erecting a lighthouse. Gallatin's letter to Benjamin Lincoln, superintendent of lighthouses for Massachusetts, sets down the requirements:

> *Treasury Department*
> *March 27th 1806.*
> *Sir*
>
> *I have the honor to enclose a Copy of an Act passed at the present Session of Congress, authorizing the erection of a Light House on Wood Island or on Fletcher's Neck, in the District of Maine and State of Massachusetts; and appropriating five thousand Dollars therefor: provided that Sufficient Land for the accommodation of the same can be obtained at a reasonable price, and the jurisdiction vested in the United States. I have therefore to request your aid in effecting the necessary arrangements preparatory to inviting proposals for a Contract.*
>
> *You will be pleased to cause an examination to be made at both the places mentioned, and the most Suitable Site for a Light House proced [?] on, designating by proper metes and bounds as much ground as may be necessary for the accommodation of the establishment.*
>
> *The great consideration in Site is the visibility of a Light House. This will depend upon its projection towards the Sea, and its elevation above the Surface of the water; but the firmness of the ground, and freedom from quick Sands.*[11]

The six owners agreed to sell six acres to the United States in May 1806. The following February 1807, another two acres were added along with a right of way that connects the government's land (now totaling eight acres) to the western end of the island, where a more suitable site for a landing could be created. By October 1807, the dwelling and tower were completed, and Benjamin Cole, the first keeper, was appointed to take control of the light station.

For more than two hundred years, the lighthouse on Wood Island reliably has signaled the way for ships to avoid the treacherous reefs and threatening shoals that lurk nearby and to point vessels toward a safe passage along the rocky coast of southern Maine. They are also years filled with stories of shipwrecks and storms; of men, women and children battling the elements of the sea. They include tales of murder, suicide and heroic rescues; of lives lived in one of the most beautiful environments imaginable and one of the most challenging. They are human stories and, in their telling, manage to capture a small slice of the history of southern Maine and its contribution to the grander history of the United States.

Chapter 1

THE UNFORTUNATE BENJAMIN COLE

1807–08

Benjamin Cole was the first keeper of the Wood Island Light Station. But he wasn't the first choice—that was Batchelor Bunker, who was one of the six investors who owned shares of Wood Island in common.

Customs collector Jeremiah Hill became the champion of Batchelor Bunker to fill the post of lighthouse keeper. In his letter of May 4, 1807, mentioning the qualities possessed by his candidate, Hill also implied a potential issue: "Probable you recollect that our friend Mr. Batchelor Bunker mentioned to you that he would like to be appointed the Keeper of this Light house when it was executed & fit for use....He is a capable man, and one who will give good satisfaction to all concerned, the *little misunderstanding about the Land matter to the contrary notwithstanding* [emphasis added]."[12]

Some four months later, Bunker's qualities were also praised in a letter to Superintendent Benjamin Lincoln by Judge George Thatcher, a Federalist and prominent citizen of Biddeford, who had served in the Continental Congress and the House of Representatives before assuming the bench. Bunker, he wrote, is a "man of peaceable, quiet disposition as a Quaker citizen I feel myself discharging a duty to the public in recommending him as a proper person to have the charge of keeping & attending the light-house."[13]

And one more time, from Jeremiah Hill: "I hope our friend Bunker will have the care of [the light] because I don't hear of any one being spoken of so well qualified for the Business."[14]

What happened? Why did the appointment go to Benjamin Cole while Bunker was passed over? The record is silent on this issue, although perhaps there are some clues in the letters themselves. First is the suggestion that Bunker may have been the cause of some tension with the decision makers during the negotiations for the sale of the land on Wood Island mentioned in the letter of May 4. Second, despite his praise for Bunker, Judge Thatcher's standing as a confirmed Federalist may not have served Bunker well in the Jeffersonian-Republican political circles dominated by Treasury secretary Albert Gallatin, who controlled all matters related to lighthouses. Third, although Bunker was described as being sixty years of age and in good health, in fact he was closer to seventy. Given the difficulties likely to arise during the first years of the operation of the lighthouse, it is understandable that a man of that age would be viewed with some skepticism.

In any case, a letter from Gallatin to Lincoln on July 30, 1807, informed the superintendent of lighthouses in Massachusetts that President Jefferson had appointed "Capt. Benjamin Cole to be Keeper of the Light House on Wood Island…and that his Salary is fixed at two hundred twenty-five dollars per annum." Ironically, this note, written at the end of July, must have passed the letters recommending Batchelor Bunker in the mail.[15]

There may have been some bitterness that persisted even after this early drama relating to the choice of Wood Island's first keeper finally played out. In a letter Jeremiah Hill wrote to General Lincoln on October 10, 1807, the customs collector reported that after the completion of the construction phase of the lighthouse project, Hill had "desired Mr. Bunker to take care of the buildings on Wood Island & see that they were not damaged and open them from time to time to air them. Probable he will expect some compensation for that service." He went on to report further discontent among the former landowners: "The Fletcher Family who owned a share of the land sold [to] the U[nited] States on Wood Island are poor, they say you have not paid for the last two acres sold."[16]

Although these tensions may have continued, by the fall of 1807, the new light station on Wood Island was ready for its first keeper.

Even before Captain Benjamin Cole assumed his role as keeper, a shipwreck a few miles to the northeast of Winter Harbor not only confirmed the need to establish a light at Wood Island but also foreshadowed the troubles that would plague the upcoming year of the first keeper's tenure.

In the early morning hours of a foggy Sunday, July 12, 1807, Captain Jacob Adams became disoriented and ran the schooner *Charles* with its crew

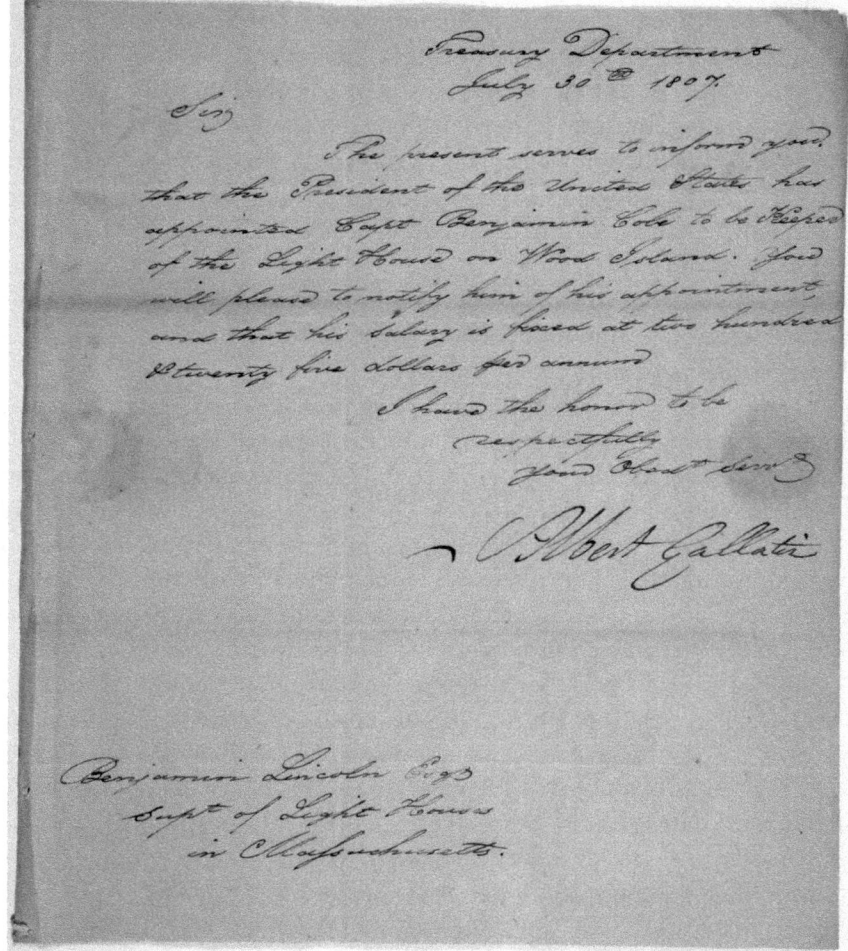

On July 30, 1807, Gallatin notified Superintendent Lincoln that Benjamin Cole was to be the first keeper of the Wood Island Lighthouse. His pay was set at $225 per annum. *NARA*.

and passengers totaling twenty-two souls onto Watts Ledge near Richmond Island. The captain had reckoned their position as being several miles south of Cape Elizabeth and the hazards presented by the ledge the *Charles* struck. "Before any aid could be afforded," reported the *Portland Gazette*, "fourteen persons were washed from the wreck, or perished through fatigue occasioned by the violence of the sea."[17]

Today, the eight-acre plot devoted to the lighthouse at the eastern end of Wood Island is connected by a wooden walkway that runs approximately one-half mile to the landing at its westernmost tip. However, in 1807, there was no established way to move from the landing to the site of the lighthouse. The cutting and hauling of the timber to be used as building materials for the wooden dwelling and tower may have created some uneven dirt pathways suitable for construction teams, but they would not have been sufficient for overcoming the logistical nightmare confronting a full-time lighthouse keeper moving supplies from the landing to the lighthouse itself. That, in combination with a dwelling whose basement was submerged under two feet of water, the absence of oil to service the lantern and the lack of a boat to transport supplies and materials from the mainland to the island, presented powerful constraints for the first keeper.

Gallatin's letter of July 30 confirming the appointment of Captain Benjamin Cole as keeper of the lighthouse on Wood Island and fixing his salary at $225 per annum was delivered to General Benjamin Lincoln, Esq., superintendent of lighthouses in Massachusetts. Although it was presumably delivered hastily to the new keeper as well in September, it did not occasion a response until November 9. In his letter, Captain Cole reported that he was indeed ready to take charge and had made the necessary preparations. However, there remained some significant issues not only delaying full-time operation of the lighthouse but also resulting in a very uncomfortable situation in the dwelling itself. Recognizing that winter was quickly approaching, one critical issue was the consequence of not having sufficient oil to fuel the lamp. Yet another was caused by the water that had accumulated in the cellar. Cole continues in his letter to plead for an advance in his pay, as well as for the government to supply a boat to allow necessary transportation to and from the mainland, about a mile away.[18]

April 1808 arrived, and still conditions had not improved. In a letter dated April 25, the keeper once again requested oil for the light, a boat allowing for transport to and from the island and his overdue salary. "I am destitute," he wrote. "I wish to be informed whether I am to receive my wages quarterly or by the year & in either case, how & where I am to receive it."[19]

By June 6, the lighthouse service had delivered the requested oil, and in a letter once again addressed to Superintendent Benjamin Lincoln, Keeper Cole agreed to take on the task of draining the cellar. However, the keeper's woes remained. Lacking the necessary supplies, he contended that he was still unable to effectively perform his duty. Cole continued in his letter: "I hope to receive a boat soon as it is inconvenient to be without one—How am I to get wick yarn   I cannot Light the lamps until Wicks are procured   I can procure them her if so directed" (original retained).[20]

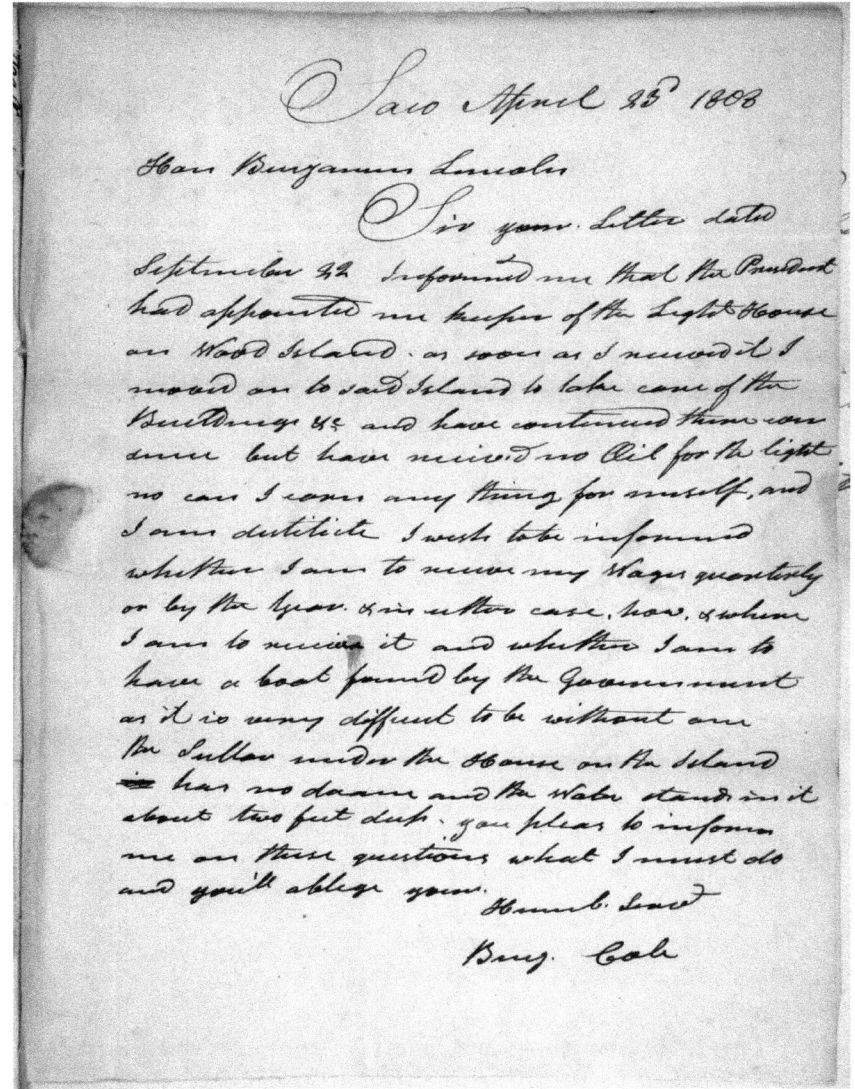

Keeper Benjamin Cole's annoyance is evident in his letter to Benjamin Lincoln inquiring about his pay and a boat in the spring of 1808. *NARA*.

Cole's two earlier letters of November 1807 and April 1808 were both dated from Saco, whereas his letters beginning in June 1808 are dated from Wood Island and suggest that perhaps it was not until the spring of 1808 that Cole took up permanent residence on the island. For more than half a year since learning of his appointment, Cole had pleaded with the

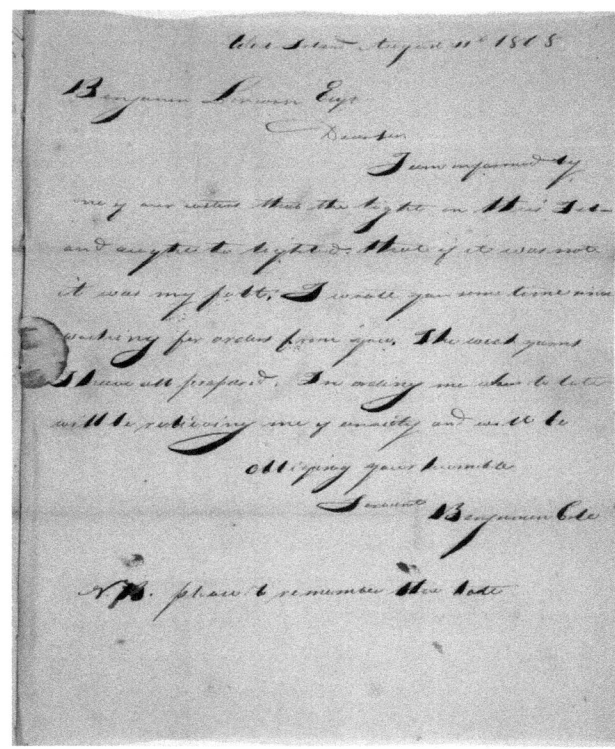

Keeper Cole's letter to Benjamin Lincoln in August 1808 expresses his continuing frustration with the lighthouse establishment. *NARA*.

superintendent for critical supplies, including a boat, as well as oil and wicks for the light. We can understand why he might be annoyed when he began to hear complaints about the light not being lit.

> *Wood island   August 11th 1808*
> *Benjamin Lincoln Esq*
> *Dear Sir,*
>   *I am informed by one of our* [cutters?] *that the light on this island aught to be lighted. that if it was not it was my fult* [sic]. *I wrote you some time since waiting for orders from you. The wick* [illegible] *I have all prepared. In* [illegible] *when to* [illegible] *will be relieving me of anxiety and will be obliging your humble servant*
> *Benjamin Cole*
>
> *N.B. please to remember the boat* [original retained][21]

Finally, by midsummer, enough was in order that Keeper Cole was able to "set the light agoing on the night of 12th August past," as well as complete the drain from the cellar. And yet, he continued to beseech Lincoln for a boat: "I am completely destitute of a boat & consequently a closely confined prisoner to the island—I do entreat you in the name of God recollect the Boat." He even provided the names of two captains in Boston by whom the boat could be sent.[22]

Captain Benjamin Cole's letter of September 9, 1808, again expressing his unhappiness in being without a boat, was the last we hear from him directly. There were no more apparent concerns coming from the superintendent's office relating to keeping the light burning, and we hear no more about the boat. In hindsight, the silence is concerning.

The merchants and town fathers of Biddeford, however, were far from silent. A letter recently discovered buried in a tray in the National Archives sheds light on the mystery surrounding the final days of Wood Island's first keeper. On October 12, 1808, a letter found its way to Albert Gallatin expressing the importance of effectively maintaining the light on Wood Island and voicing concern for the deteriorating physical condition of the present keeper while recommending his replacement:

> *To the honorable Albert Gallatin*
> *Secretary of the Treasury of the United States,*
> *Sir,*
>
> *We the undersigned, merchants, mariners and inhabitants of the town of Biddeford & Saco, fully sensible of the advantages of a lighthouse on Wood Island, knowing how much its utility depends on the steadiness and watchfulness of the keeper officially represent—that the present incumbent is now lingering in the last stages of consumption and that in all human probability that he cannot survive many weeks—and fearing lest applications may be made for this office by men who will not fully discharge its duties beg leave to suggest that Robert Patterson Junior of Biddeford mariner is an active, steady, judicious and capable man that we think him perfectly adequate to the proper management of the light house, believe him to be an honest and upright man....We take the liberty to recommend Captain Patterson to supply the vacancy in case of the decease of the present keeper.*[23]

Even given this troubling communication and the obvious difficulties confronting the isolated keeper, the entry in the diary of Biddeford resident

> District of Saco Oct 12th 1808
>
> To the honourable Albert Gallatin
> Secretary of the treasury of the
> United States,
>
> Sir,
>
> We the undersigned, merchants, mariners, and inhabitants of the town of Biddeford & Saco, fully sensible of the advantages of a light house on Wood Island, & knowing how much its utility depends on the steadiness and watchfulness of the keeper, respectfully represent, that the present incumbent is now languishing in the last stages of a consumption, and that in all human probability he cannot survive many weeks — and fearing lest applications may be made for this Office by men who will not fully discharge its duties, beg leave to suggest that Robert Patterson Junior of Biddeford Mariner is an active, steady, judicious and capable man, that we think him perfectly adequate to the proper management of the light house, and believe him to be an honest and upright man; As shipowners and mariners, we know of no person that we prefer to fill this office, and we have no hesitation in saying that we think no one will manage the property placed in his hands with more honesty and economy — he having ever conducted himself with integrity and prudence in situations with which we are personally acquainted. Interested therefore as we are that this light house should be faithfully taken care of we take the liberty to recommend Captain Patterson to supply the vacancy in case of the decease of the present keeper.
>
> With the greatest respect we are Sir Your hble Servts.

In October 1808, the merchants of Biddeford, concerned that Cole was seriously ill, recommended that Robert Patterson Jr. be appointed keeper of the Wood Island Lighthouse. *NARA*.

Samuel Merrill comes as a startling surprise. "Capt. Benj. Cole of this town died on Saturday night, Dec. 24. Died on Wood Island, had kept the light on there." Aside from this diary account, there is no official record of Cole's death in any of the formal registers of Biddeford or Saco and no mention of a cemetery stone to mark his passing.[24]

There is one additional letter, however, also recently uncovered, that seems to confirm the veracity of Merrill's diary entry and provides some insight into the three months that marked the passing of Cole and the formal appointment of Philip Goldthwait to take his place. The author, Richard Cutts, a shipmaster and wealthy partner in the family shipping business, was also a member of the House of Representatives. His letter, dated January 7, 1809, begins by verifying the death of Keeper Cole and reveals that Robert Patterson, mentioned in the previous letter, has been maintaining the light in the meantime. He seems aware of the petitions urging the appointment of various candidates but is committed to the selection of Philip Goldthwait for the position. Apparently, Cutts's support was sufficient, for on the back of the envelope, Gallatin scribbled a note: "Philip Goldthwait to be appointed; of which inform General Dearborn__A.G."[25]

The secretary of the treasury was notified of the situation, and on April 12, 1809, the formal appointment was made and the confirmation letter sent. Intriguingly, the tone and language of Albert Gallatin's letter to Henry Dearborn, Benjamin Lincoln's replacement as superintendent of lighthouses, appears both impatient and insensitive:

Treasury Department
April 12th 1809
Sir
The present serves to inform you that Philip Goldthwait of Saco, is appointed keeper of the Light House on Wood Island in the place of Benjamin Cole, who I understand is dead. You will please to notify Mr. Goldthwait of his appointment.

I have the honor to be
Respectfully,
your obedt serv
Albert Gallatin[26]

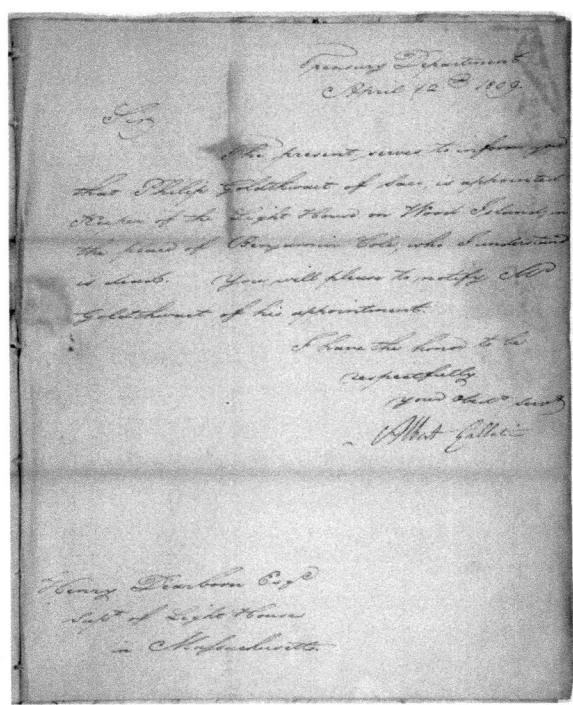

Albert Gallatin's letter to Henry Dearborn appointing Philip Goldthwait as Wood Island's second keeper displays a curious lack of compassion. *NARA.*

The sudden death of Benjamin Cole left the Wood Island Light Station without an appointed keeper for several months at the beginning of 1809. It is likely that Robert Patterson, one of the merchants mentioned in the letter of October 12, 1808, filled the role until the new keeper, Philip Goldthwait, was formally named on April 12, 1809.

Chapter 2

THE WAR OF 1812 COMES TO WOOD ISLAND

1809-32

From the moment Philip Goldthwait took control of the light station on Wood Island in 1809, he was faced with challenges at home and abroad.

Keeper Goldthwait's inventory, taken on June 1, 1809, makes it quite clear that the conditions facing Benjamin Cole, his predecessor, had not improved significantly. "I must observe," he writes regarding the quality of the station's construction overall, "the work was not well executed. The covering appears to have been put on before it was seasoned. Of course, the buildings are now leaky. The door of the Light House is broken & falling to pieces. The stone work of the Oil vault having been hove by the frost & injured the brick arching considerably." Goldthwait's assessment does, however, suggest that some progress had been made regarding one of Cole's ongoing concerns: "One boat, about 12 feet keel repaired, & now in good order."[27]

The following year, in the report submitted in 1810, the keeper found it necessary to continue to inform his superiors of matters still in need of prompt attention:[28]

- Chimney is out of repair
- Ten panes of glass broken
- Door and lock broken
- Oil vault some repairs necessary
- Lack oars for the 12-foot keel boat

Philip Goldthwait reports that the conditions at the lighthouse had not improved since Keeper Cole expressed his apprehensions a year earlier. *NARA*.

It would take the better part of three years to complete the repairs necessary to at least partially remedy the substandard handiwork of the original contractors, Thaxter and Beal. Nevertheless, by June 1, 1812, Goldthwait was able to send off a sanguine report to Henry Dearborn that revealed the progress that had been made since he took over responsibilities at Wood Island. Except for the seventeen-by-twenty-foot oil vault that was falling apart, all else had been repaired and was in good order. And now, the keeper could boast that he finally had a dependable fourteen-foot boat—with oars.[29]

THE WAR OF 1812

Abroad, the tensions between the newly established United States and opposing European powers England and France continued to escalate. The sovereignty of the United States was challenged when American vessels were attacked on the high seas by both warring nations. U.S. sailors were impressed into the British navy, as England continued to argue that "once an Englishman, always an Englishman." Jeffersonian embargoes only encouraged smuggling and created economic hardships. The costs of

Stories from the Edge of the Sea

The cannonball seen here was shot from the *Bulwark* in 1814. It passed over Biddeford Pool and was eventually recovered from the pasture of the Tarbox family. *McArthur Library.*

remaining neutral eventually became too much to bear, and so on June 18, 1812, the United States declared war on Great Britain.

The full effects of the war came to Biddeford Pool in the summer and fall of 1814. On the morning of Thursday, June 16, 1814, the *Bulwark*, a British ship of the line, approached the mouth of the Saco River, anchoring just off the western end of Wood Island. British captain Milne then fired several warning shots in the direction of Biddeford Pool, one of which passed over the Pool and landed in the field of Samuel Tarbox. A horse and rider were hastily dispatched to Saco to warn the militia but were regrettably delayed by swollen rivers and bridges damaged or destroyed by recent torrential rains.

As the morning wore on, five boats carrying 150 men were launched from the *Bulwark* under the command of Lieutenant James Symonds and headed in the direction of Biddeford Pool. They stopped briefly on Stage Island and then proceeded toward the shipyard owned by Thomas Cutts Jr. A wealthy trader, shipbuilder and property owner, Cutts had the frame of at least one ship valued at $7,000 docked and under construction and several other idle vessels moored alongside the wharf. As the British neared the landing, it is reported that Cutts, waving a white flag, attempted to head off the attack with a payment in cash. Lieutenant Symonds would have none of it, claiming that his orders were to destroy the coastal shipping industry.

Local lore suggests that what followed may have been aggravated by a personal grudge that Symonds harbored toward Cutts due to an incident that had occurred before the war broke out. In any case, the assault, lasting approximately two and one-half hours, caused much destruction, and it was Cutts who suffered the greatest damage. The British set fire to at least three ships—*Hermione*, *Catherine* and *Equator*—and confiscated another, the *Victory*. Two of the ships burned were owned by Cutts, and the *Victory*, also belonging to Cutts, was later redeemed after a payment of $6,000. In addition, Symonds's troops plundered the Cuttses' store, located near the wharf, making off with nearly $2,000 worth of goods. In all, it is estimated that the raid's cost was $25,000.

Samuel Merrill, the resident diarist and chronicler of early Biddeford history, receiving word of the raid, joined with his fellow militiamen, who

Cutts' Store, shown here in 1880, appears much the same as it did in 1814, when it was sacked by the British. *Saco Museum.*

then hastened to the mouth of the Saco River. Moving on in the direction of Biddeford Pool, Merrill described the scene when they reached Winter Harbor just as the British were departing: "Found three vessels on fire, a brig of Capt. Cutts, a schooner & a sloop loaded with lumber…that had run on shore up in the pool….After setting fire to the above vessels they [British military] took possession of the ship *Victory* belonging to Capt. Thomas Cutts and set her sail & took her away."[30]

For the next three days, the *Bulwark* stood offshore and threatened the residents of Biddeford and Saco. Although there was little further damage done to those towns, the enemy vessel continued to molest Maine's coastal settlements and attack local shipping up and down the Maine coast.

Likewise for residents along the Saco River, the harassment continued. In August, the British returned. On the twenty-sixth, a schooner from North Carolina carrying flour and tar was chased around Wood Island and eventually went aground just before finding shelter in the Pool. The American captain, seeing no escape, ordered the ship set on fire and abandoned it. The British nevertheless were able to extinguish the fire and tow the schooner and its cargo, valued at $15,000, back out to sea.

Stories from the Edge of the Sea

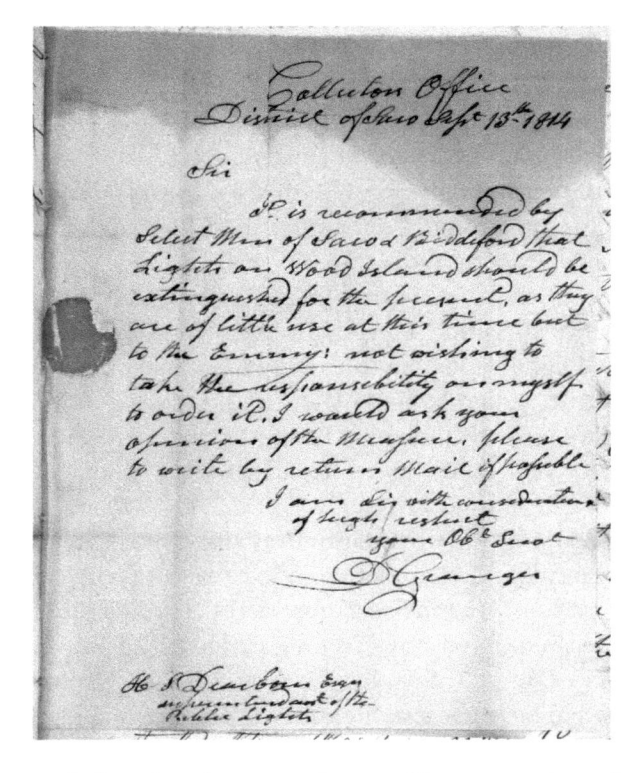

The light on Wood Island was extinguished following the British raids during the summer of 1814. *NARA.*

A few days later, on August 29, yet another alarm was sounded urging residents to hasten to Winter Harbor. This time, a schooner laden with lumber was intercepted on its route from Portland heading toward Boston and forced to drive up on the beach. When barges from the British ship of war attempted to row into the shallow water and lay claim to the schooner, the townspeople drove them away with gunshots. Eventually, the schooner was hauled off the beach and returned safely to Portland.

By September, the obvious danger posed by British privateers and ships of war led local authorities to turn concern into action. Standing at the mouth of the Saco River and Winter Harbor, the Wood Island Lighthouse came under scrutiny. Was the light contributing to the series of attacks by offering the British a clear passage into the vulnerable economic centers of southern Maine's villages and towns? The customs collector thought so. On September 13, 1814, Daniel Granger wrote to his superior, Henry Dearborn, the superintendent of lighthouses, "It is recommended by the Select Men of Saco & Biddeford that the Lights on Wood Island should be extinguished for the present as they are of little use at this time but to the enemy."[31]

Within a couple of weeks, these concerns were officially conveyed to Keeper Goldthwait, who reported on October 1 that he had "succeeded in removing all the movable articles from the Light house on Wood Island… [and had placed them] in a safe and convenient store about five miles up Saco River." Continuing, Goldthwait demonstrated his sense of dutiful responsibility by declaring his intention to "remain on the Island and take any possible care of the public property there."[32]

Notwithstanding these necessary precautions, the residents of Biddeford had not seen the last of the British. Samuel Merrill, the diarist, reports that in November, a month after the light was extinguished and moveable property taken away, a British privateer, hiding behind Wood Island, attacked and captured an American schooner inbound from Boston. Captain Andrew Spring was able to regain his vessel only after surrendering ten gallons of rum to the Brits.[33]

The war continued into early 1815, when citizens of the United States finally learned that the Treaty of Ghent, which ended the conflict, had actually been signed the previous year in December 1814. In Biddeford, where residents had felt the menace of war creeping closer and closer to home, the news of peace was cause for great joy. On Wood Island, Keeper Goldthwait's family returned to their home along with the property that had been removed. And once again, the light on Wood Island offered a safe and welcoming course to ships seeking passage into Winter Harbor and to the wharves of Biddeford and Saco.

Postwar Taxes and the Wood Island Lighthouse

The young United States had managed to survive two wars against much more powerful European nations, but after almost twenty years, the country was still at conflict with itself. Among the many issues that challenged this new experiment in federalism, none was more irksome, nor as urgent, as that of taxes, which had been aggravated by the recent war. The thorny matter of who had the power to tax created serious quarrels as institutions and struggling individuals disputed the taxing power of political entities, now especially strapped for cash following two wars. The Wood Island Lighthouse found itself in the thick of the fray.

In 1816, Winslow Lewis—prominent by that time for a reputation he acquired following the installation of his patented, fuel-efficient and

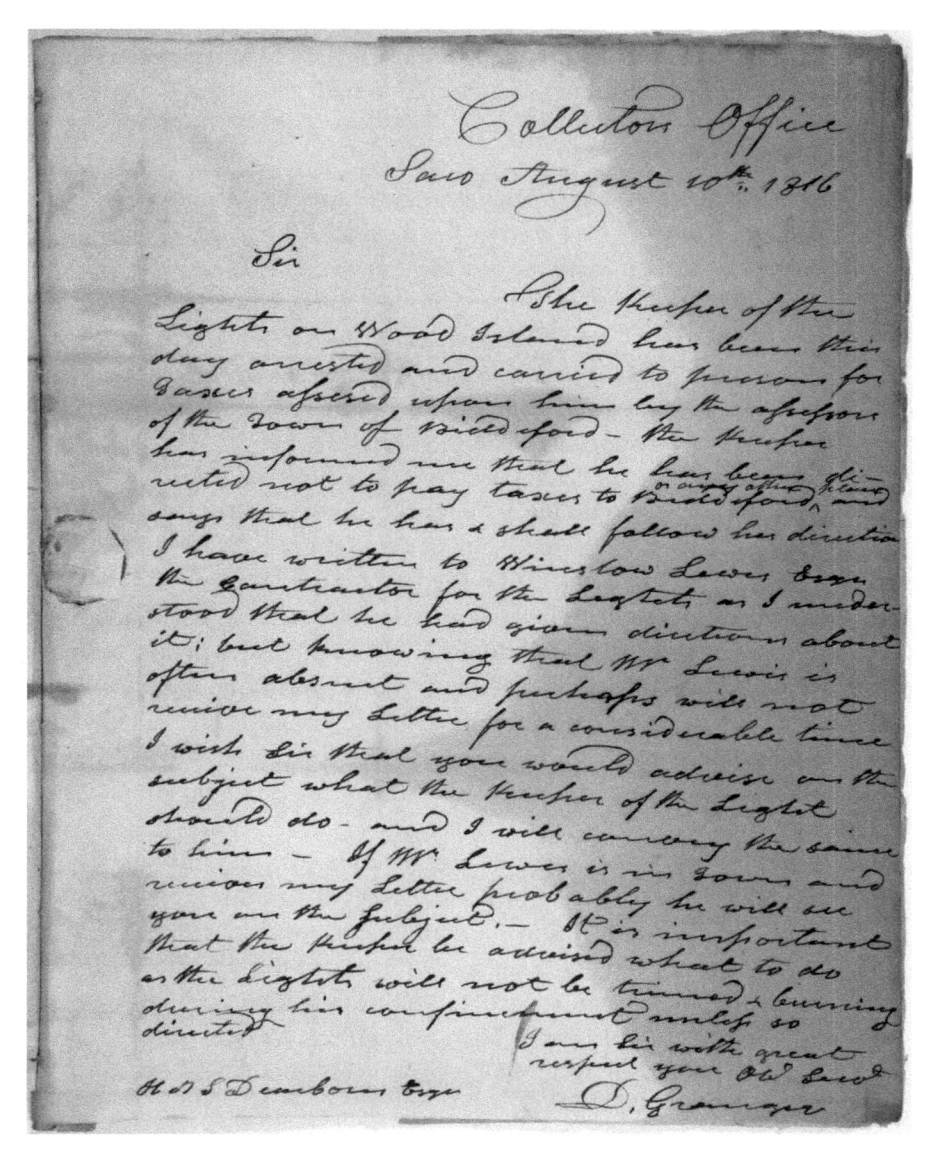

An attempt by local authorities to tax the federal property on which the lighthouse station was erected resulted in the arrest of Keeper Goldthwait on August 10, 1816. *NARA*.

brighter lamps in nearly fifty lighthouses—responded to a letter from Henry Dearborn (the original language has been retained):

> *Sir*
> *I have been wrote to since I have been engaged with the light houses by almost every keeper to know whether they were liable to pay state or town taxes. my answer has invariably been that they were not. the state having once ceded the territory to the United States they had no jurisdiction over it & in instance has a keeper of a light house been allowed to vote in the state or town affairs. when I was att wood island last the Collector of taxes from the Town of Biddeford came to the Light house & demanded of the keeper the payment of the town tax I told the keeper not to pay it.*[34]

In fact, Lewis was responding to an earlier message that Dearborn had received from Customs Collector Granger dated August 10, 1816. Granger's letter came right to the point: "The keeper of the Lights on Wood Island has been this day arrested and carried to prison for taxes assessed upon him by the assessor of the Town of Biddeford." It is not clear whether Granger was more concerned about the well-being of the imprisoned keeper, Philip Goldthwait, or maintaining the integrity of the lighthouse. He concludes his letter with these words: "It is important that the Keeper be advised what to do as the Light will not be trimmed & burning during his confinement unless so directed."[35]

Lewis was incensed and ordered Granger to hastily bail out "the keeper and send him back to the lighthouse." Keeper Goldthwait apparently survived the humiliation of his incarceration, and we learn from Lewis that "the Light has never been out & the keeper is now home."[36]

For the next fifteen years, Keeper Goldthwait, along with his family, tended the light at Wood Island. His twenty-three years of service ended with his sudden death in 1832 while still on the island. He was the light station's longest-serving keeper.

Chapter 3

POLITICAL PARTISANSHIP AND ACRIMONY IN THE LIGHTHOUSE SERVICE

1841–61

A scornful letter written in 1842 by I.W.P. Lewis to the Honorable Robert C. Winthrop of Massachusetts, member of Congress, reflected the attitude of contempt that was held throughout the ranks of the lighthouse service. Lewis, a civil engineer and contractor hired to supervise a number of projects by the lighthouse authority, expressed his dismay at the frauds that resulted in the waste of "enormous sums." He went on famously to point to "236 witnesses, in the shape of lighthouses, that all order, economy, and utility, in the construction, illumination, and administration of the light-house service is set at utter defiance by the rule of ignorant and incompetent men, who are still pursuing the same career."[37]

At the Wood Island Light Station, the nature of the incompetence alluded to by Lewis was felt firsthand. The experiences of the lighthouse keepers whose service spanned most of the first half of the nineteenth century are testimony to the ineffectiveness and ineptitude of the system that controlled their livelihood.

JOHN ADAMS: 1841–45

Captain Goodrich had no apparent cause for concern on March 16, 1836, as he made his way toward the northern tip of Long Beach Island in New Jersey. His barque, the *Galaxy*, was returning from an extended and profitable voyage to Canton, China, loaded with more than $50,000 in goods to be imported into the United States. Suddenly, he met with calamity when his ship ran onto a shoal near Barnegat Lighthouse. During the inquiry that followed, the commissioners determined that the light at Barnegat had been "erected and lighted during his absence; the captain made the light [and] shaped his course believing it another and a well-known light." Simply put, the lighthouse had been erected during the *Galaxy*'s voyage. Captain Goodrich was not made aware of this new marker and mistook it for another, resulting in the disastrous consequences that followed.[38]

For Edmund and George W. Blunt, brothers and publishers of the *American Coast Pilot*, this unfortunate incident illustrated the lack of communication and general neglect that characterized the American lighthouse establishment. It was but one in a long list of grievances that the international and local coastal shipping community had against the incompetence that typified the management of an organization vital to the commercial success of the United States. In their report of 1837, the Blunts argued that the lighthouses along the coasts of the United States were far inferior to those of England and France. In reporting their findings, they offered specific evidence that focused on poorly constructed buildings; insufficient well systems; poor supervision of contractors; improper maintenance of lamps and machinery; infrequent inspections and supervision; and shipwrecks resulting from poor dissemination of information relating to the erection of new lights, as well as the extinguishing of existing lights during alterations.[39]

It was into this environment of conflict and controversy that the new keeper began his tenure at the Wood Island Light Station. Shortly after his selection, the *Daily Eastern Argus* reported that "Mr. John Adams of Saco, has been appointed Keeper of the Light house, Wood Island, in Biddeford, in place of Mr. Abraham Norwood, removed."[40] He would be the fifth keeper of the Wood Island Lighthouse and earn an annual salary of $350. When he took over the position of keeper, Adams was thirty-nine years old; had been married to Elizabeth Pike Kendrick for sixteen years; and was the father of eight children, four boys and four girls.

His appointment during the acrimonious early years of the Whig presidency of William Henry Harrison was made doubly complicated when the new president died a mere thirty-one days after his inauguration. Harrison's vice president, John Tyler, embattled by partisanship as he set about assuming the full powers of the presidency, was forced to confront a citizenry filled with the usual ire that followed political appointments made as a result of a patronage system that provided the "victor" with the "spoils." The rancor and ill will on this occasion was fueled by Democratic commentators in York County who wrote, for example, that voters "have been duped, cheated and deceived—the promises made to them violated—their hard labor made to enure [*sic*], not to their benefit, but to that of a set of office holders chosen from among the favored few—their remonstrances against bad appointments sneered at and derided—their whole expectations of good from the Harrison 'change' totally disappointed."[41]

Democrats in Biddeford and Saco were clearly not happy. Nor, apparently, was Norwood, the previous keeper and landowner, who had been maintaining the light since 1833. Due to his persistent efforts, in 1839, a new granite keeper's house and tower were erected to replace the leaky, cold, wood-frame residence that the government had previously provided. He also erected a barn on the lighthouse acreage. Now, he learned that he was to surrender the fruits of his efforts to the new keeper, John Adams. The frosty relationship that followed was made clear in the report later submitted by Keeper Adams on August 15, 1842:

> *On leaving here, he* [Norwood] *demanded of me $200 for the barn, 50 cents a rod for the walls and fence; he also claims a portion of the old keeper's house, which he cut off therefrom, and converted into a cow-house and pigstye.... This keeper, Abraham Norwood, has since complained of me, because I decline buying the barn, walling, fencing, and other improvements.*[42]

This difficult relationship continued to deteriorate over the course of the months following his appointment to the point where Adams's superior was forced to intervene. However, by March 1843, it appears that this personal quarrel was resolved. In his report of March 2, 1843, Inspector Nathan Cummings, the current superintendent of lighthouses in Maine, wrote that the "difficulty between the present and former keeper, in relation to improvements and division fence [has persisted]; I recommended an arrangement, which appeared to be satisfactory to both parties."[43] Other matters, however, were not so readily fixed.

By 1842, conditions within the lighthouse establishment had reached another point of crisis. Ironically, Isaiah William Penn Lewis (the nephew of Winslow Lewis, the patent holder and a staunch supporter of the lens systems used in lighthouses throughout the United States) was asked to lead the congressional inquiry into the administration of the Lighthouse Service. I.W.P., as he was known, was about to investigate his own uncle and his uncle's boss Stephen Pleasonton. These latter two were mainly responsible for the design, construction, maintenance and oversight of the 236 lighthouses that operated within the boundaries of the United States in 1840.

Wood Island Lighthouse

In the summer of 1842, John Adams had been the keeper at the Wood Island Light for just over a year. He was still smarting from the disparagement leveled at him by his Democratic critics and the surly attitude and inhospitable welcome he received from his predecessor when he, along with other lighthouse keepers throughout New England, received the order to assess and then describe in an official statement the day-to-day conditions at the lighthouses under their supervision. Adams's report was to become part of a larger document offering evidence ultimately used to condemn the incompetence of the establishment's management and its head, the fifth auditor in the Treasury Department, Stephen Pleasonton. Adams's comments are representative of those reported by light keepers throughout New England:

> *I was appointed keeper of this light July 6, 1841, upon a salary of $350. This island contains about thirty acres of land, six of which belong to the Government. My dwelling house is built of rough stone, with brick gables. It leaks about thee windows and chimneys; the plastering has dropped off of one chamber entirely, and also in several other parts of the house. There is no floor in the cellar, which* [is] *always muddy and wet, the water from the sink leading* [sic] *into it. The joints of the masonry want pointing, being filled now with sand instead of mortar. The house was built by J. Berry, of East Thomaston.*
>
> *The tower is in pretty good order, except about the windows which are leaky. The clock which carries the lamps round is very badly fitted, so that it frequently stops; the rope by which the clock weight is suspended saws against the staircase. The arch supporting the lantern deck is cracked away, and is now supported by a wooden framing. The lantern sweats a good deal. I am allowed a boat, though there is no landing place or slip, nor shelter for the boat. The right of way and landing place are allowed by the owners of the island. A barn was erected here by the late keeper; also a fence, stone wall, etc....I can raise about ten tons of good hay on the six acres belonging to the Government. From the light of Saco we estimate the distance as nine miles; I obtain all my supplies from Saco.*
>
> *There is no rain water cistern belonging to the establishment. The light has ten lamps, and revolves once in two minutes, or should do so; but owing to the clumsy manner in which it is fitted up there is no regularity in its movements. My oil has been of good quality.*
>
> *JOHN ADAMS, Keeper*[44]

Although the reconstruction project, authorized three years earlier in 1839 and completed just prior to his appointment at Wood Island, had resulted in newly constructed buildings, Keeper Adams's report echoes those of other lighthouse keepers who testified to the inadequate living conditions that they were confronting. While the efforts of the reformers brought about some minor modifications and small adjustments to the system as a whole, the overall response of the Congress at that time was to ignore the report's recommendations and to uphold the status quo. As a whole, lighthouse historian Eric Jay Dolin suggests, any changes "to the system were marginal, and the technology of America's lighthouses at the time remained a sorry affair at best."[45]

JOTHAM PERKINS: 1845–49

The election of James K. Polk to the presidency in 1844 set off a new round of politically charged patronage appointments. Now it was the Democrats' turn to choose which party loyalists would be rewarded. The choice for the Wood Island Light Station was announced in the *Saco Union* on June 6, 1845: "Jotham Perkins, of Biddeford, has been appointed keeper of the Light House on Wood Island, at the mouth of the Saco River."[46]

The actual living conditions confronted by the new keeper in 1845 had not improved since the assessment submitted by Keeper Adams some three years earlier. Following up on Adams's appraisal, Superintendent of Lighthouses Nathan Cummings submitted his own report to the Congress in 1843, commenting on the broken and loose plaster, the stonework in need of pointing and the woodwork throughout that required whitewashing. Cummings's comments, in turn, were folded into the report later submitted to Congress by I.W.P. Lewis and offer a description of the station Keeper Perkins inherited:

> *Dwelling-house…laid up in bad lime mortar; roof shingled; three rooms on first floor, and three chambers in attic; walls open at joints of masonry, which appear to be filled with sand instead of mortar; windows leaky; plastering dropped entirely off one chamber, and some in other rooms; cellar wet and muddy; no drain to kitchen sinks; whole construction very defective in materials and workmanship.*[47]

Challenging living conditions resulting from the substandard management that characterized the lighthouse service were not the only issues confronting Jotham Perkins. A year after Keeper Adams handed the key to the Wood Island Lighthouse to his successor, Jotham Perkins, the new keeper found himself embroiled in controversy. During July 1846, the *Middletown Constitution* joined the *Saco Union* in condemning the keeper of the Wood Island Light for "outrageous carelessness." The paper reported sources that included several shipmasters and fishermen "whose word can be relied on" who asserted that the light on Wood Island had been permitted to go out for several nights within the last fortnight, with the consequence that several vessels came near to going on shore. The *Union* went on to charge that "there must be great negligence somewhere—either with the light-house keeper or in those whose duty it is to supply the light with oil." Although political opponents continued to hurl accusations in order to gain partisan advantage, the real offender in this case was likely to have been the lighthouse establishment itself. Lack of proper funding, coupled with poor management policies and political cronyism, continued to inhibit the ability of lighthouse keepers to effectively perform their duties.[48]

Stephen P. Batchelder: 1849–53

The election of the Whig candidate Zachary Taylor as president of the United States in 1848, which created a new round of applications for federal office, once again focused attention on the controversial patronage system. The debate that was sparked in local papers highlighted yet again one of the several problems plaguing the lighthouse establishment. Stephen Pleasonton, himself under fire from the voices favoring lighthouse reform, defended himself and his organization by drawing attention to the flaws inherent in the "spoils system": "It must be apparent to all who reflect upon the subject, that I have had much inconvenience and difficulty to encounter from the frequent changes incidental to our form of government, in the [politically appointed] keepers, who for a time do not understand the management of their lamps and consequently keep bad lights and waste much oil."[49]

At the time of Keeper Batchelder's appointment, apprehension about the patronage system only scratched the surface of the concerns being leveled at the lighthouse establishment. Accusations of fraud, corruption and mishandling continued to be hurled at Pleasonton and his assistant, Winslow Lewis. The recent war with Mexico had confirmed America's place as a continental power with industrial and technological progress everywhere evident—except in the lighthouse establishment.

Two years into the tenure of Keeper Batchelder, the concerns expressed earlier by Adams and his colleagues played a decisive role in the reorganization of the lighthouse establishment. In May 1851, after more than ten years of agitation for change, the *Maine Democrat* reported that "under the provisions of an act passed at the last session of Congress, the Secretary of the Treasury has appointed…a board of commissioners to inquire into the conditions of the light house establishment of the United States [in order to] guide legislation in extending and improving the present system of construction, illumination, inspections and superintendence."[50] Early the following year, on January 30, 1852, the board was prepared to present its findings and, in so doing, offered what amounted to a powerful rebuke of the current lighthouse establishment. "At one fell swoop," reported the *Maine Democrat* nine months later, "Congress had ordered a change in the whole light-house system of the United States."[51]

On Wood Island, the response of the newly constituted Lighthouse Board to the conditions described in 1842 by Keeper John Adams was to provide $5,000 for the reconstruction of the lighthouse. The funding, which was the equivalent of approximately $150,000 in today's dollars, was to be used for repairs and alterations to the tower and lantern room, largely intended to allow for the fourth-order Fresnel lens, which was eventually installed in 1858. In addition, a new dwelling would replace the existing granite residence with a one-and-one-half-story, wood-frame structure, which would hopefully provide a more comfortable house for the keeper. Unfortunately for the family of Stephen P. Batchelder, who would leave Wood Island in 1853, the new construction was still a year into the future and would not provide relief for the current keeper.

Nathaniel Varrell and Lyman Frank Verrill: 1853–57

In November 1852, political power in the United States shifted once again. The Whig appointees were swept out of office and replaced with those preferred by the new government. On May 4, 1853, the *Saco Union* announced that Keeper Batchelder had been removed from his post.[52] The new keeper at the Wood Island Light Station was to be Nathaniel Varrell (later changed to Verrill), currently residing in Biddeford but, like the new

Left: Keeper Nathaniel Varrell later changed the spelling of his last name to Verrill. *Friends of the Wood Island Lighthouse (FOWIL) Archives.*

Right: Lyman Frank "L.F." Verrill assumed the light-keeping duties when his father passed away in 1856. *FOWIL Archives.*

Democratic president, originally from New Hampshire. With civil service reform still decades away from realization, once again, custom had dictated "to the victor belong the spoils."

When Keeper Verrill and his family viewed the dwelling that would be their residence for the near future, they were not greeted by a welcoming sight. The dwelling left behind by Keeper Batchelder had suffered the ravages of time, aggravated and intensified by mid-century gales. When combined with the ever-present deterioration caused by constant exposure to wind, sea and salt, conditions had created a desperate need to repair and rebuild the structures on Wood Island.

Under the authority of the newly constituted Lighthouse Board and the appropriation in 1854 of $5,000, the Wood Island Light Station was among those singled out in the first district to be rebuilt. In addition to a new wood-frame keeper's house, the improvements were to include a "new reflecting lighting apparatus," adhering to the admonition that "at the close of the fiscal year ending June 30, 1858, there will be in this district no lights fitted with expensive and inefficient reflectors and lamps of the old system."[53]

In fact, the new renovation was constructed so as to accommodate a fourth-order Fresnel lens. The new lens, which would be more than two feet high and weigh approximately five hundred pounds, could now cast a useful beam up to fifteen nautical miles out to sea.

Keeper Nathaniel Verrill was not able to take full advantage of the improvements to the light station made during his time of service on Wood Island. He was sixty years old when he was appointed, recently widowed and of uncertain health. On April 29, 1856, after only three years at the Wood Island Lighthouse, Nathaniel Verrill passed away. He was sixty-two years old. His son, Lyman Frank Verrill, stepped up briefly to complete the remaining years of his service.

JAMES BRYANT: 1857–61

On May 14, 1857, Keeper L.F. Verrill was removed from his post, and fourteen days later, once again adhering to the tradition of political patronage, James Bryant was formally appointed as keeper at the Wood Island Lighthouse. His salary was to be $350 per year. During his four-year tenure, Keeper Bryant would benefit from changes to the organization of the lighthouse establishment, as well as the important renovations made to the station on Wood Island itself.

In 1852, the autocratic system created under the leadership of Stephen Pleasonton had given way to the new Lighthouse Board, which met officially for the first time in October of that year. By the time Bryant assumed his duties at Wood Island, the board had firmly established its authority by issuing a detailed set of instructions for keepers, who would be required to be both literate and physically capable of effectively performing their assigned duties. The keeper's performance would be assessed and enforced through unannounced periodic visits by lighthouse inspectors. Lighthouse design and construction would be undertaken only by skilled contractors agreeing to use the best available materials and whose plans were reviewed and approved by engineers. And perhaps most important of all, the lenses currently in use would be gradually replaced by new, more effective Fresnel lenses. In Maine, this meant that the old lantern would be replaced by June 30, 1858.

By June 1857, as Bryant was settling into his new post, plans for reconstructing the dwelling and light tower had already been set in motion. A photo that dates from 1859 shows the newly renovated dwelling connected to the granite tower by a covered wooden walkway. The residence was a

The first known photograph of the Wood Island Light Station, circa 1859. *FOWIL Archives.*

one-and-one-half-story, three-bay frame structure, and the tower required an interior reconstruction in the lantern room to accommodate the new, weighty fourth-order Fresnel lens.

While the efforts of reformers in the previous two decades had resulted in significant improvement in the administration and operation of the nation's lighthouses, tensions within the country as a whole were threatening to shatter the fragile bond that bound the states to one another. As Keeper Bryant prepared to leave his post at the Wood Island Lighthouse, the republic was confronting its most consequential trial since the War for Independence. Managing affairs at the Wood Island Light Station during these trying times would fall on the capable shoulders of Ebenezer Emerson.

Chapter 4

OF GALES, QUAKES AND A WOODLESS WOOD ISLAND

1849–1906

The storm that would eventually be called the "Lighthouse Storm" was the worst of several gales that struck the southern Maine coast in the middle of the nineteenth century during the service of Keeper Stephen Batchelder. The first of these occurred in October 1849, six months after Keeper Batchelder was appointed. It was followed by a second ferocious tempest in November of that same year. Referring to the second November storm, the *Maine Democrat* on November 13 announced that the "storm of last week was the most severe one that has visited us for a long time." The paper continued to report that two schooners, the *Grape* and the *Minor*, were "driven upon the beach a little to the eastward of the mouth of the Saco River [and] lie upon the sand above high water mark." Happily, the crews were saved. Pieces of additional vessels went ashore nearby with no report of the fate of the crews involved. Eastward of Wood Island, in Bath at the mouth of the Kennebec River, the *Hanover* struck on Pond Island Bar and immediately went to pieces, littering "the beach for nearly two miles with…fragments of the wreck." The entire ship's company of seventeen persons perished.[54]

Yet the Lighthouse Storm that battered the New England coast in April 1851 appears to have been far worse than any of the other mid-century storms. It struck the New England coast with a fury seldom experienced, bringing a tragedy that would shake the lighthouse community to its core.

In an era before weather alerts were commonplace, the awesome power of the rain, hail, snow and violent winds surprised coastal communities on April 14 as these elemental forces combined with the full moon to create historically high tides. This dynamic continued over the next five days to wreak havoc inland as well as along the shoreline. On Thursday, April 18, while the gale was still raging, the *Saco Union* was able to report "a heavy fall of rain, which has swollen the river....And at the Pool, the lower floor of Mr. Bickford's new house, which...stands some rods above the beach, and on comparatively high land, was flooded, and the inmates were obliged to take refuge in the second and third stories."[55] The following week, the *Union* assessed the damage in southern Maine. In Portland, the "tide rose to great height, and Vaughan's Bridge had been swept away on the Cape Elizabeth side of the harbor."[56] Closer to Biddeford, the schooner *Augusta* went ashore at Wood Island, with no crew on board at the time. The editors of the *Maine Democrat* expressed hope that the men had been on shore at Richmond Island, where the vessel first went adrift.[57]

By far the storm's greatest violence was felt along the coast of Massachusetts, where dozens of vessels were lost, along with significant human casualties. The gale's tragic designation as the "Lighthouse Storm," however, is the result of the destruction it inflicted on the lighthouse at Minot's Ledge, located about twenty miles southeast of Boston.

The *Boston Journal* on April 17 sadly informed its readers of the destruction of Minot's Rock Light House and the death of two assistant keepers. "The last time the Light was seen standing was about half-past three o'clock yesterday [Wednesday] afternoon....The light was not seen burning last night."[58] Evidence of the tragedy was apparent, as the wreckage from the lighthouse was seen strewn all along the beach, and from the battered bodies of the assistant keepers that were eventually recovered. Two months later, on June 17, the *Maine Democrat* reported: "The last words from Minot's Ledge—A gentleman picked upon the Beach at East Boston, yesterday a bottle in which was enclosed a letter from Joseph Wilson, one of the under keepers at Minot's Ledge Lighthouse, [when] it was swept away, and states that it has just received a terrible shock, and that another as terrific would destroy it." When the handwriting was later compared with other letters written by Wilson, it was believed to be authentic.[59]

The distress expressed in the final words of Keeper Wilson captures the terror and anxiety that all those who make their livelihood on the sea must feel on occasion. The winter storms that hammered the entire New England coast during the mid-nineteenth century most certainly had an effect on Wood Island's keeper, Stephen Batchelder. But it was the entire lighthouse community that suffered when it learned that two of their colleagues, alone in a cramped, ten-foot octagon approximately sixty feet above the rocks on a ledge one mile off the coast of Cohasset, Massachusetts, would experience the darkest moments of a lighthouse keeper's worst nightmare.

Following his retirement from the lighthouse in 1853, Stephen Batchelder and his wife spent their remaining days in Saco, Maine. After twenty-seven years of marriage, in 1866, Hannah passed away. One year later, on April 21, 1867, Stephen also died. He was sixty-seven. Today, both are buried in the Laurel Hill Cemetery on Beach Street in Saco, Maine.

WOODLESS WOOD ISLAND

Edwin Tarbox, Wood Island Lighthouse keeper from 1865 to 1872, was witness to some of the most devastating storms of the century during his assignment to the station. In fact, observers of Wood Island's history, referring to that period, point to a tempest in 1869 that stripped the island of the trees, which at one time had been the source for its name. Waldo Stillson Verrill, the "Biddeford Pool Poet" whose uncle L.F. Verrill kept the light just prior to the Civil War, recalled in an interview in 1928 that Wood Island "was covered from one end to the other with a dense growth of firs. They were so thick that vessels coming out of the Saco River at night found difficulty in locating the light." He goes on to report that "in 1869 there was a terrific winter gale. It centered its wrath on Wood Island and mowed a pathway through the beautiful trees....[The] wind blew them down right and left. This made openings through which subsequent gales could sweep and each heavy one took its toll."[60]

Another essayist, Alan Casavant, in a short unpublished paper, "Wood Island Light Station: Keepers of the Light," also pointed to 1869 as the year that a "strong storm sent waves crashing on Wood Island...[and] leveled numerous trees....The ferocity of the storm," he stressed, "and associated winds, [traveled] in a tornado-like path that stretched from one end of the island to the other."[61]

The assertion that a single storm is responsible for stripping the island of its celebrated wooded landscape has no doubt been aided by an obscure legend. The tale appeared in an article published in the magazine section of the *Lewiston Journal* by Alfred Eldon on February 15, 1936, and gained traction when it was reproduced in the *Biddeford Daily Journal* a week later. The story is a strange one involving a light keeper, an angry traveler and a vengeful curse and, in all likelihood, never happened in quite the way it was related by Eldon.[62]

Wood Island Lighthouse

The Gypsy Curse on Wood Island

In 1869, a tribe of Gypsies established themselves in Old Orchard Beach. Edwin Tarbox, the keeper of the Wood Island Lighthouse at the time, was enjoying his day off there when he was swindled out of his month's pay by some gypsy pickpockets. The keeper, infuriated by the scam, informed the local police, who arrested the culprits and forced them to return the unlawful loot. Reporter Elden goes on to relate the enigmatic threat proclaimed by the leader: "To you and yours, to all who ever occupy your accursed island, there shall come a blight. I henceforth put the Gypsy curse on you!"

While the keeper shrugged and smirked triumphantly as he left with his returned money, it may well be that the last laugh actually belonged to the gypsies. For that very night, the legend continues, the infamous gale that targeted Wood Island struck with giant waves that pounded its shores and "swept through the dense woods from which the island received its name. Like ten pins the tall spruces and firs crashed right and left....More than half the woods had been razed." The "Gypsy's Curse," so the myth concludes, will not be lifted as long as the light station on Wood Island remains.[63]

Edwin Tarbox, the eleventh keeper of the Wood Island Light Station (1865–72), was the object of the "Gypsy Curse" in 1869. *FOWIL Archives.*

Alfred Elden, like so many other authors intent on telling a good story, is silent regarding the sources that provide the substance for this compelling tale. There is no question that Wood Island has experienced more than its fair share of tragedy and heartbreak, but it may be a stretch to assign these unfortunate events to an irritated lighthouse keeper, a wrathful gypsy and a vengeful curse.

Relentless Gales

Local newspapers during the period of Keeper Tarbox's service certainly confirm the unsettled weather patterns from 1865 to 1872. In 1866, for example, the *Union and Journal* reported that a storm occurring late in November "was among the most violent of those which rarely happen." Roofs were detached, tarring was stripped from the city building and a post office window crashed in. There were also reports that a steamer had gone ashore near Wood Island. In all, thirty ships were wrecked along the Maine coast due to the storm.[64]

The gales of September and October 1869 seem to have been even more devastating. "But few in this section ever witnessed anything equal to the 'gale' of Wednesday night the 8th inst.," reported the *York County Independent* on September 14, 1869. "It is safe to state that it was the heaviest since 1815." Winds with "tremendous destructive power" were reported to have been terrible at sea and on land, responsible for demolishing buildings and uprooting trees. "Injuries to orchard and gardens were very great throughout the state....Branches were broken off and trees torn up without number." In York County, at least one tornado was spawned.[65] The *York County Independent* reported that the steeple of the Second Parish Church was blown over and that the roof and side of Mr. Verrill's barn at the Pool were blown off. The report continued: "A number of vessels have been stranded; one on Stage Island, one Ram, one Bluff, one sunk on Richmond, one on a reef, bottom up, on Stratton, and three on Old Orchard Beach." The *Maine Democrat* added that "one sloop and two schooners are ashore on Wood Island."[66]

Less than one month later, New England newspapers turned their attention to yet another ferocious storm. The so-called Saxby's Gale on October 4, 1869, brought a strong storm surge that affected rivers and tributaries fifty-five miles inland. Heavy rains of up to six inches created floods and extensively damaged homes throughout the state. The *Maine Democrat* called the harm done by the storm "immense." At the Isle of Shoals, just a few miles down the coast from Wood Island, an "immense tidal wave" did more damage there "than has ever been known before," with the loss of boats being "considerable."[67]

Two years later, on November 14–15, 1871, another fierce gale struck the coast of southern Maine. The *Union and Journal* acknowledged, "The storm that set in about midnight Tuesday, has proved one of the heaviest known hereabouts for many years....This storm has caused the highest tides known for ten years, there being one in 1861 said to have been higher." A schooner laden with 140 tons of coal was dashed onto rocks at Stage Island Point when the gale, reaching near hurricane strength, caused the vessel to drag her anchors. Only the heroic action of local pilots—who included Jacob Verrill, Daniel Charles, Harrison Goldthwait, Charles Hussey and Simon Bunker—risking their own lives, managed to save the crew even while "the sea was making a clean sweep over [the vessel] from fore to aft."[68]

Wood Island Light Station, circa 1880.

The *Union and Journal* reported that the same storm drove three other schooners through the "Gutt" and into the Pool and onto the beach. In addition, the excursion boat *Augusta* broke from her moorings at the Pool and nearly drifted onto the beach before being brought under control, likely undoing much of the finishing work accomplished earlier in May.

Today, the belief persists that the island, once covered with trees and vines, was vastly altered by a single mighty gale (perhaps aggravated by a gypsy's curse) during Keeper Tarbox's tenure. While there is some evidence to underscore this idea (well, not the curse), it nevertheless seems probable that there was no one dramatic storm that caused the entire change. More likely, a series of weather events over a period of several years caused the devastation to the trees that once stood proudly there. Powerful winds and strong surges from the sea, combined with the long-standing practice of cutting trees for both lumber and firewood, all contributed to the transformation that resulted in a "woodless" Wood Island and elicited the comment of the Biddeford Pool Poet during his interview in 1928.

Stories from the Edge of the Sea

An Earthquake Rattles the Glass

A HEAVY SHOCK AT THE POOL.
Wood Island Also Quivered and Shook Like a Huge Jellyfish[69]

A sudden shift in the tectonic plate between five and ten miles below the surface of the earth created an inaudible rumble that rapidly assaulted the earth's crust and announced itself to the terrified inhabitants of Biddeford Pool. Windows and dishes rattled, buildings rocked and houses trembled, providing what their frightened occupants could only describe as a "peculiar sensation." In Mr. F.O. Goldthwaite's grocery store, shelves clattered and the goods on the cases were thrown to the floor and boxes upset. In nearby Portland, a temporary highway bridge spanning the upper harbor made an odd cracking sound, began to sway and eventually gave way with a lurch and sank about six feet.

On Wood Island, the disorientation provided by the earthquake was no less pronounced. Charles Albert Burke had replaced Thomas Orcutt as keeper nearly a year earlier and, like Orcutt, came to his new assignment from Saddleback Ledge Lighthouse, where he had served three years as assistant keeper. Burke was born in Portsmouth, New Hampshire, on February 10, 1877, and was twenty-nine years old when he arrived at Wood Island. His father, James Monroe Burke, was the light keeper at the Nubble Light in 1912. For two years (1912–14), both father and son were attending lighthouses at the same time, approximately thirty miles apart. Wood Island's recently appointed keeper and his new wife, Carrie Emma, were fully aware of what life on a light station entailed, but probably nothing could have prepared them for this unexpected act of nature.

"Wood Island Rocks and Keeper Rows to Biddeford Pool" read the headline in the *Boston Globe* on October 21, 1906. Indeed, following the tremor, Burke took to his dory, rowing the better part of a mile to the Pool, where he described the sensation as different from anything he had ever experienced and

Keeper Charles Albert Burke (1905–14) reported that the island shook like a leaf during the earthquake of October 1906. *FOWIL Archives.*

"declared that the island shook like a leaf" for one to two seconds. He went on to report the rocking to and fro to be like "the shaking of gelatin pudding" before settling back into place again.[70]

Although earthquakes are not as rare in Maine as one would expect, most are minor and go unfelt. The quake of 1906 was an exception. And although there were no lives lost and very little significant damage resulted, it served as a rude welcome to the fourteenth keeper of the Wood Island Light Station.

Chapter 5

THE HEROISM OF EBENEZER "EBEN" EMERSON

1861–65

Residents of Biddeford were undoubtedly saddened to wake up on the morning of March 12, 1897, and read the obituary that appeared in their morning paper announcing the death of Ebenezer "Eben" Emerson (1814–1897).[71] "Uncle Eben" had been a fixture in Biddeford for the better part of his life and played a critical role in its evolution from a sleepy town to the fourth-largest city in the state. He began his early working life as a sailor, turning later toward farming and then lumbering. Several years following his marriage in 1836, he moved to Biddeford, where he established his family and distinguished himself first as a constable in the town and eventually as a deputy marshal. His ardent support of William Henry Harrison (Old Tippecanoe) in the election of 1840 and passionate advocacy of abolitionism confirmed his loyalty to the Whig and Republican Parties and generated a reputation that ultimately reached the office of President Lincoln, who appointed him the tenth keeper of the Wood Island Lighthouse in 1861.

As keeper of the light during one of the most trying periods in our history, Eben Emerson's role was affected by matters stretching far beyond the reefs and ledges of York County. The bitter campaign and eventual election of Abraham Lincoln to the presidency in 1860 made the national rupture that followed inevitable. By 1861, with the onset of the Civil War, Maine's political landscape reflected those national tensions and was characterized equally by turmoil and confusion. Divisions over prohibition, abolition, states' rights and nativism had sown discord throughout the state. And because much of

Maine's prosperity had come from commercial shipping interests that were heavily invested in transporting southern cotton to New England textile mills, there was a good deal of support and sympathy for the Confederate cause. Consequently, the Union's "Anaconda Policy," calling for a blockade of southern ports, caused serious disruption to Maine's economic well-being. Bath shipyards were launching half the number of vessels in 1861 when compared to each year during the decade of the 1850s. As the war at sea continued, the Confederate steam sloop of war *Alabama* sank over fifty U.S. vessels—eleven of them from Maine.

As the residents of Biddeford continued to read his obituary on that March morning in 1897, many would have been reminded of Keeper Emerson's heroism during his tenure at the Wood Island Lighthouse. At 1:00 a.m. on the morning of March 16, 1865, Eben Emerson had just completed trimming the lamps in the lantern room when he stepped outside to appraise the state of a rapidly intensifying storm. In the distance, he heard the sound of voices in distress and recognized immediately that a ship had gone aground on Washburn Ledge, about five hundred yards southeast of the lighthouse. Perhaps he was thinking of the tragedy that befell the *Bohemian*, a brig that wrecked on Cape Elizabeth the previous year with the loss of forty-two souls, as he launched into action.[72]

The *Union Journal* of March 31 described the daring rescue as follows:

> *Mr. Emerson, keeper of the light house on Wood Island, got up to trim his lamp, and going to the door to observe the weather he thought he heard amid the roar of the breakers a human voice. Hastily dressing himself he launched his wherry, but found his utmost strength unable to pull the boat through the surf. Arousing a neighbor they pulled through the thick fog in the direction of the sounds and finally came alongside the brig, which he boarded after many vain attempts owing to the breakers, which ran nearly forty feet high. One of the brig's boats was launched and immediately swamped. The other was hung up on the davits into which the crew were placed with the captain at the fore and the mate in the stern with orders to cut loose when the order should be given. Mr. Emerson's comrade then attempted to bring the wherry near to the brig to take him off. The tenth attempt was successful by a leap of about ten feet. They then pulled as near as they could to the hanging boat and swinging a rope to the boat's crew, as a high sea came the order was given to cut loose, and fortunately they arrived safe to land, but before landing the brig went to pieces....*

Stories from the Edge of the Sea

>...*Just before leaping from the wreck he thought he heard a sound in the cabin, and going below he found two white little Guinea pigs which he hastily thrust into his pocket and rescued.*[73]

The harrowing rescue was formally recognized the following month by the British government. Keeper Eben Emerson was honored for his intrepid courage with a gift of binoculars contained in an inscribed wooden case. "The glass is the most powerful of any we have ever seen," reports the *Union Journal*, which then goes on to quote a portion of the letter that the British minister wrote to the secretary of state:

> *Her Majesty's Consul at Portland has reported to my Government the humane and gallant conduct of Mr. Eben Emerson, keeper of the lighthouse at Wood Island, near that port, who rescued the master and crew of the British brig "Edyth Ann," of Digby, in Nova Scotia, from a situation of imminent danger on the night of the 16th of March last. The "Edyth Ann" had gone on shore near Wood Island, and shortly became a total wreck; and, had it not been for the timely aid rendered by Mr. Emerson, would probably have perished.*[74]

The British consul's official recognition of Emerson's bravery is contained in the following letter that accompanied the gift and was addressed to the collector of customs in Portland with a request to pass it and the binoculars on to Emerson:

> *Sir; I have caused to be transmitted to you by Hamden and Co., Exporters, a box containing a binocular glass which the British Government desires to present to Mr. Eben Emerson the Keeper of the Lighthouse on Wood Island, on account of services rendered by him to the Master and crew of the British Brig "Edyth Ann" of Digby, Nova Scotia on the night of the 16th of March, last. Enclosed herewith a copy of a note from Sir Frederick W.A. Bruce, her Britannic Majesty's Minister residing here, which, together with the Glasses, I will thank you to forward to Mr. Emerson without unnecessary delay.*
>
> *I am, Sir, Your Obedient servant*
> *W. Hunter, Acting Secretary*[75]

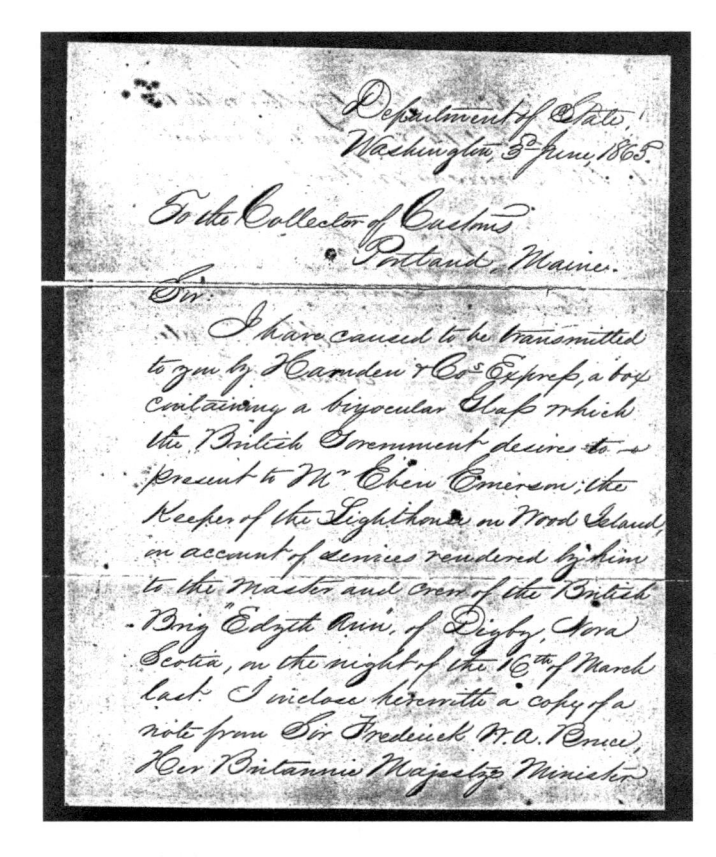

Left: The British consul commended Keeper Eben Emerson for his actions on the night of March 16, 1865. *FOWIL Archives.*

Below: Keeper Emerson was presented with a pair of "binocular glasses" in recognition of his heroic actions that saved the lives of crew members on the brig *Edyth Ann*. *FOWIL Archives.*

Eben Emerson left Wood Island after five years. He and his wife returned for a time to a life of farming and lumbering and dedication to his family. Even as a farmer, Emerson's inclination to assist in municipal and civic affairs constantly called him back into service to his community.

During his retirement, Emerson continued to advocate for his principles, never reluctant to "raise his voice in enunciation of any subject." In December 1896, shortly before his death, his followers and friends celebrated his life and advocacy by presenting him with a hat and a pair of gloves: "Uncle Eben Emerson wears a brand new hat today, the gift of 'the boys' who presented it to the Tippecanoe veteran as a campaign souvenir."[76]

When Emerson's long life and commendable career finally came to an end in March 1897, his admirers remembered him primarily as "a man of sterling character [who] enjoyed the respect and esteem of many friends."[77] Today, he rests with his wife, Susan, in a family plot in the Greenwood Cemetery in Biddeford, Maine.

Chapter 6

TRIALS AND TRIUMPHS OF ALBERT NORWOOD

1872–86

It would seem like his advantages would provide a promising start for Albert Norwood, the twelfth keeper of the Wood Island Light Station. Albert, second-to-youngest son of Abraham, was born on December 13, 1823, and likely was among the five youngest children who came to the lighthouse when his father assumed his role as keeper in 1833. For the next eight years, he would live the life of a lighthouse keeper's son. Like many such lads, Albert would have aided his father in setting lobster traps and fishing to supplement their family's livelihood. He would also have assisted with the routine maintenance and repairs to the buildings, sheds and walkways required by the constant exposure to sun and sea; the splitting and hauling of wood; chores related to the family's small island farm; and other general work around the grounds and living spaces. When his father was replaced as keeper in 1841 by John Adams, young Albert chose to set out for the next thirty years to make a living from the sea as a fisherman.

Albert Norwood was fifty years old in 1872 when he and his wife, Mary, moved from their family home on Pool Road just below Ferry Lane to the light station's residence on Wood Island. Prior to his lighthouse service, he appears on the Civil War Draft Registration as a sailor. Later, the U.S. Census indicates that he returned to fishing for his livelihood. Little is known of his life prior to coming to Wood Island, but records compiled by his descendants indicate that he was introduced to tragedy when he was quite young. By the age of ten, he had experienced the death of his brother Edwin and two of

Stories from the Edge of the Sea

This detail of the Wood Island Station includes the granite light tower, toolshed and pyramid-shaped bell tower. *Maine Maritime Museum.*

his sisters, Ann and Mary. At age fourteen, he lost another sister, Eleanor. His parents both passed away before he reached the age of thirty. Four other sisters—Augusta, Susan, Abigail and Hester—would all die before Albert received his appointment to Wood Island.

As the son of a former lighthouse keeper, it would have been expected that Norwood might have impressed his supervisors as he set about tending the light on Wood Island. And yet, a report filed three years after Norwood assumed his duties unfortunately concluded, "The station is neglected. Keeper not keeping it in the order it should be."[78] Despite this inauspicious review, for the entire fourteen years of his appointment, Keeper Albert Norwood's actions would demonstrate a pattern of dedication to duty that would wholly contradict this early assessment and bring honor to himself and the Lighthouse Service.

Norwood's performance evaluation was part of a larger report submitted in 1875 that offers a description of the station and reservation to which the new keeper and his family were assigned. This official account suggests that the tower and residence had not changed since the reconstruction in 1857–58, with one notable exception: "a pyramidal frame structure, painted white, [which] stands East of tower 15 feet, on the East face of which is a bell struck by Steven's Machine."[79] The *Biddeford Daily Evening Times* had earlier alerted its readers about the new addition on August 4, 1873: "The government have [*sic*] the fog bell in successful operation on Wood Island, and it can be plainly heard at the Pool. The bell is rung by machinery located in a pyramid shaped building between the lighthouse and the water. The bell strikes every fifteen seconds—or rather strikes once, then after fifteen seconds strikes twice."[80]

For the Norwood family, this new development must have generated a bit of excitement and relief. Prior to the development and widespread use of clockwork mechanisms, fog warnings were first indicated with cannon shots and later with hand-struck bells. The latter required the presence of the keeper or an assistant to physically strike the bell periodically with a sledgehammer until the fog lifted. During extended periods of fog, family members were often enlisted to assist in this arduous task. Now, with the introduction of the automatic striker, Keeper Norwood and his family helpers needed only to wind the clock mechanism—generally a ten-minute undertaking that would allow for approximately four hours of operation.

Three Vessels Went Ashore Southeast of Wood Island

Often, family members were called upon to participate in the life of the lighthouse keeper in ways that could not be anticipated. Such an occasion occurred as Christmas approached in the first year of Keeper Albert Norwood's appointment. On December 26, 1872, the *Daily Times* in Biddeford reported, "Three vessels went ashore on Beach Island, east of the Pool and southeast of Wood Island last Tuesday evening about 7 o'clock."[81] Apparently, the mishap resulted when the Wood Island Light was confused with the Cape Elizabeth Light in the heavy mist. The three vessels originally were thought to have been the *Credit*, the *Virginia* and the *General Tuttle*. However, the following day (December 27), the paper corrected its report: "It was the *Intrepid* of Portland and not the *Credit* that went ashore on Beach Island Tuesday night." Further, the reporter writes that "when the light house keeper at Wood Island was informed that a sick lady was on board one of the wrecked schooners, he immediately went to her assistance and she was brought into his house and sat in a chair." Over the course of the next few days, the uninsured *Intrepid* broke apart, with only her rigging and chains being saved. The two other schooners that went ashore on the night of December 24 came off without serious damage or loss of cargo.[82]

On Wood Island, however, matters were becoming quite complicated. Shortly after bringing the captain's wife into the keeper's house, Norwood was asked if there were any children in the house. "Upon being answered in the affirmative he [the captain of the *Intrepid*] informed his benefactor that the lady had the small pox! This undoubtedly created some trepidation as the lady was immediately placed upon a sled and taken to a building at some distance from the lighthouse. An overcoat worn by one of the gentlemen was destroyed soon after."[83] When it was learned that two members of the crew of the *Intrepid* had made their way to the city of Portland, the *Daily Times* editorialized that "the Portland authorities had better look out for them."[84]

The situation could not have arisen at a worse time. In recent weeks, rumors of a smallpox outbreak had spooked residents in the Portland area. At one point, the local paper reported as "unqualifiedly false" allegations that a retail proprietor and one of his clerks had contracted smallpox. As a follow-up to this evident falsehood, a letter from one alarmed citizen cautioned, "It has been falsely reported by some evil-minded person, that we have the small-pox again in our city….How careful people should be in repeating assertions unless properly authenticated."[85]

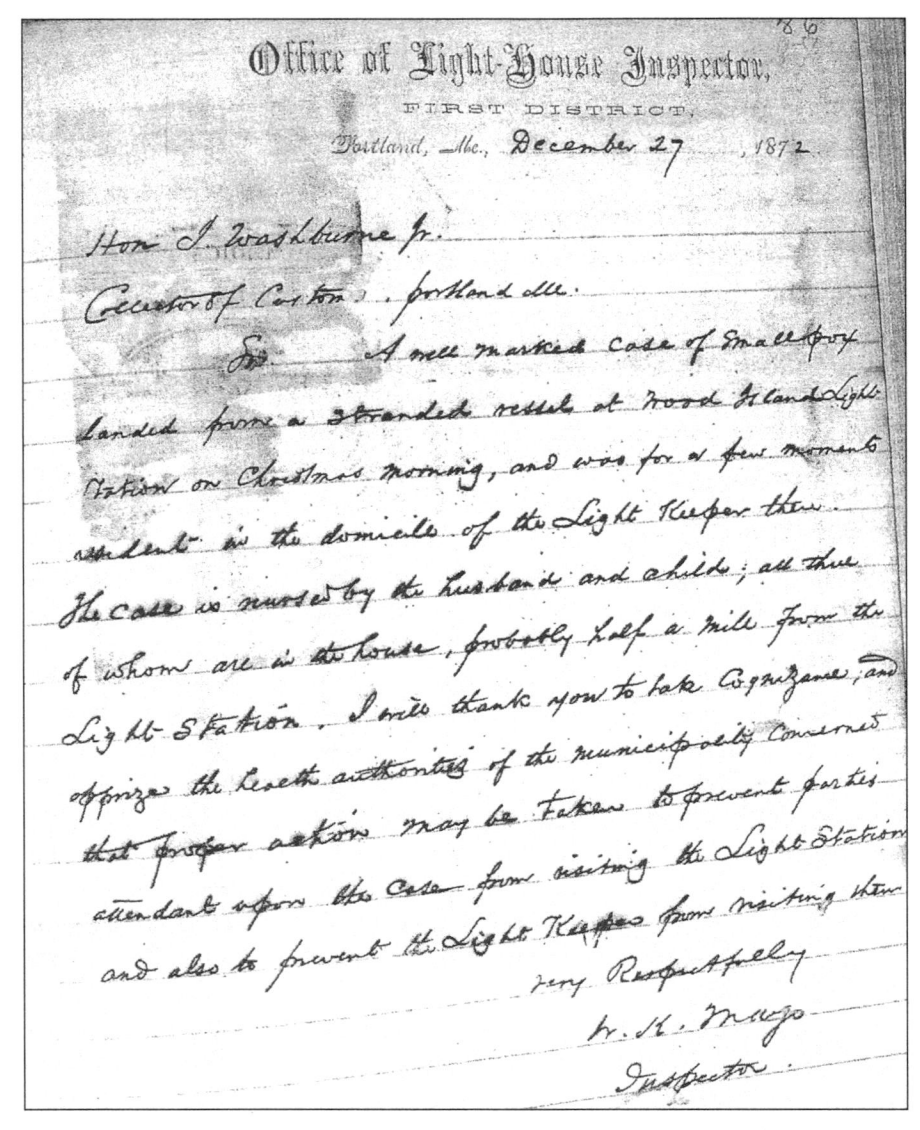

> Office of Light-House Inspector,
> FIRST DISTRICT,
> Portland, Me., December 27, 1872.
>
> Hon. I. Washburne Jr.
> Collector of Customs, Portland Me.
>
> Sir — A well marked case of small pox landed from a stranded vessel at Wood Island Light Station on Christmas morning, and was for a few moments resident in the domicile of the Light Keeper there. The case is nursed by the husband and child; all three of whom are in the house, probably half a mile from the Light Station. I will thank you to take cognizance, and apprize the health authorities of the municipality concerned that proper action may be taken to prevent parties attendant upon the case from visiting the Light Station and also to prevent the Light Keepers from visiting them
>
> Very Respectfully
> W. K. Mayo
> Inspector

Inspector Mayo's letter praising Keeper Norwood and the other "big-hearted coast watchers" who came to the assistance of others while often risking their own well-being. *NARA*.

In such an atmosphere of evident fear fueled by gossip and outright falsehood, it is little wonder that the lighthouse establishment moved quickly to get ahead of this potentially tragic situation. Commander William K. Mayo, inspector of lighthouses for the First District, hastily informed his superiors on the Lighthouse Board in Washington, D.C., as well as the superintendent of lighthouses in Portland, of the incident. "Sir," he wrote to Israel Washburn Jr., the collector of customs, "a well-marked case of smallpox landed from a stranded vessel at Wood Island Light Station on Christmas morning, and was for a few moments resident in the domicile of the Light Keeper there....I will thank you to...aprize [sic] the health authorities of the municipality concerned that proper action may be taken to prevent parties attendant upon the case from visiting the Light Station." In his letter, the inspector was also quick to recognize the courage of Keeper Norwood and all the men employed in the occupation as a whole: "It will be remarked that the hospitality of the Light Keeper was asked for 'a woman freezing to death' in the biting bitter cold. No man could refuse such an appeal. These big-hearted Coast watchers identify themselves with such suffering."[86]

As far as can be determined, neither the keeper of the Wood Island Light, his wife, nor any of his children were negatively affected by this event.

"Captain Norwood Went to the Assistance"

Although smallpox made the situation involving the schooner *Intrepid* somewhat unusual, marine accidents near the lighthouse were not all that uncommon during the years when Albert Norwood tended the light at Wood Island. For example, in March 1874, the schooner *Ossian E. Dodge* went ashore and eventually was dashed to pieces on Beach Island. In June 1875, an unmanned boat came ashore at Wood Island. It was determined that the boat belonged to a man recently drowned off Cape Porpoise. The schooner *Annie Frye* dragged her anchor in October 1878, went ashore and was pounded for four hours on Lobster Rocks, halfway between the Pool ramp and Stage Island. The schooner *S.H. Poole* broke in two when she was wrecked on Stage Island in December 1878. In March 1884, the coal schooner *Abbott W. Lewis* struck a shoal off Wood Island.

It is not always clear what, if any, role the lighthouse keeper played during these unfortunate maritime events. However, one notable exception involved a heartbreaking incident that occurred on September 5, 1877, and received extensive coverage in the *Daily Times*. On that day, five men set out from Factory Island in a nine-foot sailboat, reaching the Pool about noon and, following a noontime snack and a quick swim, decided to "sail around Wood Island and take a look at the lighthouse from the southeastern side." Tragedy followed when they were simultaneously struck and overturned

> **Boat Capsized.**
>
> *Man Drowned off Wood Island.*
>
> A sad accident occurred yesterday afternoon by which John Maloney, a young man well known in this city, lost his life. Yesterday morning a belt broke in one of the York mills, Saco, and five of the men employed in the glazing room—John Maloney, his brother James, Michael Higgins and Patrick Dean of Biddeford and William McLellan of Saco—thought a good opportunity was afforded them of having a sail, so one of them procured a boat and they started down river and reached the Pool about noon. After dining, bathing and enjoying themselves until about three o'clock they started for home. A desire seized some of the occupants of the boat to sail around Wood Island and take a look at the lighthouse from the southeastern side. This was agreed to and there being a good stiff breeze they went along well and passing between the Pool and the Island were soon abreast of the light and heading northeasterly. Observing breakers ahead they attempted to bring the vessel about when the sail hung loose, and there being a heavy swell at the time, before it filled again one of the waves or else a sudden puff overturned the boat and the five men were in the ocean about half a mile outside of the Island. The boat was round bottom with center board and afforded little chance for the men to cling to it. However, McLellan and Higgins caught hold of it, while the other three started to swim ashore. John Maloney was an excellent swimmer and took the lead, followed by

An article from the *Daily Times* (September 6, 1877) reporting the accident that resulted in the drowning of John Maloney.

by a strong gust of wind and a heavy swell. Struggling in the frigid Maine water, two of the men tenuously grasped the centerboard of the craft, while the other three started to swim the half mile to the shore of Wood Island. John Maloney and his brother James "continually shouted for 'help' and John threw his arms out of water and endeavored to signal persons at the light-house. A boy was observed to come out and then start off across the island. It afterward appeared he went across to the wharf where Capt. Norwood was with the boats and summoned him to aid the men and he started in his boat." Fatigued and likely suffering from near-hypothermia, three of the men managed to struggle to safety while Captain Norwood "went to the assistance of William McClellan who declined to swim ashore and instead managed to cling to the swamped boat. Taking him on board and making fast to the overturned craft, [they] soon reached the shore [where] Capt. Norwood and family cared tenderly for the men [and] procured dry clothing for them." Later, they were taken by boat to the Saco Ferry.[87]

John Maloney, the fifth sailor, while attempting to swim ashore, disappeared under the water. "It was thought that the man must have become exhausted and sunk through his frantic efforts to summon aid." A few days after the incident, on September 12, this gruesome notice appeared in the *Daily Times*: "The body of John Maloney was found off Wood Island yesterday forenoon by a son of Capt. Norwood, the light house keeper. The body was first discovered very near where Maloney was seen to disappear and Mr. Norwood put out in a boat for its recovery. It was fast being floated away from the island. The face and head was very much battered, indicating that the heavy sea had beat it about upon the rocks."[88]

A month later, on Tuesday, October 9, 1877, in the "Jottings" section of the *Daily Times*, this short notice appeared: "Capt. Norwood, light keeper on Wood Island, has been presented with a heavy whale bone cane." Although it is not specified, we might assume that the gift was in recognition of his valiant response during the tragedy that occurred on September 5.[89]

"Compass Was of Little Account"

Another harrowing, though less tragic, affair occurred nearly two years later in April 1879. A heavy fog and mist set in during the overnight period leading into the morning of Sunday, April 6. Three seamen from the Philadelphia brig *Lige Houghton* arrived on Wood Island in a small boat and alerted Keeper Norwood that their ship "lay about two miles to the eastward and was in distress." The *Union and Journal* reported what happened next: "Captain Norwood and his two sons went out with them. The men gave the locality of their brig as near as they were able and they succeeded in finding her. Her compass was of little account. The brig had shifted her cargo between decks, and lost her anchor. After some trouble they worked her into the lower harbor where she was taken to Portland by a tug."[90]

Family Matters

By the spring of 1886, with his health increasingly becoming an issue, Keeper Albert Norwood decided to pass the torch. On May 13, 1886, readers of the *Biddeford Daily Journal* would have seen this notice: "Capt. Albert Norwood, who has so faithfully attended to the Wood Island Light for the last thirteen years, has resigned and moved back to his old homestead. May his future pathway be lighted as bright as day even to the pearly gate."[91]

Albert Norwood, the twelfth keeper of the Wood Island Light Station, passed away just a little over two years after leaving his post on Wood Island. On August 11, 1888, he was sixty-four years old. For the Norwood clan, however, the lighthouse-keeping legacy would continue.

Abraham and Albert, father and son, were followed in their role as lighthouse keepers by later generations of Norwoods who also found they were similarly called to the service. Albert's grandson Ralph C. Norwood, born in 1904, later became an assistant to the keeper of the nation's oldest lighthouse on Brewster Island in Boston Harbor. When the Coast Guard took over responsibility for maintaining the nation's light stations in 1939,

Ralph immediately enlisted, and when Keeper Babcock, the primary keeper, retired in 1941, Norwood was appointed keeper in his place. His large family later gained notoriety when Norwood's wife gave birth to their seventh child. The little girl, Georgia, became a sensation when author Ruth Carmen dramatized her birth in a novel titled *Storm Child* (1937).

Finally, by the time Ralph Norwood's son LaForest (Gail) Norwood became the keeper of a lighthouse in Nova Scotia, the impressive Norwood family had contributed four generations of lighthouse keepers to a selfless profession dedicated to saving lives and property. Truly, their descendants can proudly declare that keeping a lighthouse has, for the Norwoods, been a family affair.

Chapter 7

OF DOGS AND MEN

1886–1905

The gentle fog misting along the top of the rock-bound island's shoreline did little to obscure the bright summer sun casting its warmth on the napping dog. Without warning, Sailor's nostrils flared and his ears perked to attention. His intelligent brown eyes snapped open as if called to order, yet no obvious provocation had induced his awareness. Still, here he was, now on all fours, readying himself thoughtfully for the task he was obligated to perform—one he had grasped years ago and had executed dozens of times.

Thomas Orcutt, Sailor's master and the thirteenth keeper of the Wood Island Lighthouse, smiled at his four-footed longtime companion in anticipation. Keeper Orcutt took over the light station duties in 1886 and had remained there until this late summer day in 1905. He was fifty-three years old when he moved onto the island with his forty-five-year-old wife, Hannah, and five children, who ranged in age from seven to nineteen. He had been a sea captain and, just prior to his appointment to Wood Island, served as first assistant keeper at the Saddleback Ledge Lighthouse, one of the "loneliest, most miserable assignments of all." Wood Island must have been a significant improvement, as his extended service of nineteen years there proved to be the second-longest term of any keeper.

Of his five children, it is unlikely that in 1886, the oldest two—Annie, age seventeen, and Nelson, age nineteen—lived with their parents on the island for very long, if at all. The other three—Mattie (eleven years old), Minnie Estelle (nine years old) and George (seven years old)—grew up under the watchful eyes of their parents and the lighthouse, which guarded the bustling community that thrived around them. Like the lighthouse keepers who came before, the Orcutts supplemented their $600 yearly salary by tending the farm and barn animals contained on the government reservation and by fishing the abundant waters of Saco Bay.

A letter written by Minnie in 1889 when she was about twelve years old reveals some detail regarding their life at the Wood Island Light Station. She describes her island home as consisting of forty acres, eight of which belong to the government. The light, she writes, is a "red flash light," and the granite tower is forty-eight feet high and has sixty-two steps going up to the light where "there are two lamps weighing 16 lbs. each, we burn them one at a time, change in the middle of the night."[92]

Portrait of a youthful Thomas Orcutt dressed in the formal uniform of the Lighthouse Service. *FOWIL Archives.*

Minnie remarks that the boathouse is "half a mile" from the station and that the shore, where they go for the mail, is a mile away. "My sisters and I," she declares, "…have a boat of our own….In the summer, we often go over and get our mail by ourselves. We enjoy going in the boat very much." Apparently, the young men of Biddeford Pool enjoyed the occasion as well. Carol Orcutt Bassett, a descendant and family biographer, commented, "It is said that the three girls were beautiful, and pictures of them as young women attest to that. When they would row to the mainland the Pool residents would gather to watch and comment, 'Here come the three jewels.'"[93]

Sailor was a lighthouse dog whose reputation reached far beyond the limits of the thirty-five acres (Minnie slightly overestimated the total acreage) that made up his "canine estate" on Wood Island. His sixty pounds were covered mostly in dark brown and black fur ending in a broad, bushy tail. However, his four paws, ankles, elongated nose and throat were an attractive tannish-brown color. His remarkably intense and intelligent eyes were complemented by three fashionably white markings on his chest. Some would call him a mutt, but those who grew to know him recognized his proud Scotch-Collie heritage.

The puppy was barely two months old in 1890 when he was adopted and brought to the island from a milk farm in Westbrook, Maine. Sailor was forced

Stories from the Edge of the Sea

The attractiveness of the Orcutt daughters was not lost on the local fishermen, who nicknamed them the "Three Jewels." *From left*: Minnie Estelle, Mattie and Annie. *FOWIL Archives.*

to quickly shed his farming legacy and adapt to a life surrounded by rocks, seagulls and pounding surf. Although the puppy was originally intended to be a playmate for Orcutt's young children, little Sailor nevertheless decided that the keeper himself was to be his master and "role model." In an interview with the *Philadelphia Inquirer*, Orcutt reported, "I brought him here when he was but a few weeks old and for want of better amusement he would follow me around the place as I performed my various duties."[94]

Now at the keeper's feet, Sailor began to wag his tail. Keeper Orcutt was well aware that the dog's intuition and long years of service had once again alerted him to the approaching ship—this time the lighthouse tender *Geranium*—now clearly visible in the sea smoke as it advanced from the west. Sure enough, as soon as the ship was within a few hundred yards of the island, the tender's captain saluted the lighthouse by blowing his steam whistle three short blasts. In response, Sailor charged toward the pyramid-shaped wooden structure that housed the mechanism for the shiny 1,200-pound bell that hung a few feet above the partially covered timbered platform. Grabbing the cord in his strong jaw, he gave the passing tender one, two, three gongs in response to the captain's salute.

One summer day in 1901, several years after Sailor had become proficient and dependable in his bell-ringing skills, a small yacht approached and signaled the lighthouse in the usual fashion. Keeper Orcutt, fully expecting

Sailor leads Keeper Orcutt and companion as they approach the station, circa 1890. *NARA*.

Sailor to take charge, sent his dog to salute with the fog bell. George Orcutt, the keeper's son, continues the story:

> *The dog was gone several minutes and my father, not hearing the bell, which never failed to ring started to go and see what was the matter. He had not reached the door before Sailor was upon him, looking up at him in mute appeal. I happened to be in the room and I heard and saw what occurred. "Sailor," said my father, reaching for a stick in the corner, "if you don't go and ring that bell this minute, I will whip you." My father shook the whip in Sailor's face as he spoke, and the dog slunk off down towards the station with his tail between his legs. Father hadn't more than returned the stick to the corner before the dog was back again. This time Sailor hung his head and would not look up until my father had again reached for the stick when he went away as before. We were wondering what could have happened to poor Sailor that he could have so lost his wits, when all at once we heard him at the door whining to be let in. My father left his chair, and what do you suppose we saw? There was Sailor looking as if he had lost his best friend, and holding the broken bell rope between his teeth. The rope had been parted in some way during the previous night and this was the way Sailor had of informing us.*

Keeper Orcutt looks on as Sailor rings the fog bell in greeting as a ship enters Wood Island Harbor. *FOWIL Archives.*

Hastily, the cord was repaired, grasped firmly in Sailor's teeth, and the bell was finally rung. Undoubtedly, that evening Sailor received an extra serving of his favorite dog food![95]

Sailor, Wood Island's lighthouse dog, stood at the forefront of a considerably long list of Maine's other lighthouse dogs that managed well-earned reputations. For example, in 1902, Smut, the keeper's pooch at Two Bush Lighthouse near Vinalhaven, Maine, managed to alert his master that the fishing schooner *Clara Bella* had driven onto the rocks in a raging storm. His efforts came just in time to save the two sailors who had become stranded on the rocks surrounded by the pounding surf. And Spot, another canine with an uncanny ability to ring the fog bell, resided at Owl's Head Light near Rockland, Maine. One frightful snowy evening, the bell had become

Sailor's reputation stretched across the Atlantic. The *Strand Illustrated Magazine* of London portrayed the lighthouse dog as a "blurred mass of fur" when he rang the bell. *FOWIL Archives.*

hopelessly muffled and inaudible because of the piles of snow surrounding it. The sound of the noisy mailboat's familiar motor alerted Spot as the boat became dangerously close to shore. The dog bolted from the house, discovered he could not ring the bell and began barking nonstop. Captain Ames, who had become disoriented in the storm, heard the barking dog, determined his position and was able to steer well clear of the rocky island. Captain Ames and his thankful wife credited Spot with preventing a disaster.

Sailor's dazzling skills created a popular following and a reputation that only intensified over the fifteen years that he and Keeper Orcutt tended the lighthouse together. The *Weekly Standard* in Biddeford, Maine, proudly announced that "Captain Orcutt, keeper of the Wood Island light, has a

Keeper Orcutt and Sailor take a break from lighthouse duties as an unidentified observer watches in the background, circa 1890. *NARA*.

dog whose intelligence borders on the human."[96] In 1896, the *Stevens Point Journal*, a newspaper in central Wisconsin, featured Sailor in an article and an accompanying, though fanciful, illustration titled "Clever Canine Employed at Wood Island Lighthouse." The reporter quipped, "The patient animal rings the bell without complaining [and]…has never been known to desert his post."[97] In 1900, the *Atlanta Constitution* also celebrated Sailor's talents when it ran an article reporting "a real 'dog watch' is kept on Wood Island Lighthouse, of Biddeford Pool, Me. Sailor is the name of the faithful collie who keeps vigil there for passing craft."[98] Even London, England, was not too distant to recognize Sailor's extraordinary gift. In the spring issue of the *Strand Illustrated Magazine*, an image of Sailor ringing the Wood Island fog bell accompanied an article that began, "The blurred mass of fur seen in the accompanying photograph represents a shepherd's dog at Wood Island, Maine, ringing the fog bell with a rope held between his teeth."[99]

In 1905, after nineteen years as keeper of Wood Island Light and with Sailor beginning to show signs that he also was ready for retirement, Thomas Orcutt sensed that it was time to step down. The partnership enjoyed by the keeper and his four-legged companion had endured nearly every circumstance and occupational hazard that could confront a lighthouse keeper and his valued canine assistant. With his family in agreement, Thomas Henry Orcutt handed responsibility for the lighthouse over to his son-in-law, Levi Jeffers, at the end of September 1905. Then he, Sailor and Hannah left the island to live in Biddeford Pool. Less than one month later, Sailor, no longer able to ring his beloved fog bell as a welcome to passing ships, died in the arms of his master and longtime companion. The *Lewiston Journal* suggested in Sailor's obituary "that he lived and died true to his name from early watch till late at night when the fogs gathered dungeon thick about the little fog station."[100] A few years earlier, in 1900, Orcutt had said of his canine assistant, "Sailor and I are old comrades. Wood Island would be a lonely place if I hadn't had the dog to keep me company."[101]

Six short months later, Thomas Henry Orcutt was taken to his bed complaining of ailments described at the turn of the century as "the grippe." A week and a half later, on March 10, 1906, he passed away. He was seventy-three years old at the time of his death and today rests with other members of the Orcutt family in Laurel Hill Cemetery in Saco, Maine. He is remembered in his obituary as being "well known among the sea faring men and was well liked by all."[102] However, perhaps the most fitting epitaph is attributed to his grandson, who, shortly following Orcutt's funeral and noticing the light in the lighthouse, said, "There's the Lighthouse. That's the old home and I guess that's where Grandpa is."[103]

A portrait of Keeper Thomas Henry Orcutt (1886–1905), the thirteenth keeper of the Wood Island Lighthouse. *FOWIL Archives.*

Chapter 8

THE MURDER HOUSE ON WOOD ISLAND

1896–1921

A handwritten note just below the photograph that appears on the following page reads:

The "Murder House" on Wood Island, Biddeford, 1921. This house stood on the end of Wood Island nearest Biddeford. It was known as the "Milliken House" but was abandoned before 1870. It was the scene of the murder of a Biddeford Pool lobsterman sometime in June 1896, and the murderer committed suicide nearby. Thereafter it was known as a haunted place.
J. Vaughan Dennett[104]

The scorched remains of this old house, staring out from a small rise on an island in Saco Bay, convey the eerie impression that there is something sinister hiding behind those blackened walls. Titled "The Murder House," the photograph taken in 1921 resides in an archival box in the company of other vintage images stored in the McArthur Library in Biddeford, Maine. The muted gray tones feature a soulless, deteriorating structure on the verge of collapse despite its commanding presence in the composition atop a slight incline. Below, a hauntingly sparse foreground is dotted with lifeless trees, which threaten an anonymous ghost-like figure apparently hesitant to move any closer to the building itself. It is an intriguing photograph whose sinister title and spectral atmosphere invite an exploration into events that have greatly impacted the history of Wood Island and its frequently visited lighthouse.

The Murder House. *McArthur Library, photo by J. Vaughan Dennett.*

Almost as well known as the light station are the essential elements that form the basis for the tale of the unfortunate murder and suicide that occurred there in 1896. Memory of the details of the fateful incident that happened in the shadow of the "Murder House," however, has faded with time. And even less is remembered of the heartbreak that followed in the next twenty-five years. It's in the telling of the full story that the viewer comes to appreciate the unsettling feeling that stalks the image residing in the McArthur Library.

"Rum Did It"

Frederick W. Milliken was thirty-three years old in 1892, about seven years younger than his new bride, when he established his home on the southwestern end of Wood Island. Milliken's wife, Isabella, brought along her three teenage sons from a previous marriage. Her first husband, Freeman Doane Rich, had been a popular and successful Biddeford Pool fisherman who passed away in 1892. Milliken was also a fisherman who earlier had been appointed as a special officer and game warden. He was a large and powerful man, capable, it was said, of carrying his dory on his shoulders.

Fred Milliken's new family would live in the house that had been erected on a small knoll looking out at Gooseberry Island and the harbor leading to the entrance to Biddeford Pool.

The home likely belonged to Michael Milliken, a distant relative who had purchased the property in 1887 from his deceased brother Francis's wife, Margaret. Aside from the government buildings attached to the lighthouse, the dwelling stood alone on Wood Island, save for a hennery about two hundred yards away. It was in this transformed and rickety living space that Frederick Milliken's two tenants, William Moses and Howard Hobbs, made their home.

Milliken's renters were each about twenty-three years old. Their livelihood was scraped together by combining fishing and seal hunting with odd jobs, some obtained with the assistance of Hobbs's half-brother Wylie in Old Orchard Beach. Both Hobbs and Moses had reputations as vagabonds and were described by the local newspaper as "intemperate" in their drinking habits.

On Sunday, May 31, 1896, Hobbs and Moses left Wood Island in their dory and headed for the pier at Camp Ellis. From there, they made their way to Old Orchard Beach determined to celebrate their "day of rest" with an ample amount of alcohol. By evening, they had created enough of a disturbance to attract the attention of Deputy Sheriff Duff. The officer confronted the two men and threatened to lock them up but eventually gave in to their entreaties and dismissed them on the condition that they would cause no more trouble. They agreed and were not heard from again during the rest of the night.

The following morning, Monday, June 1, the pair began making their way back to their shanty on Wood Island, but not without picking up where they left off the night before in the consumption of alcohol. They left Old Orchard Beach around noon and followed the route of the "Dummy Railroad" paralleling the beach on their return to Camp Ellis. Once again giddy under the influence of liquor, they reached their boat and began rowing back to the island, stopping along the way at Hill's Beach. It was between 3:00 and 4:30 p.m. when they reached the boat landing on the western end of Wood Island.

William Moses was a witness to what happened next. He told a reporter from Biddeford's *Evening Record* that shortly after their arrival at the island, he accompanied Hobbs to their henhouse dwelling. While there, Hobbs told Moses that he wanted to see Milliken and picked up his .44-caliber repeating rifle, claiming that he might be able to shoot a bird. Despite being urged to leave the weapon behind, Hobbs took it with him as he left to knock on the door of the home of Mr. and Mrs. Frederick Milliken. Mrs. Milliken informed the men that Fred was not at home but would be returning soon.

Hobbs met Milliken a few seconds later just outside the fence in front of the Milliken house. According to Moses, Milliken asked if the gun was loaded. When Hobbs responded that it didn't matter, Milliken went into his house, returning a few minutes later with his vest displaying his policeman's badge. "I'll see whether the gun is loaded or not," announced the deputy. When he had come to within a few yards of his tenant, Hobbs raised his rifle, and it discharged. Moses was not able to say if it was intentional or an accident. He could only say, "I know he wouldn't have shot him if he hadn't been drunk and I don't believe he would if Fred hadn't come for him as though he meant to take the rifle away from him."[105]

Isabella Milliken, hearing the shot, ran from her house "and got to the gate just as my husband staggered to the ground and helped him into the house." Hobbs followed Mrs. Milliken into the house. When the wounded man's wife threatened to take the rifle, Hobbs became aggressive, saying, "If you come a step toward me I'll put a hole through you." When his demeanor suddenly turned and he became remorseful, Mrs. Milliken asked that he make his way to the lighthouse and inform Keeper Thomas Orcutt of what had transpired.[106]

Hobbs arrived at the keeper's doorstep and found him at home. He hastily provided an account of what had occurred and then hurried back to the scene of the shooting. It took only a few minutes for Hobbs's return from the lighthouse. When he arrived, he immediately inquired as to the condition of Mr. Milliken, proclaiming that "he wouldn't have shot him if he hadn't been drunk." Mrs. Milliken reported that he then left again, only to return about a half hour later and ask once more how her husband was. "'My husband is dead,' said I, and he walked off towards his house and that was the last I saw of him."[107]

In the meantime, Keeper Orcutt, responding to Hobbs's alarming story, followed Hobbs from the lighthouse only to arrive at the Milliken home to find the wounded man in his last dying moments. Orcutt was helpless to assist except in giving comfort to Mrs. Milliken. A report filed the following day in the *Biddeford Evening Record* suggests that Orcutt's involvement was anything but routine. "That Hobbs was in a murderous mood," writes the reporter, "is further shown by his threat to shoot Mrs. Milliken and similar threats which he made upon the lighthouse keeper's life."[108]

Meanwhile, William Moses, who had gone to Biddeford Pool with one of the Milliken sons to telephone for medical assistance, returned to the island. When asked what happened next, he recounted that he immediately went to their shack "and looked into the house. I couldn't see Howard and I called out his name. I didn't get an answer and I came up here into the loft and found him laying as you see him now, dead, with the rifle beside him and the bullet hole through his head."[109]

Dr. O'Neil arrived just before seven o'clock expecting to attend to the victim of an accidental shooting. Instead, when he discovered that there were two corpses, he contacted the deputy marshal, who later made his way to the scene of the tragedies, joined by W.I. Dennett, the undertaker. Evidence obtained by the interviews they conducted was confirmed by the examinations made by the coroner the following day. Milliken's life was ended when a bullet fired by Howard Hobbs entered his abdomen, struck a rib and lodged near his liver. His killer had later returned to his dwelling and, lying on his back, placed the muzzle of the gun near his temple and pulled the trigger. The officials concluded that there was no need for an inquest.

The version of the story told by Mrs. Milliken was consistent with that of William Moses, the only witnesses to the event. In spite of vague, unsupported rumors of previous tension, Isabella Milliken affirmed that there had not been any trouble between her husband and Howard Hobbs, with the possible exception of overdue payments for the rent.

Because the coroner declared no need for an inquest following the murder-suicide, William Moses was not held and has disappeared from the pages of Biddeford history.

Isabella married her third husband, James McCune, in Biddeford on January 18, 1900. She passed away in 1919 and is buried at the Laurel Hill Cemetery in Saco, Maine.

Thomas Orcutt continued in his role as lighthouse keeper on Wood Island for nearly ten more years until his retirement in 1905.

The photograph residing in the McArthur Library in Biddeford was a gift of Mr. J. Vaughan Dennett. The Biddeford coroner, originally under the impression that the case involved a single victim of an accidental shooting, did not immediately make his way to Wood Island but sent a local undertaker in his place to take charge of the body. The name of the undertaker was Walter I. Dennett, a first cousin of J. Vaughan Dennett.

Hobbs's body was transferred to Old Orchard Beach on the evening of June 2 and, after a funeral the following afternoon, was interred.

"Leaps from Window of Saco Hotel"

Following the events of June 1896, the "Murder House" likely stood unoccupied for several years.

In 1905, the heirs of Michael Milliken transferred ownership of the property at the western end of Wood Island to William H. Webber. The new owner purchased two parcels, one consisting of fifteen acres, for $500. For the other, Webber paid just $1 and "other valuable considerations." By 1910, according to an article that ran on September 16 of that year in the *Biddeford Weekly Journal*, Webber could claim ownership of "all of the [island] except for the part owned by the government and occupied by the lighthouse plant."[110]

William H. Webber, his wife and his mother-in-law shared their solitary life on the island with their poultry and sheep. However, Webber's professional life was not limited to raising stock. He was a follower of several other professions, but chief among them was as an agent for the Redpath and Eastern Lyceum Bureau of Boston. As an agent for the Lyceum Bureau, Webber was responsible for arranging Chautauqua-style lectures and, in the course of his professional life, may have come in contact with prominent luminaries of the time including Mark Twain, Edward Everett Hale, Susan B. Anthony, Elizabeth Cady Stanton and others.

Nor was his social life apparently a lonely one. In 1910, the *Biddeford Weekly Journal* celebrated the Webber family's jovial and generous hospitality to be found at their island home. "Friend Webber," the author wrote, "thinks everybody who calls on him is hungry." On one occasion when a party of stranded fishermen was brought ashore, they were treated to a first-class lobster lunch and warned, "Don't spoil your appetite for dinner." Sure enough, after a one- to two-mile walk around the island, they were served a "Rhode Island Red chicken banquet by Mrs. Webber and Mrs. Colwell, her mother."[111]

What seemed on the surface to be an idyllic existence for the family of William H. Webber obscured a darker, more unhappy reality. Periodically, Mr. Webber would suffer from bouts of "derangement." Not long after the article commending his hospitality appeared, Webber found himself in the hospital in Saco following a violent episode in which he made "a good deal of trouble for his attendants [and] was kept in close confinement for about 24 hours." Eventually, he was declared in good health and sent home, where he remained stable until the middle of August 1911.[112]

On Friday evening, August 18, 1911, the doctor was called to Biddeford Pool following concern created by Mr. Webber's behavior. Webber left his

Stories from the Edge of the Sea

Leaps From Window of Saco Hotel

SACO, Aug 21.—William H. Webber, aged 49, jumped from the second story window of the Saco House early today and died three hours later from internal injuries received. He lived on Wood Island and owned all of the island except that part occupied by Wood Island lighthouse.

Mr. Webber while suffering from a mental trouble was taken to a local hospital Friday night and escaped from the institution last night. He went to the Saco House, registered and was assigned to a room. Shortly after midnight he became violent and smashed most of the furniture in his room. Then he broke out a window and jumped to the ground, a distance of about 20 feet. He wore very little clothing. A police officer heard his moans and located him between the hotel and an adjoining building. He was conscious and was taken into the hotel where two physicians attended him. He leaves a widow and one sister.

"Leaps from Window." This short article reveals the circumstances of the unfortunate death of William H. Webber in 1911. *Collections of the Maine Historical Society.* Coll. 2025.

home on Wood Island and, after meeting Dr. Hird at Biddeford Pool, was transported to the Trull Hospital in Biddeford, where he remained for treatment until he slipped away in the early evening two days later. Webber subsequently made his way to the Saco House, where he registered without incident and was assigned to a room on the second floor.

What happened in the next few hours remains unclear, but suddenly, around midnight, Webber became agitated and began to smash the furniture in his room. Whether by accident or intention, he crashed through the window and fell twenty feet to the ground. Two officers standing nearby heard the breaking glass and, following a somewhat circuitous search, discovered Webber, in a sitting position, wearing only a shirt and mumbling that he had slipped on the water and fallen overboard. Hastily, the patrolmen took the victim back to his room and summoned Drs. William and Robert Maybury. The examination revealed no broken bones, and the doctors left with instructions to watch the patient and make him comfortable. The end came about 3:30 a.m., a few hours after the mishap. Webber's death resulted from internal injuries caused by the fall.

Immediately following Webber's death, his remains were taken to the undertaking rooms of Mr. W.I. Dennett, where they were prepared for burial. His funeral was held the following Thursday, August 24, 1911.

The 1911 logbooks of Wood Island Lighthouse keeper Charles Albert Burke have been lost, and therefore, we have no documentary record from that source of the tragedy that befell the keeper's neighbor on Wood Island. There is, however, a scrapbook at the Maine Historical Society that was created from a Wood Island logbook and bears the dates 1905–06. The written entries on many of the pages have been obscured by various newspaper clippings, which evidently contain some meaning and relevance for the scrapbook's creator. On one of the sheets is an article covering the

Webber incident and titled "Leaps from Window of Saco Hotel," suggesting that members of the Burke family were well aware of the misfortune that ended the life of their neighbor.[113]

"House Owned by Mrs. Webber Destroyed Last Sunday Night"

Mrs. Webber continued to spend time at her property on Wood Island following the tragic death of her husband. It appears, however, that increasingly her practice was to limit her stays to the warmer summer months. A notice appearing in the "Home Personals" column of the *Biddeford Weekly Journal* of October 9, 1914, informs us, "Mrs. W.H. Webber has closed her Wood Island home for the winter."[114] And, again, on May 12, 1916, when the region was struck by an electrical storm, Mrs. Webber was reported to be in Watertown, New York, having spent a "part of last summer on Wood Island."[115]

On May 7, 1916, Clifford Blanchard Staples had spent the last year and a half as the lighthouse keeper on Wood Island. His dwelling, located at the far eastern tip of the island, was approximately one-half mile from the property owned by Mrs. Webber. On that day in early May, the light keeper made the most extensive entry into his logbook during his two and one-half years of service on the island (original language retained):

> *May 7. Sunday had extensive thunder storm in afternoon between 4 pm and 6 pm. Quite heavy   first one of season   hit Mrs. Wethers* [sic] *house at western end of island and burnt it to the ground. Fire didn't break out until about 11 pm   Coast Guard crew came over but it was too far gone to save any of contents. Fire didn't spread any   good thing   everything was wet   it would have swept the island and would have been a question about saving the property*[116]

On May 7, a thunderstorm early in the evening hurled rain and lightning in the direction of the western end of Wood Island and the infamous house belonging to Ann C. Webber. It appears that a spark ignited a small blaze and, with the house unoccupied, was allowed to smolder for some time. Later, around 11:00 p.m. that Sunday night, an on-duty member of the lifesaving crew at Fletcher's Neck spotted the fire and notified Captain Staples, who happened to be the light keeper's father. Members of the

Detail of a photograph from 1912. The Webber home and property at the west end of Wood Island can be seen four years prior to the destructive fire of 1916. *McArthur Library.*

lifesaving crew arrived by boat in time to save the Webbers' barn and outbuildings, but the home was engulfed in flames when they arrived and was described as a total loss.

The burned-out shell that remained of the Webber home is the subject of the photograph from 1921 titled "The Murder House."

"It Was Known as a Haunted Place"

The brief commentary that accompanies the photograph of the "Murder House" in the McArthur Library suggests that the incidents that occurred there made it into a "haunted place." Today, all evidence of the structure that once stood at the western end of the island has disappeared, but the rumors of ghosts and unexplained phenomena persist. In the early years of the twenty-first century, the Friends of the Wood Island Lighthouse undertook to investigate these disquieting tales and contracted with the New England Ghost Project to examine lingering allegations of paranormal activity.[117]

On two occasions—September 30, 2005, and again on September 30, 2006—the Ghost Project team arrived on Wood Island fully equipped with digital recorders, heat-sensitive cameras and electromagnetic scanners to aid in their research. They were joined by Maureen Wood, a medium who had hopes of making a connection to any spirits that still reside on the island.

The investigations reported in local newspapers and the *Boston Globe* joined coverage in tabloids as far away as Pennsylvania to deepen the island's characterization as a "haunted place." The report submitted by the New England Ghost Project following their explorations offers an intriguing addition to the island's widespread reputation and the description accompanying the "Murder House" photo itself.

With no prior specific knowledge of the events that originated from the "Murder House," Maureen Wood and her colleagues followed the half-mile path that leads from the boat landing to the site of the Wood Island Light Station. During the course of the late afternoon, the project's researchers explored the lighthouse buildings and deployed their equipment. Then, sometime approaching midnight, Maureen and Ron Kolek, the project's leader, made their way to the lantern room at the top of the tower. There, while Kolek tracked the room temperature as it plummeted, Maureen made contact with the first of several "entities" that the team would greet during their stay at Wood Island.

"I didn't mean to do it," murmured the spirit who had taken possession of the medium, "I didn't mean to do it." Later, a shaken Wood was able to describe the feeling that emanated from the spirit as remorseful and raised the unanswered question of whether the disembodied voice was that of Howard Hobbs, the murderer of Fred Milliken, who later took his own life.

During their investigations at Wood Island, the New England Ghost Project encountered several instances of unexplained phenomena, which included black shadows, bright green lights drifting in the darkness and the image of a human female form captured by the infrared camera. The *Boston Globe*'s interview with Ron Kolek concluded with the inevitable question, to which the Ghost Project's leader responded: "Oh there are ghosts here… can't you feel them?"[118]

"A Picture Is Worth a Thousand Words"

The scorched, disintegrating structure captured by the photographer of the "Murder House" appears intent on keeping its secrets—hiding the tales of life and sorrow that took place in its shadows. But stories of the tragic homicide that played out in the Milliken home, the troubled soul that leaped from a second-story room in Saco and the blaze that brought an end to the legendary dwelling on Wood Island are worth the telling. The solitary figure standing at the bottom of the rise in the photograph appears to be asking the relevant questions. And to reply, spirits have taken up residence in the Wood Island Lighthouse.

Chapter 9

THE FARMER IN THE LIGHTHOUSE

1819–1933

Wood Island Lighthouse keeper Philip Goldthwait had been thinking about a barn for some time. Unlike so many of the lighthouses built in Maine during the nineteenth century, the Wood Island Lighthouse did not include a barn as part of the original plan and construction in 1806–07. But in 1819, after a bit more than ten years of tending the light, Keeper Goldthwait wrote to Henry Dearborn, superintendent of lighthouses, that he had gotten James Ramsey, a local builder, to agree to erect a barn, eighteen by twenty-eight feet, for the sum of $175. It is unclear whether the barn proposed by Goldthwait was ever built. However, when Keeper Goldthwait passed away in the early winter of 1832, Tristram, Philip's son, petitioned to remain on the island because "he had some stock and hay on the island and could not get it off until spring." It is evident that the keeper's letter in combination with Tristram's later request confirms that Wood Island light keepers were at least part-time farmers and that a barn would make an important contribution toward fulfilling that function.[119]

The first visual representation of the light station on Wood Island appears in the cropped photograph shown here. The barn structure in this 1859 photograph may have been constructed during the service of Philip Goldthwait but was more likely built by Keeper Abraham Norwood. That the barn was raised as a result of expenditures made by Norwood is suggested by his successor, John Adams, who wrote in his 1842 report, "A barn was erected here by the late keeper [referring to Norwood]; also a fence, stone wall, etc." In addition, the new keeper credits Norwood with converting a portion of the old keeper's house into a cow-house and a pigsty.[120]

Wood Island Lighthouse

This detail of the 1859 photograph is cropped to feature the wooden barn and hennery. *FOWIL Archives.*

Adams continues, while complaining of Norwood's apparent enmity, to confirm the important place farming activities held for the early nineteenth-century lighthouse family. Even after Adams had been appointed, the previous keeper had cut all the hay grown on the island, taken it away and then charged the new keeper at a rate of fourteen dollars per ton for the one and one-half tons he needed for his cow.

There is no record relating to Ebenezer Emerson's agrarian activities while serving as the light keeper on Wood Island during the years of the Civil War (1861–65). It is certain, however, that Emerson spent a significant portion of his life farming. His obituary recalls Emerson's life as a "farmer and lumberman." After he retired from the lighthouse, jottings in the *Biddeford Daily Times* report that "Mr. Eben Emerson lost a valuable horse the other day…from some throat disorder."[121] And in 1884, "during a heavy thunder shower that passed over the city…lightning struck a barn belonging to Eben Emerson." In the blaze that resulted, "eighty tons of hay were consumed, besides a hog, several harnesses and a lot of farming implements," totaling an estimated $1,600. It would seem entirely likely, given his occupational background, that Keeper Emerson would have found ways to apply his farming skills while at Wood Island.[122]

An official report issued in 1875 provides a description of the lighthouse station and continues to imply the importance of lighthouse farming. The commentator describes the keeper's barn as a bare wood-frame structure in need of whitewashing and located about 250 feet from the bell tower. The property on which it sits is pictured as "about six acres, good grass land, no garden, all in meadow. A fence runs N. and S. across the point on line of reservation."[123]

In 1882, a short note in the personal column of the *Union and Journal* suggests that the property on Wood Island offered more than just an opportunity to gather hay. "Mr. A. Norwood," observes the writer, "the Keeper of the Lighthouse on Wood Island, has in constant use two pairs of drawers the wool for which was grown on the island, and spun and the garments made by his mother over ten years ago. He also uses occasionally a pair of mittens which were knit by his mother over thirty-six years ago. The wool for them was also grown on the island and spun by his mother."[124]

The time frame implied by these comments indicates that the breeding of sheep on Wood Island had been continuing for close to forty years. Some thirty years later, in 1910, when William Webber inhabited the home at the western end of the island, the local paper again commented how the owner benefited from the wool resulting from raising sheep on the acreage not owned by the government.

The extent of ownership and cultivation of sheep by the lighthouse keepers on Wood Island during the latter half of the nineteenth century remains unclear. The barn existing at that time would certainly have been useful for that purpose. In any case, it is fascinating to speculate about whether the 750 feet of barbed-wire boundary fence with cedar posts built in 1892 and again in 1905 was intended to pen creatures in or keep them out.

In 1887, the lighthouse authorities conducted an assessment of the government land and property on Wood Island. In the survey that resulted, the barn appears as an L-shaped structure approximately 150 feet from the dwelling, and roughly measured, the size is 20 by 30 feet.

Five years later, a new barn was built. It is described as being somewhat smaller, "18 by 25 feet in plan," and is likely the structure that is pictured in the photograph from 1900 reproduced on the following page. Two years earlier, documents indicate the building of a boundary fence, but there is no mention of the small corral that seems to appear in front of or just beside the barn itself. There is also very little discussion of the use Thomas Orcutt, the keeper until 1905, made of this barn; however, photographs found in the family album of Charles A. Burke, his successor, do provide significant insight.[125]

An iconic view of the Wood Island Light Station circa 1900 is made even more stunning by the three-masted schooner passing in the background. *FOWIL Archives, photo by Belinda Dapice.*

The Wood Island Light Station can be seen in the distance in this detail of a photograph from 1912. The treeless setting appears to contradict the island's name. *McArthur Library.*

Charles Burke became the lighthouse keeper at Wood Island in 1905 and remained in service there until 1914. It is his home that has been replicated by the Friends of the Wood Island Lighthouse, and many of his possessions are contained therein. In the distance, the light station on Wood Island creates a picturesque backdrop for the clambake held by Knights Templar in June 1912. In the photograph, the barn appears in front of and to the right of the two-story Dutch Colonial keeper's dwelling. The structure contains a second floor, perhaps a loft. Windows now appear on the side and the eastern end facing out to sea; another window or perhaps a door is visible below. A ventilator protrudes from the roof. The ledge in the foreground obscures a full view of the western side.

Burke's twin boys, Wyatt and Wallace, were born on Wood Island during their father's appointment and are pictured here feeding the chickens beside the barn. It appears that the barn has no foundation but rather is supported by stones. Where the boys are standing at the barn's more westerly end, two windows appear. The fenced corral pictured in the earlier 1900 image no longer exists. The barn's orientation indicated by its base creates a sightline pointing directly at the old bell tower.

Twins Wallace and Wyatt Burke, sons of the keeper, feeding the chickens beside the station barn, circa 1910. *FOWIL Archives.*

Additional images provided by the family of Keeper Charles Burke unmistakably point to the importance of family farming. The top image to the left features the keeper's wife, Carrie Emma Greenleaf Burke, standing alongside a visitor, probably one of her brothers. She is holding a milk pail and seems hopeful for what her cow is about to provide. Directly behind her, chickens can be seen pecking in front of the barn.

Carrie Emma Greenleaf Burke holds a milk pail as she stands beside the family cow and an unidentified visitor in front of the lighthouse barn. *FOWIL Archives.*

And the image on the following page suggests that animals kept on the lighthouse property possibly served more

The trek from the boat landing at the western end of Wood Island may have been made somewhat less taxing when aided by this mode of transportation. FOWIL Archives.

than just one purpose. The cow harnessed to a cart may have been one solution for the need to transport materials and supplies in the years before a half-mile boardwalk connected the boat landing to the lighthouse property.

In the twentieth century, the keeper's logbooks provide ample evidence for the continuing role that farm-related activities played in the day-to-day schedule of the lighthouse keeper and his family. The records indicate that haying, butchering pigs and cows, caring for stock, working in the garden and transporting grain from the mainland all contributed to making up the keeper's work schedule. Occasionally, direct reference is made to the barn: "Cleaning up barn and shed," "Repairing doors to barn," "Cleaning barn and hen house." One comment reveals the purpose of the structure on top of the barn's roof: "Repairing and painting ventilator on barn." And another reminds us of the strenuous labor that farming entailed: "Wheeling manure out from barn to field."[126]

Storms in early 1933 finally caused the barn to be torn down. Keeper George Woodward in January of that year reports that a gale pounded the region for several days. Local news coverage described heavy damage in Biddeford Pool, and the keeper's log recounts the substantial destruction to the boathouse. For the next several months, Woodward was clearing rocks and making repairs. By the beginning of August, having fully restored the functionality of the boathouse, he was able to turn his attention to tearing down the henhouse (August 2–3) and then the "old barn" (August 7–19).[127]

There seems to be little question that the henhouse, shed and "old barn" were essential components of the lighthouse station for over one hundred years. Recognizing that the light keeper on Wood Island was as much a farmer as a mariner adds a significant dimension to the full telling of his story.

Chapter 10

WRECKS AND RESCUES, PART I

1898–1909

GALES AND WRECKS: THOMAS ORCUTT

During Thomas Orcutt's nineteen years serving as keeper (1886–1905), no fewer than twenty-seven shipwrecks or maritime accidents occurred in the waters around Wood Island, many the result of some of the most powerful storms in memory.

Keeper Orcutt's duties did not take a holiday when tempests howled their way east along the coast of Maine. His duties, clearly detailed by the government in the *Instructions to Light-Keepers* (1881), emphasized that his primary responsibility was to maintain a good light and fog signal. Orcutt was undoubtedly mindful that mariners were most in need of his services when circumstances produced foul weather. When these conditions developed, Keeper Orcutt knew he was required to spend the entire night in the tower protecting the vulnerable light and keeping it aglow. While these powerful storms, which occurred throughout the year, were howling and creating near-hurricane conditions, the valiant keeper periodically found himself scrambling outside onto the narrow platform, sixty feet above the rocks of Wood Island, to clean accumulated salt, snow or ice from the glass panes. Orcutt was certainly all too aware of upsetting stories of lighthouse keepers whose efforts during conditions such as these led to terrible tragedies.

On the Saturday following Thanksgiving in November 1898, two low-pressure areas converged on coastal New England, surprising weather forecasters and creating conditions that would result in more than 400 deaths and the sinking of 150 vessels. On that fateful day in November, Portland's newspaper blared, "Terrible Storm Strews Coast with Wrecks with Many Lives Lost." The following day, the *Eastern Argus* confirmed, "Shipwrecks and Disasters Reported on All Sides." Eventually, the storm came to be known as the "Portland Storm" because of the terrible tragedy that befell the steamship *Portland*, which disappeared near Cape Cod along with an estimated 180 passengers and crew.[128]

In the vicinity of Wood Island, the storm was no kinder to property, but luckily there was no recorded loss of life. Earlier that same summer in June 1898, the captain of the *Grecian Bend* became disoriented in the midnight fog and confused the lights on the seaward end of the recently completed Old Orchard Beach Pier for the lights of residences on Ram Island, close to two miles away, near the mouth of the Saco River. He had intended to go up the Saco River to have some repairs done on his ship but, unaware of the new, recently completed pier, had miscalculated, causing the vessel and its cargo of 360 tons of plaster rock to be driven onto the beach just north of the new pier, where it became permanently stuck.[129] A few months later, in November 1898, and then again in early December, near–hurricane force winds from two more powerful nor'easters produced high winds and huge waves that gradually caused the stranded schooner to break apart. When large sections detached from the ship and pounded against the world's longest steel pier, the pilings eventually gave way, and the pavilion at the end of the structure fell into the sea.[130]

Another schooner, *The Queen of the West*, went aground in 1898 just off Biddeford Pool and within sight of Wood Island. Orcutt fought the howling winds and blowing snow as he attempted to keep the light burning and the fog bell signaling. Meanwhile, a valiant team from the Fletcher's Neck Life Saving Station was able to save the crew.[131]

Two years later to the day, on December 4, 1900, southern New England was blasted by yet another gale. Newspapers once again proclaimed the power of the storm: "It was the worst night that has been experienced at [Biddeford Pool] since the one on which the *Portland* was lost."[132]

The coaster *Thomas B. Reed* was caught in the storm while heading toward Gardiner. Her captain attempted to seek shelter in the harbor behind Wood Island when she ran onto the rocks on Stage Island Point. Although she resisted early attempts to save her, the schooner was eventually salvaged. Neither the schooner *R.P. Chase* nor the steamer *Fanny and Edith*, which went to pieces on Prout's Neck during the same storm, was recovered. A fourth vessel, the *Sea Bird*, went aground at Biddeford Pool but was eventually floated.

Stories from the Edge of the Sea

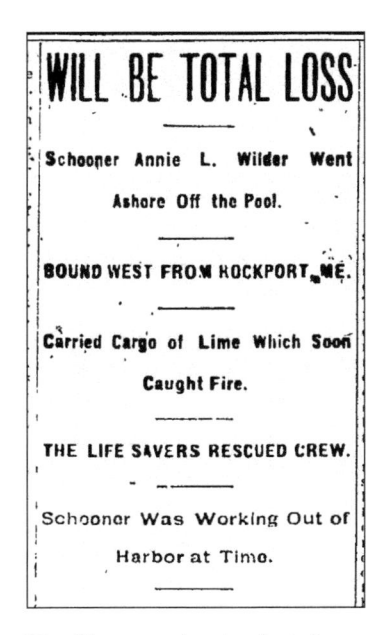

> **WILL BE TOTAL LOSS**
>
> Schooner Annie L. Wilder Went Ashore Off the Pool.
>
> BOUND WEST FROM ROCKPORT, ME.
>
> Carried Cargo of Lime Which Soon Caught Fire.
>
> THE LIFE SAVERS RESCUED CREW.
>
> Schooner Was Working Out of Harbor at Time.

Headline reporting the *Annie L. Wilder*'s mishap and the lime fire, which resulted "in setting the harbor aglow." *Biddeford Weekly Journal*, April 14, 1905.

And just six months before Orcutt's retirement, an unusual accident occurred that is noteworthy for its spectacular result. The seventy-six-foot, two-masted schooner *Annie L. Wilder* missed stays in shallow water and grounded as she left the harbor at Biddeford Pool on the morning of April 13, 1905.[133] There was some early hope that the vessel would float at high tide, but optimism proved to be an illusion as she began to go to pieces on the ledge.

"The Harbor Was Aglow" reported the *Biddeford Daily Journal* when, late in the afternoon, the schooner began to leak and caught fire.[134] Although lime in and of itself is not necessarily flammable, the chemical reaction that occurs when the substance comes in contact with water does create a sufficient increase in heat to ignite combustible materials. In this case, as the *Annie L. Wilder* began to break into pieces, it created a dazzling display for residents and onlookers along the nearby coast. Although the vessel proved to be a total loss, the captain and crew were saved by the Pool lifesaving crew and returned to Rockport, their home port, where, it was reported, they would soon ship on another schooner.[135]

As Keeper Orcutt was preparing to retire from his stint at Wood Island, debris deposited by the advancing waves along the rocky shoreline continued to serve as a reminder of the shocking disaster that had occurred just two short years before. On June 11, 1903, the *Washington B. Thomas*, the largest schooner ever to wreck on the Maine coast, went aground one storm-plagued, foggy night and was "pounded to pieces" on Stratton Island.

The *Washington B. Thomas*, 286 feet in length, nearly 50 feet in breadth and boasting five masts, was returning to Portland from Virginia on her very first voyage. The massive ship was laden with 4,226 tons of coal when she ran into thick fog that had settled in just off Wood Island. The captain decided to drop anchor off the eastern end of Stratton Island and wait until the fog lifted. As the storm intensified, however, the schooner began to drag her anchor. Heavy seas washed over the ship and ultimately pushed the stern onto the reef at Stratton Island. Captain Lermond, honeymooning with his bride of just a few months, Hattie May, warned her to stay below. Unfortunately, during the height of the storm, a massive wave caused a beam to collapse on Mrs. Lermond and crushed her skull. Eventually, she was washed overboard by the surging torrent and lost in the darkness as the ship itself began to disintegrate. For two days, the storm dumped thirteen inches of rain on Old Orchard Beach and vicinity, which hampered rescue attempts.

For days, wreckage washed up on the coastal beaches and islands of southern Maine. But particularly gruesome was the body of the captain's twenty-four-year-old bride, who was discovered on the beach about a half mile from the mouth of the Saco River several days after the tragedy itself. Nevertheless, eventually all fourteen crew members, the disconsolate captain and his son were brought to safety.

Shipwrecks and Death: Charles A. Burke

Marshall Perrin

Keeper Charles Albert Burke (1905–14) barely had time to recover from the earthquake that occurred on October 21 when, on Thursday, November 16, 1906, terrible circumstances thrust him again into the midst of misfortune. The 103-foot schooner *Marshall Perrin* was returning to Rockland, Maine, and had anchored at Richmond Island when a furious gale parted the ship's anchor chains around 11:00 p.m., and the craft was blown eight miles in the direction of Wood Island. The strength of the storm made it impossible for the three crew members to control the vessel, and as they approached the ledges near the island, they made their way to the bowsprit, thinking that they could jump to safety when the ship struck. And strike it did, launching the ship's cook, William Jarwin; the captain, Herbert Bray; and Seaman John Burke into the frigid, rocky water.

In the early morning hours on Friday, Seaman Burke (no relation to the keeper of the lighthouse) regained consciousness on the rock-bound shore. He noticed the beam from the lighthouse about seventy-five yards away and, as quickly as he could, made his way to the tower to give notice of the disaster. Seaman Burke hastily returned with Keeper Burke to the scene of the wreck only to find the schooner already breaking apart with merely a few timbers still visible and washing up on the rocks.

It was not until daybreak when the thick weather began to moderate that the crew at the Fletcher's Neck Life Saving Station noticed the signal hoisted by the lighthouse keeper. Although a search finally resulted in the discovery of the bruised and battered body of the deceased Captain Bray, the cook was never found.

A week later, on November 21, 1906, Waldo Stillson Verrill, the Biddeford Pool Poet, a grandson of Nathaniel Verrill and nephew of Lyman Frank Verrill, both previous keepers of the Wood Island Light, immortalized the calamity in his poem titled "The Wreck of the Marshall Perrin":

THE WRECK OF THE MARSHALL PERRIN
By Waldo Stillson Verrill

Across the bay, the Perrin *lay,*
At both her anchors riding,
Her chains were long and large and strong,
In which they were confiding.

A north-east gale with sleet and hail,
Was making great commotion;
And heavy seas before the breeze
Were rolling in from ocean.

She pitched and rolled, quite uncontrolled,
'Till chains were snapped asunder;
Then drifted off "mid breakers" froth,
From Richmond's Island under

The seas were wild and combed and piled
Upon this frail craft drifting
Across the bay—eight miles they say,
No sign of storm-cloud lifting.

The breakers roar; brave hearts are sore,
They know there's land to leeward;
Through fierce gale, no stress of sail
Can forge their vessel seaward.

Wood Island Lighthouse

Nor can they steer, though doom is near,
Their fated craft to haven.
While hope is dim, they trust in Him,
Who hears the cry of raven.

Still on they drift, but through a rift,
They see a red light flaring;
No hope is there, it brings despair
To sailors bold and daring.

The beaming light reveals a sight
To seamen's hearts appalling;
A leeward shore, where breakers roar,
And billows high are falling.

She soon must strike, but they will fight
The waves 'mid roar and rattle;
Although it snows, they cast their clothes,
And wait the dreadful battle.

She strikes; a shock, the billows mock
And dash with mighty power
Across their craft, the beam abaft,
Oh, dismal, fateful hour!

Out on jib-boom, they wait their doom,
And think of those that love them.
Drenched by the spray, they hug the stay,
With threatening waves above them.

A thunderous crash, and down they splash
In waters rough and chilling;
By dint of strength, they hope, at length,
To reach the shore, God willing.

A moment more and all is o'er;
No harm can come nigh them.
Two seamen sleep beneath the deep

No more can tempest try them.
But one is saved—on rocks storm-laved,
Benumbed by cold, nigh fainting,
'Mid spray and rain he waits in vain,
A scene too sad for painting.

Two widows weep; oh dreadful deep!
How many now are sleeping
In watery graves, beneath the waves,
While loved ones dear are weeping.[136]

Schooner Maple Leaf

Of course, not all shipwrecks ended in tragedy. On February 7, 1907, less than a year following the *Marshall Perrin* disaster, Keeper Burke logged this entry: "Sch ashore on Sharps Rocks name unknown." The following day, he was able to identify the unfortunate vessel: "Sch proved to be the *Maple Leaf* of Harrisboro, NS. Came off uninjured."[137] Although the final rescue of the schooner proved to be a challenge, the *Daily Eastern Argus* reported on February 9, 1907, that all had ended well: "The tug *Priscilla*…returned to this port yesterday morning towing the two-masted British schooner *Maple Leaf* which went on the rocks at Sharp's Point at Biddeford Pool.…The vessel was but little damaged." The newspaper went on to comment that the storm that passed through coastal Maine earlier in the week had carried away two buoys, resulting in miscalculation and the ship's eventual grounding.[138]

Schooner Valetta

Burke's rather unassuming logbook entry on October 28, 1909, heralds yet another near tragedy: "Sch Valetta ran ashore on Washburn Shoal at 7 P.M. Floated later and was towed to Biddeford Pool." The keeper's comment, however, obscures the tensions that resulted when the crew decided to immediately depart the ship and row to Wood Island and safety.[139]

Later, around 10:30 that same evening, the *Valetta*, which was carrying a cargo consisting of 122,000 feet of lumber and nearly twenty thousand shingles, the total value of which was approximately $8,000, floated off the ledge at high tide. At that moment, it was boarded by two men from

Biddeford Pool who claimed the right to salvage since the vessel was adrift and apparently abandoned. The captain and three men who made up the crew maintained their belief that the schooner was fast on the ledge and could not be floated except by a tug, thereby representing that the vessel was not abandoned and subject to the salvage laws.

Apparently, there was no easy resolution to these opposing claims. Although each of the Pool men and the tug captain were offered $100 each to settle their claims, they refused the proposition, contending that it was not enough. It is unclear how this issue was finally decided.[140]

The Launch Item

On at least three occasions, Keeper Charles A. Burke noted in his logbook the passing of the presidential yacht, *Mayflower*. On July 17, 1908, he wrote, "Str Mayflower passed East at 9.30 A.M." And then again in July 1910, the keeper spotted the USS *Mayflower* as it "passed in Harbor at 2:30 P.M. with President Taft on board." The next day, July 28, he noticed that the "*U.S.S. Mayflower* left Harbor at 9:30 A.M. going west."[141]

In 1909, sightseers aboard the doomed launch *Item* hoped to get a close-up view of the presidential yacht *Sylph* (pictured here). *Collections of the Library of Congress.*

When President Taft was inaugurated in March 1909, the residents of Biddeford Pool were hoping that they would be treated to a visit from the first family because Mrs. Taft's sister Eleanor More had a summer cottage in Biddeford Pool. Unfortunately, President Taft's wife became the victim of a stroke later that spring, and her sister was called upon to nurse her during her illness and take her place beside the president on official occasions. Toward the end of July, as Mrs. Taft began to show some improvement, Mrs. More decided to spend a few days at her summer home in Biddeford Pool. In order to assist her, the president placed his official yacht, *Sylph*, at her disposal for the journey. When Mrs. More arrived at her cottage, the citizens of Biddeford and Saco were delighted to look out into the bay and see that the presidential yacht had anchored near the mouth of the Saco River.[142]

Keeper Burke's logbooks for July 30 and 31, 1909, remain silent, however, regarding the awful catastrophe that resulted when a group of sightseers set out on an overcrowded launch in the evening on July 30 to get a closer look at the president's yacht anchored in the harbor of Biddeford Pool. Local newspapers covered the incident extensively, and the headline of the *Biddeford Record* blared in oversized type:

TWO GIRLS DROWNED,
LAUNCH ITEM *CAPSIZED.*

TWENTY-SEVEN CLUNG
TO OVERTURNED BOAT

And Were Picked Up by the
President's Yacht and Launch Nimrod

Twenty-nine passengers boarded the little forty-foot gasoline-powered launch *Item* around 7:30 p.m. on Friday evening, July 30, in anticipation of an exciting moonlight excursion down the Saco River culminating in a close-up look at the president's yacht, *Sylph*. According to the testimony of Captain Ernest E.E.M. Vinton, in charge of the launch, the trip downriver to that point was without incident. As they neared the mouth of the Saco River, the captain agreed to sail out and around Wood Island. "It was a nice party," he said, "they were singing and apparently enjoying every minute of the sail."[143]

Testimony from the inquest held over the following few days revealed what happened next. As the little boat left the protection of the Saco River and entered the Atlantic, some of the passengers became alarmed as the

Thirty-one passengers and crew were cast overboard when the launch *Item* was swamped in Saco Bay. *McArthur Library.*

long, rolling swells caused the *Item* to become "cranky," listing first to one side and then the other. Captain Vinton assured everyone that they were not in danger but that they should remain seated.

As confidence returned to the young merrymakers, they confirmed their desire to continue past the presidential yacht and cruise around Wood Island. Although they continued nervously to contend with the boat's rocking motion, all appeared to be content as their voyage continued. After rounding the east end of the island, Captain Vinton was making his way back by way of steering a course between Basket and Stage Island. It was as the *Item* was approaching the mouth of the river that the little craft, once again encountering sudden swells, began to tip. This time, instead of righting itself as it had previously, the boat capsized, casting its occupants into the frigid water.

Amid the near-panic and confusion, reports later confirmed the many acts of bravery that were performed, especially by the young men who sought to aid the women who were seriously hindered by their clothing. One report heralded the efforts of an unnamed youthful hero who "dived under the upturned boat three times and each time brought a girl to the surface of the water, where she grabbed hold of the clothing of some person who was clinging to the craft."[144]

The screams and shouts of the men and women in the water were heard by the seamen on board the *Sylph*, which was anchored approximately one hundred yards away from the site of the disaster. The sailors immediately launched the *Sylph*'s tender and brought it alongside the overturned *Item*. Able Seaman Cummings, one of the rescuers, tells what happened then:

> *Commander Williams gave orders to turn on the searchlight, and then we saw them hanging to the bottom of that boat....We told the men to keep quiet and that we would get them after the women were hauled aboard our launch. The men didn't dispute what we said, but took it in just a matter of fact sort of way and appeared mighty glad that help had come to them. We took the women off the upturned boat on the first trip, and then went back and got the rest, together with the men.*[145]

Within minutes, other boats appeared at the scene, anxious to help. One of these was the *Nimrod*. Captain Piper of the *Nimrod* had been following the *Item* as it was returning to Saco and, therefore, arrived on the scene of the accident within minutes. As rescuers pulled the *Item*'s passengers from the water, they deposited them on the *Nimrod*, which eventually carried them back to Factory Island Wharf in Saco. One rescued passenger, however, was suffering so badly from her injuries that she was transported immediately back to Biddeford Pool and carried into the Goldthwaits' restaurant. Her name was Florence Ellis Cutts.

Cutts, age twenty-nine, was crushed when she became tangled in lines and gear as the *Item* rolled over. She was unconscious and suffering from internal injuries and hemorrhaging when she was rescued. For the next day and a half, she lingered, occasionally regaining consciousness, first at the restaurant and then in a comfortable room in a private cottage in Biddeford Pool. At 1:30 a.m. on the Sunday following the accident, she passed away from her injuries.

As one by one the victims were pulled to safety, it became shockingly apparent that not all could be accounted for. The cry was shouted: "O where's Katie Lynch?" In fact, two of the young women, Katherine Lynch and Margaret Harvey, were missing and, despite the best efforts of the searchers, could not be found. Meanwhile, the *Item* was towed to nearby Basket Island and beached. While attempting to retrieve the personal belongings of some of the victims, Hiram Dolby put his hand through one of the windows and touched the foot of a human being. It turned out that he had discovered the body of Katherine Lynch.[146]

It was not until later that evening that it was determined that there was a likely third victim. The brother of Margaret Harvey telephoned just before midnight to ask whether his sister was still at the Pool. No one had seen her, and by 2:00 a.m., it was feared that she had drowned. Efforts to find her body proved unsuccessful, and it was the prevailing opinion that her body would be washed out to sea and never recovered.

A little less than two weeks later, two young men discovered her body washed up on the beach near South Point, well over a mile from the scene of the tragedy. Harvey's body had been trapped in currents that prevented it from being washed out to sea and instead carried it around the peninsula and eventually cast it ashore. Margaret Harvey was just twenty-five years old.[147]

In all, three women perished as a result of the accident. After hearing testimony from a number of witnesses, the coroner's jury that had been convened to investigate the tragedy demanded to see the *Item*, which had been brought to Saco. As one of the jurors stepped from the wharf onto the recovered launch, the boat keeled over quite suddenly. It was reported that perhaps this incident was critical in the jury's final determination.

On August 5, the jurors returned with a verdict. They found that the *Item* was "unstable, easily capsized and entirely unfit to carry passengers." In spite of their finding, they recommended that no further action be taken.[148]

Chapter 11

A LIGHTHOUSE EDUCATION

1872–1963

Large lighthouse families inevitably meant that there were children in need of schooling. When the local public school was nearby and within reach, this usually did not present a problem. However, when the school was inaccessible to the light station, the education of the keeper's children could pose a serious challenge. In many cases, especially in the early nineteenth century, the children were homeschooled. When the offshore keeper's residence was of sufficient size, or if there were several families posted at the station, the lighthouse service occasionally would provide a stipend permitting a teacher to live at the station. In other cases, it was up to the lighthouse keeper and the local community to negotiate an acceptable solution.

At Wood Island, documentation relating to the education of the keepers' children is spotty at best. What evidence does exist suggests that lighthouse tasks were undertaken collectively and that parents schooled their youthful learners in the essential three Rs, along with the practical arts needed to sustain their livelihood on a remote island.

Little is recorded regarding the schooling of girls and young women at the Wood Island Light Station during the nineteenth century. Still, we know that at similar postings, daughters would assist their mother with chores that involved cooking and baking and maintaining the household by learning the skills of knitting, crocheting and sewing. An illustration is provided in a surviving letter written by Keeper Albert Norwood dated November 30, 1873. Here, Norwood writes that although his son Nelson (age two) is in bed, his youngest daughter, Mary (age eight), is making a shirt, while an older daughter, Ida (age twenty-three), is busy making a dress.[149]

Lighthouse chores were not always gender specific. Lighthouse history is filled with reports of women as well as sons and daughters who learned alongside the keeper how to fully maintain the light. Wives and older children were often called on to tend the light when their husband or father left the island, became ill or for some other reason could not perform his duties. Ida Lewis and Abbie Burgess are just two examples of the many women who heroically took control of their light station during exceptional times.

Keeping a lighthouse could more often than not be a solitary and lonely occupation. In fact, some assignments, referred to as "Stag Stations," were considered too remote and far too dangerous for women and children. Even though Wood Island is located approximately one mile from the mainland and was considered to be a family station, during severe weather and throughout the winter months, making contact with members of the larger community was treacherous and too often highly uncertain. In 1876, four years into Keeper Norwood's tenure, the Lighthouse Board began to distribute "traveling libraries" in an effort to promote learning and battle this sense of isolation. Each of the "mini" libraries contained about forty titles housed in a wooden box and remained with the keeper for about six months. The library would then be exchanged for another box containing a new set of forty books.

The traveling libraries were provided primarily to satisfy the needs of the adults and older children. A clearer understanding of the educational experience encountered by younger children of school age is suggested by a notice appearing in the *Saco Union and Journal* in May 1878: "Albert Norwood resident on Wood Island, asked the city [for] the amount of school money his children were entitled to in order that he may hire a teacher to instruct his children on the island. He represented that his residence made it very inconvenient for his children to attend school on the mainland. Previous to last year a portion of the school money had been allotted to him." Norwood's plea confirms the ongoing educational challenge faced by Wood Island families and suggests that the solution was to arrange for a teacher to come at least intermittently to the island for instruction.[150]

Three of the children of Keeper Thomas Orcutt—Mattie (eleven years old), Minnie Estelle (nine years old) and George (seven years old)—grew up on the island under the watchful eyes of their parents. Like the lighthouse keepers who came before, the Orcutts supplemented their $540 yearly salary by tending the farm and barn animals contained on the government reservation and by fishing the abundant waters of Saco Bay. The Orcutt children no doubt learned the skills necessary to contribute to these agrarian activities.[151]

The lighthouse tower and dwelling are shown, circa 1880. The keeper (likely Orcutt) is standing to the right; his wife and two girls are seated in the doorway; three young boys are seated on the white retaining wall. *NARA.*

The letter written by Minnie Orcutt in 1889, when she was about twelve years old and partially quoted in an earlier chapter, briefly outlines her educational experience. In it, she informs us that she and her brother George were schooled on the island. Minnie mentions studying reading, spelling, writing, geography and history. She also reports that she has "been through physiology once."[152]

LILLA B. SEVERANCE: LIGHTHOUSE TEACHER

When Keeper Wilbert Freeman Lurvey (1917–23) and his wife took control of the light station on Wood Island, their son Wilbert Jr. was five years old, and their daughter Edith was four. Consequently, in addition to his lighthouse chores, Keeper Lurvey needed to consider issues related to the education of his children. On February 25, 1919, with both children now of school age, Lurvey's logbook reports that Lilla B. Severance, the state teacher, arrived and remained until March 5. She returned in May for a week and again in July for two weeks. When Severance left Wood Island on August 7 following her third visit of the year, Lurvey records that she was bound for Boon Island, apparently following a lighthouse circuit prescribed in her contract.[153]

Lilla Bernice Severance was the first of the professional educators approved by the State of Maine in accordance with a new plan for educating the state's lighthouse children, slated to begin in 1915. Maine's innovative educational program (which would eventually offer a model adopted by the U.S. Congress in 1918) provided for an instructor, called the "lighthouse teacher," who would visit school-age children in those lighthouses considered remote enough by the state to eliminate the possibility of access to any other source of educational opportunity. The plan was for the lighthouse teacher to provide regular instruction to the children living with their light-keeping families on Maine's rocky outposts. She would provide an outline of work to be completed before her return several months later. To accomplish this task, the itinerant teacher would remain on site for a week to ten days at a time to deliver the appropriate instruction. The women would often be required to travel significant distances in a tender provided by the lighthouse service, braving the unpredictable and often challenging conditions offered up by Maine's fickle weather. Usually, following the long trip between lighthouses, the teacher would find it necessary to transfer cautiously to a smaller dinghy for the final leg of the trip onto the island itself.

Severance quickly discovered that her job went well beyond the instruction of her young charges. In a presentation before the Portland Phi Beta Club in November 1949, long after the lighthouse teacher program had come to an end, she told the story of one of her first assignments. When she arrived at the Petit Manan Lighthouse, about thirty kilometers northeast of Bar Harbor, Maine, the keeper informed her that his pregnant wife was about to give birth to their eighth child. Young Severance, lacking any medical training, was nevertheless called upon to assist in the successful delivery of the new baby. Presumably during her stay, she also found time to provide instruction to the keeper's children.

Two more lighthouse teachers spent time with the Lurvey children before his family left the island. In March and June 1920, Miss E.A. Salsman called on the island for a two-week instructional visit. And then, in October 1921, we learn from the keeper that "Miss Julia Hancock arrived to teach the children."[154] For the young learners living in isolated conditions on remote islands, the arrival of the lighthouse teacher must have provided a welcome relief from their usual routines. Unfortunately, the lighthouse teacher program ended in 1922, even before Keeper Lurvey left Wood Island and moved with his family to Bar Harbor.

Stories from the Edge of the Sea

SCHOOLING THE CHILDREN OF KEEPER GEORGE WOODWARD

More than any other light keeper at Wood Island, George E. Woodward allowed his logbook to provide glimpses into his personal life. Comments made during his time of service are reminders that lighthouse keepers were also fathers and husbands.

A glance at Woodward's logbook reveals that on numerous occasions, he was charged with making arrangements for transporting members of his family to the mainland and destinations beyond. Most of these are at least partially related to managing the formal instruction of his children. While at Wood Island, Keeper Woodward was challenged at various times by a continually growing family, which included an infant in constant need of attention; a wife overcoming a bout with pneumonia, as well as the effects of giving birth; two school-age teenagers requiring transportation to and from school; and his own susceptibility to illness—all while living in a somewhat isolated condition on an out-of-the-way island. The added dilemma posed by the need to educate their children merely compounded the problems faced by George and Hazel Woodward and indeed required a creative solution.

Mr. and Mrs. Walter Church had already graciously offered their home on Yates Street in Biddeford Pool to Hazel Wass Woodward when she was recovering from her hospital stay in the fall of 1927. Walter Church was Hazel's great-uncle, her grandfather's brother. Curiously, two of Walter's siblings were named Coleman and Charlotte, the names of the Woodward children born to George Woodward's first wife, Ida Church Woodward. On February 26, 1933, Woodward's logbook indicates that "Mr. Church came out to get daughter." It is clear that there was a close family connection between the keeper, his family and Mr. and Mrs. Walter Church. It is this close connection that provided the solution for the Woodwards' educational dilemma.

Keeper George Woodward's logbooks contain nearly one hundred family references, and close to one-half of these are connected to transporting his school-age children back and forth between Wood Island and the mainland. His records indicate that nearly all of these trips occurred on or around the weekend and only during the months when school would have been in session. Representative logbook submissions from 1928 will illustrate: "Took daughter to school" (January 8, 1928); "Took son ashore" (February 4, 1929); "Went ashore for supplies; also took daughter to school" (March 12, 1928); and "Went ashore after son—PM" (January 4, 1929). On Saturday,

September 15, 1928, the keeper "Went to Pool After Family." Then, the following Monday, September 17, he "took family ashore."[155]

While dividing his time between attending to his chores on the island and providing for his family, it appears likely that his wife and children lived at least part time in Biddeford Pool. On several occasions, Woodward tells us that he "went to Pool to get wood for family" (December 6, 1928). At other times, he is even more direct: "To Pool to see family" (October 19, 1929) or "To Pool after wife and provisions" (January 7, 1931). The implication is that the keeper's school-age children were living away from the island while they attended school and that his wife and newborn son were with them for a good portion of the time.[156]

The Coast Guard Era

In 1939, when administrative responsibility shifted to the Coast Guard, a new brand of lighthouse keeper was ushered onto the Wood Island Lighthouse scene.

From 1807 to 1939, a period of 132 years, eighteen lighthouse keepers watched over the Wood Island Lighthouse. These men and their families were New Englanders hailing from coastal communities in Maine, New Hampshire and Massachusetts. The average length of service for each keeper was about eight years. During that period, Philip Goldthwait remained in his role for twenty-three years, Thomas Orcutt for nineteen years and Earle Benson for seventeen years.

From the time that Earle Benson departed Wood Island in 1951 until the last Coast Guard light keeper left the station in 1986, thirty-five years later, approximately twenty men were assigned to watch over the light. As members of a branch of Uncle Sam's military, the geographical diversity represented in their backgrounds increased. These lighthouse keepers now often represented inland communities and hailed from states such as New York and Nebraska. Each of them served an average of less than two years. Only Edward Frank, Coast Guard keeper from 1952 to 1956, served for more than three years.

The Coast Guard keepers were younger as well. The average age of the Wood Island Lighthouse guardians during the nineteenth century was just over fifty years of age. Generally, their families were large. Abraham Norwood and his wife had twelve children; Edwin Tarbox, eleven; Philip Goldthwait and John Adams, seven and eight, respectively. In contrast,

Coast Guard families never included more than three children while they were stationed at Wood Island, and the age of the keepers and their wives was usually in the early to mid-twenties. Understandably, the children of these Coast Guard families were young as well, seldom of an age requiring formal schooling.

    Jackie Netherwood Kennedy, the oldest daughter of Jack Netherwood, had just reached the age where schooling was required when her family took up residence on Wood Island. Today, she remembers bits and pieces of her life as a five-year-old when her father was the lighthouse keeper (1962–63). Mostly, she recalls spending her active summers with her cousins and winters romping in the snow with her brothers. As for school, Jackie recalls that the Coast Guard would send a boat to take her back and forth to Biddeford, where she attended kindergarten. Although her cousins were very envious, she recalls that the trips "were a little bit difficult because I would get deadly sea sick." She went on to mention that the "Coasties" had a galvanized bucket with Jackie's name painted on it that became a required and necessary addition to the uncomfortable, sometimes stomach-churning passage.[157]

Chapter 12

THE SCRAPBOOK[158]

1905 AND 2019

Beginnings

In the late fall of 1905, Charles Arthur Burke replaced Thomas Orcutt, who had been the lighthouse keeper on Wood Island for nineteen years and just recently retired. In an effort to better chronicle Keeper Burke's years of service, the small history team at the Friends of the Wood Island Lighthouse requested the logbooks that all keepers were required to maintain from the National Archives and Records Administration. Surprisingly, only the years from 1907 to 1914 were extant. What happened to the logbook(s) that included the period 1905–06?

Further research at the Maine Historical Society turned up an oversized book with a cover that revealed it to be a lighthouse keeper's logbook similar to those found at the National Archives. And since the early years (1905–06) of Keeper Burke's service were missing from those volumes, this promised to be a valuable find. Unfortunately, someone had misused the logbook by turning it into a scrapbook of sorts. Pages originally containing the entries of Keepers Burke and Orcutt had been overlaid with clippings glued from newspaper articles and other writings of interest to the scrapbook creator. What a tragedy to lose the opportunity to reconstruct the record of an entire year of a light keeper's life during the tenure of two of Wood Island's very consequential keepers.

Stories from the Edge of the Sea

The Logbook

A closer look at the artifact, however, not only offered a peek into the interests and concerns of the scrapbook creator but also provided intriguing insights into the life and times of the Wood Island Lighthouse keepers themselves. On the one hand, the entries of both Thomas Orcutt and Charles A. Burke were partially visible on some pages and wholly readable on others. On the other hand, there remained the mystery of who "inherited" this Wood Island logbook and how and why they chose to transform it into a scrapbook.

The cover of the scrapbook makes known that it is an official document of the United States Lighthouse Establishment and contains a record of the daily expenditures made for oil, wicks and chimneys at the Wood Island Light Station in Maine. And indeed, each page is filled with a daily accounting that details the time each evening when the light was lit, the time each morning when the light was extinguished and the number of hours and minutes that the light was operational. In addition, each day the keeper was required to provide "remarks" on the weather during the twenty-four-hour period. So, the right-hand side of the logbook page is filled with a steady, if somewhat monotonous, chronicle of meteorological conditions of interest primarily to mariners.

The scrapbook cover indicates its origin as an official record of the United States Lighthouse Establishment. *Collections of the Maine Historical Society. Coll. 2025.*

Lighthouse keepers in the nineteenth century were held strictly to account for the amount of oil they used. It was not unheard of for more unprincipled employees to increase their somewhat meager salaries by selling the oil provided by the lighthouse establishment for their own benefit. This was more common in the early and middle years of the nineteenth century, when the politically appointed lighthouse keepers were unable to resist the opportunity presented to them when the price of sperm oil rose dramatically from $0.55 per barrel in 1841 to $2.25 in 1855. The manic concern for accuracy can almost be felt in the calculations made by Thomas Orcutt in February 1905,

Left: Another typical log page, this time showing Keeper Orcutt's calculations of oil usage. Collections of the Maine Historical Society. Coll. 2025.

Below: The bottom of the log page with the keeper's signature confirms that the light in the early twentieth century was flashing red. Collections of the Maine Historical Society. Coll. 2025.

which can clearly be seen on the left-hand column of his logbook. At the bottom of each page, the keepers accounted for the amount of oil consumed during the month both in the light tower and the keeper's dwelling.

Each month, the keeper was required to sign the page and attest to his entries. Because several of the scrapbook pages still retain the original notes, the signatures of both Thomas Orcutt and Charles A. Burke have been saved. In addition, Burke informs us that in 1905–06, the light was generated from a fourth-order Fresnel lens with one wick and a flashing red signal. On later pages, the keeper wrote *Harbor* in the space for "Kind of Light."

THE SCRAPBOOK

But most of the pages in this keeper's logbook are covered with clippings glued over the log entries of Orcutt and Burke. Many of these items contain romantic poems or illustrations similar to the one on the first page of the scrapbook reproduced to the left.

Other pages, however, seem to include newspaper stories having some meaning for the scrapbook creator. Several of these seem to indicate a continued attachment to Wood Island. For example, an old photograph of the lighthouse and dwelling also shows the bell tower, which has since disappeared. The caption reads, "Fixed red with red flash every minute. Bell. Double and single blows alternating; intervals, 25 sec."

The logbook was used as a scrapbook. The creator pasted news articles and other "sweet thoughts" over the keeper's logbook entries. *Collections of the Maine Historical Society.* Coll. 2025.

Two other pasted articles relate to aspects of Wood Island's past. The first refers to the "monument" on Stage Island and describes the tragedy that took place when the tower collapsed during its construction in 1825. The other references the suicide of William H. Webber, a resident of Wood Island whose struggles with mental illness and suicide are explored in an earlier chapter.

In all three clippings, the references to Wood Island were unmistakable but did little to clarify questions relating to this curious artifact. Who was its creator? What relationship did he or she have to Wood Island's lighthouse?

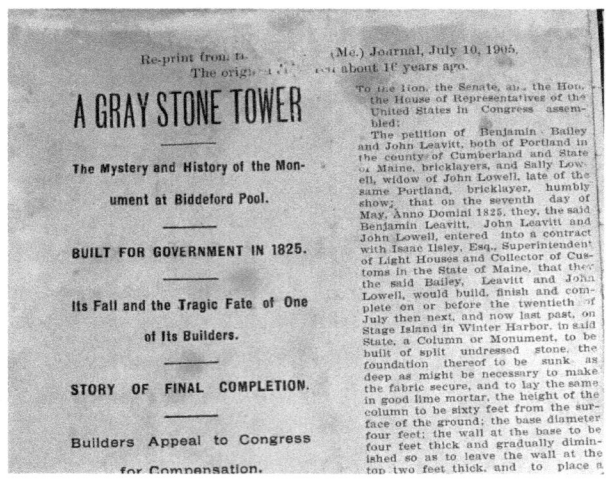

Above: A newspaper clipping of the Wood Island Lighthouse, pasted into the scrapbook, describes the characteristics of the light and fog signal. *Collections of the Maine Historical Society. Coll. 2025.*

Left: The scrapbook includes an article tracing the history of the Stage Island "monument." *Collections of the Maine Historical Society. Coll. 2025.*

And how did it end up in the hands of the Boothbay Region Historical Society, which ultimately contributed it to the Maine Historical Society.

One clue to unraveling the mystery appeared as a faint scribble on the front page of the logbook. Written in pencil and suffering from the one hundred–plus years since its creation, there appears to be a name: *Josephine*. A search of the records available for Keepers Burke and Orcutt—and even an attempt to track down the family records of other keepers of the era—

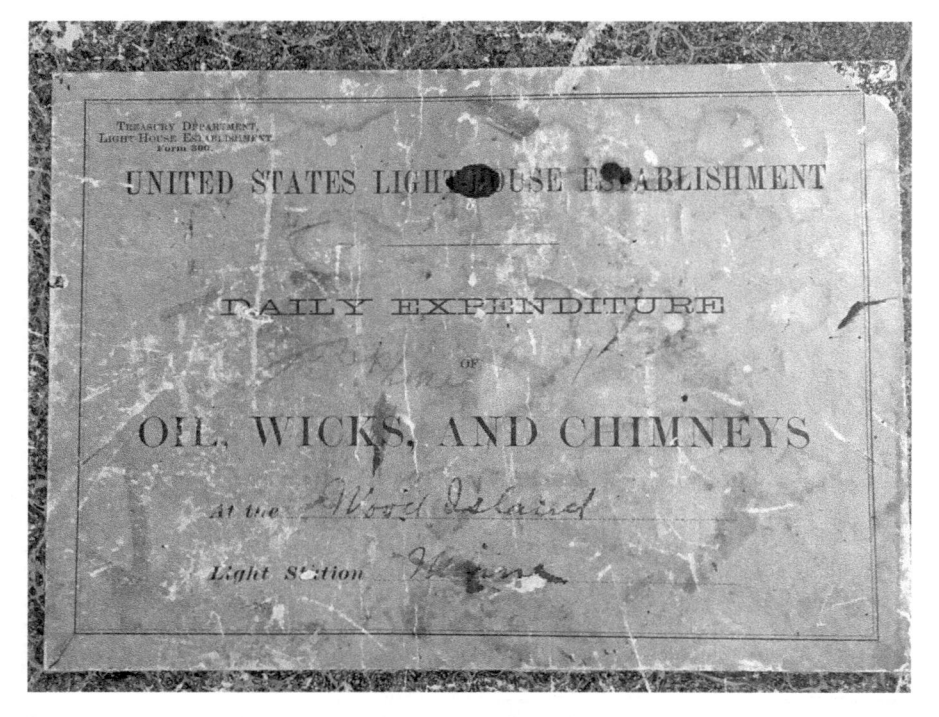

Detail of the scrapbook's cover reveals the name "Josephine" faintly written with a pencil just below the words "DAILY EXPENDITURE," but still visible. *Collections of the Maine Historical Society. Coll. 2025.*

turned up nothing. However, the name *Josie* does appear in the caption to one of the photos pasted in the scrapbook.

The top image on the following page was clipped from the *Portland Sunday Press and Times* of January 2, 1910, and was titled "Western Maine Pythian Tournament." Josie Skillin is standing in the middle of the second row, fourth from the right. Elsewhere in the scrapbook, the name Skillin appears and is often found near items associated with the name Greenleaf. One of these reports that "a very happy event took place at the home of Capt. Edward K. Greenleaf on Wednesday evening last, in the marriage of his daughter L. Josephine to Mr. Frank H. Skillins of Portland."

Another intriguing group of items included in the scrapbook contains references and images relating to Captain George W. Greenleaf. One article reports that the government was becoming alarmed at the declining population of cod and haddock and had therefore enlisted the assistance of Greenleaf's steamer, SS *Gannet*, to participate in a conservation effort to restore the numbers of these and other fish so critical to the commercial fisheries in Maine. In

Above: "Western Maine Pythian" includes an image of Mrs. "Josie" Skillin (*center row, fourth from the left*). Her maiden name was Josephine Greenleaf. *Collections of the Maine Historical Society. Coll. 2025.*

Left: "The Cod" is an article reporting on the important work of Captain George W. Greenleaf, the brother-in-law of Charles Burke, keeper at Wood Island. *Collections of the Maine Historical Society. Coll. 2025.*

Stories from the Edge of the Sea

1912, it is reported that the SS *Gannet* put 150 seed lobsters (10 million lobster fry) into the water between Wood Island and Biddeford Pool. Another article chronicles that on one occasion while serving just outside Portsmouth Harbor in New Hampshire, the *Gannet* encountered a severe southeast gale that "got the better of the little craft and her rudder and rudder post were carried away and she began leaking badly." A lobster boat managed to tow the *Gannet* into port for repairs, and no one was lost or injured during the incident.

Finally, with the information gleaned from the items in the scrapbook, it became possible to search for a family tree that would link some of the key names included in this old keeper's logbook. The result is reproduced below.

GREENLEAF FAMILY TREE

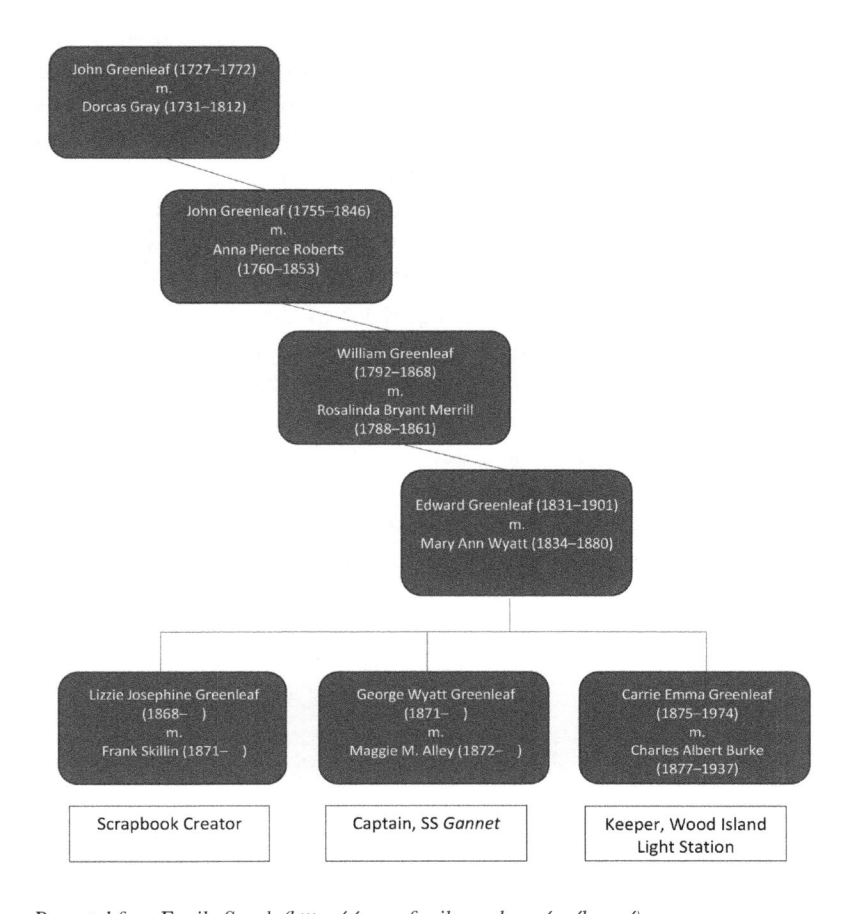

- John Greenleaf (1727–1772) m. Dorcas Gray (1731–1812)
  - John Greenleaf (1755–1846) m. Anna Pierce Roberts (1760–1853)
    - William Greenleaf (1792–1868) m. Rosalinda Bryant Merrill (1788–1861)
      - Edward Greenleaf (1831–1901) m. Mary Ann Wyatt (1834–1880)
        - Lizzie Josephine Greenleaf (1868–) m. Frank Skillin (1871–) — Scrapbook Creator
        - George Wyatt Greenleaf (1871–) m. Maggie M. Alley (1872–) — Captain, SS *Gannet*
        - Carrie Emma Greenleaf (1875–1974) m. Charles Albert Burke (1877–1937) — Keeper, Wood Island Light Station

Recreated from Family Search (https://www.familysearch.org/en/home/)

The Greenleaf family tree strongly suggests that Josephine Greenleaf, the daughter of Edward and Mary Ann Greenleaf, was probably the creator of the scrapbook. She was the sister of Captain George Greenleaf, commander of the SS *Gannet*, and also the sister of Carrie Emma Greenleaf, the wife of Wood Island Lighthouse keeper Charles Albert Burke. It is likely that the logbook that Josephine used to create her scrapbook was obtained somehow from her younger sister.

Afterword

Captain George Wyatt Greenleaf continued to command the *Gannet* and pursue his dedication to the cause of conserving Maine's fisheries. His sons, Luther and Arthur, following a similar calling, were appointed warden and commissioner, respectively, for the Department of Sea and Shore Fisheries, the state's organization for enforcing the laws as applied to the fishing industry. Captain George Greenleaf died in 1953 and is buried in the Greenleaf plot at the Oceanview Cemetery in Boothbay Harbor.

Josie Greenleaf was employed as a clerk at the famous Portland department store Owen, Moore and Company on Congress Street before her marriage to Frank H. Skillin in September 1893. Skillin is described as "one of Portland's best young citizens having been in the chocolate confectionery manufacturing department of I.A. Goudy and Goudy & Kent's for the past ten years." Their daughter Gladys was born in 1894. They lived in Portland for nearly twenty years before moving back to Boothbay Harbor. Josie, who died in 1953, and Frank, who passed away two years later, both rest in the Oceanview Cemetery, not far from Josie's sister, Carrie.

The scrapbook still resides on the dusty shelves inside the Maine Historical Society on Congress Street in Portland, Maine.

Chapter 13

UNEXPECTED ENCOUNTERS
1925-82

In keeping the journal, two pages (the right and the left) are to be used for one month. The events of the day must be written on one line across both pages...any item of interest occurring in the vicinity, such as the state of the weather, or other similar matter.
—Instructions to Light-Keepers, *July 1881*

"Any Item of Interest..."

As was required of him by the *Instructions* of 1881, Keeper Albert Staples made careful note of matters of interest during his years of service at his Wood Island Station. One such item began to catch the attention of faithful readers of the *Biddeford Weekly Journal* as early as January 16, 1925:

>BIDDEFORD AND SACO PEOPLE
>MAY GET A GOOD VIEW
>OF ECLIPSE OF THE SUN

The headline was intended to generate excitement and alert potential viewers to the rare astronomical event that would occur on January 24. Readers were warned of the dangers of directly viewing the eclipse and to prepare a viewer of "smoked glass" by taking a piece of "clear glass and put it over a lamp or candle wick until it is thoroughly covered with a deep coating of soot." Teachers, while encouraged to give their students a chance to view the spectacle, should be especially cautious and urge their charges to take care to properly shade their eyes.[159]

SHENANDOAH OFF FOR MAINE NEXT FRIDAY

Leaves Jersey at 8 A. M., Reaches Bar Harbor Before Night.

Lakehurst, N. J., July 1.—(AP).— The dirigible Shenandoah will be taken to her mooring mast tomorrow night in preparation for her trip to Bar Harbor, Me., which, if weather conditions are favorable, is to begin on Friday morning at 8 o'clock.

The ship will fly over Bridgeport, Conn., Providence, R. I., Boston, Cambridge and Lawrence, Mass., and Portland, Me. She is expected to arrive at Bar Harbor before sunset, Friday.

She will remain anchored to the mooring mast on the cruiser Patoka until Saturday evening.

Leaving Bar Harbor that night, the dirigible is expected to reach Lakehurst before daybreak, Sunday.

Navy officials were unable to give a definite schedule of times for the Shenandoah's passage over New England cities en route to Bar Harbor, but indicated that it would take about three hours to reach Providence.

Left: Albert Staples and his wife, Emily. Keeper Staples was fondly called "Gramps." *FOWIL Archives, courtesy Elaine Jones.*

Right: Headline announcing the schedule for the *Shenandoah*'s appearance in Maine. *Biddeford Weekly Journal,* July 3, 1925.

The following week, a detached Keeper Staples wrote, "Partial eclipse of the sun @ 8 AM. Eclipse clear 10:10 AM."[160] The *Biddeford Weekly Journal*, however, was a bit more enthusiastic. "The eclipse was wonderful," it exclaimed. And even though it was partially obscured by clouds and the cold made it somewhat uncomfortable for viewing, the event offered the opportunity of a lifetime.[161]

Six months later, the keeper made note of another "item of interest":

SHENANDOAH
TO PASS OVER
THE TWO CITIES

On Friday, July 3, 1925, Staples reported that he was not feeling well but had managed to attend to his general duties. He went on to write, "Large Dirigible, *Shenandoah* passed by W. of this station 5 PM standard time bound E. to Bar Harbor, Maine." The following day, the Fourth of July, "the same air ship, *Shenandoah*, passed East of this station bound W. this day at 6:45 PM standard time." The airship, which had left New Jersey early on the morning of the third, was scheduled to make the trip to Bar Harbor, Maine, and then return the following evening, flying overnight back to its base in Lakehurst, New Jersey.[162]

Along the coast of southern Maine, anticipation of the dirigible's flight created quite a stir. Onlookers were not disappointed. An airplane taking off from Old Orchard Beach appeared to be "a mere fly beside the giant balloon," whose 680 feet was more than twice the size of two football fields. So large and unprecedented was the sight that observers on rooftops in Biddeford thought the craft traveled directly overhead when in fact its course was well to the east, flying above Fletcher's Neck and directly over Camp Ellis and Old Orchard Beach.[163]

"Wonderful Sight to See"

Just short of ten years following Keeper Albert Staples's logbook entry commenting on a partial eclipse of the sun, the public once again prepared for an astronomical treat, on this occasion a total eclipse of the sun. On August 31, 1932, it was Keeper George Woodward's turn to look up in amazement and write, "Total eclipse of sun 3:30 p.m. Visible and a wonderful sight to see."[164] Residents of New England lucky enough to find themselves along a one-hundred-mile-wide belt stretching from Canada along the White Mountains, through Fryeburg and Biddeford, were warned to protect their eyes with darkened glass or photographic film negatives. Observers were informed that the sensation of the dimming sky would even bring a noticeable coolness to the air.

Although in Vermont two spectators became so frightened that they required medical attention, strong reaction to the unusual event was not limited to humans. Dogs were reported to begin whimpering, crickets chirping and roosters crowing as the sun slowly darkened their world. On dairy farms, cows returned to their stalls for milking, while puzzled birds returned to their roosts, presumably under the assumption that the day was over.[165]

News of the total eclipse created excitement and wonder along its path in Maine. *Biddeford Daily Journal*, September 1, 1932.

"A Beautiful Late Spring Day..."

Coast Guard keeper Russ Lowell's "item of interest" took a somewhat different form. In 2006, twenty years after his assignment to Wood Island, he related this story in an interview:

> There was this time that I headed for the boathouse going to get the mail. And I had noticed that the seagulls were up and flying. It was a beautiful late spring day, early summer. I came over the little rise and there are these two women walking up the boardwalk "boliky bare assed." I am pretty surprised. They had been out canoeing and they were all wet and they didn't know that anyone was on the island. They were from Canada.[166]

Not to be outdone, the keeper's wife, Terry Lowell, launched into an even more "R-rated" tale. "There was that boat which was moored off the point and they were sunbathing in the nude." "Well [interjects Russ] they were doing more than just sunbathing in the nude." Terry continued without missing a beat: "You went up the tower to see what was going on to see if they were in distress. And then didn't you hit the foghorn?" Russ takes the story from there. "The foghorn gives a blast and this young couple in the bottom of this little boat look up and see me with a pair of binoculars hanging around my neck hollering, 'Are you in distress? Move along!' They were pretty shocked."[167]

"Waterboro Man Feared Drowned at Pool"

Keeper Michael McQuade (1976–79) credits his predecessor Jerry Murray (1973–76) with preparing him for the surprising twists that are an integral part of the keepers' life on Wood Island. "I do have to thank Jerry Murray, the previous keeper," he said, "for alerting me to the hazards involved in landing the peapod at the boathouse." Murray made him "well aware about the swells coming in, the waves, the wind coming in. Don't just look one way, look all around. Look to the left. Look to the right. See what was ahead of you, see what was behind you. Because the swells might be coming in one way and the next second you might be getting a swell coming in from another. Make sure you time it."[168]

Murray's advice to McQuade to be aware and observant originated during the new keeper's weeklong training period and followed a particularly unnerving experience. "Patsy and I lived here with the previous keeper and his wife to learn the ropes," said McQuade. "He started me in the habit of scouting the shoreline once a week to see what has washed up. During that week the resident keeper and I discovered a body that had washed ashore after a boating accident a week before."[169] The unfortunate incident, described in the *Biddeford Saco Journal* on July 26, 1976, involved five men who were cast into the sea when their fifteen-foot boat was swamped. Four of the five were able to swim to Wood Island and were rescued by the Coast Guard. The body of Kenneth MacCorison, age thirty-two, however, was not recovered until it was discovered nearly a week later by Murray and McQuade.[170]

"…Must Have Gotten Fresh…"

Not all stories of stranded boaters are tragic, nor do romantic encounters always end with the groan of a foghorn. Lily Burnham, wife of Keeper Laurier Burnham (1959–62), recalled during an interview the tale of a local girl and her male guest "speeding around the harbor in her speedboat. He must have gotten fresh," she suggested, "because Laurier spotted him from the tower clutching onto the bell buoy east of the island and had to call Fletcher's Neck to rescue him."[171]

"Seventeen and Just About Done For..."

There was nothing remotely romantic about the story Eloise Frank reported, which also highlights the lack of responsibility that can so often lead to tragedy.

> *We came back from town one day and there was this boat floating by out by the bell buoy and we heard somebody yelling and screaming. So, my husband* [Keeper Edward Frank, 1952–56] *launched the boat and he went out and picked up this kid, seventeen years old and was just about done for. His boat broke loose from the mooring and instead of staying with the boat, he jumped overboard to swim.*
>
> **(Interviewer) Was he clinging to the buoy?** *No, he was in open water.*
>
> **(Interviewer) Did he have a life vest on?** *No nothing.*
>
> *The Saco River was coming strong, it took him. We just happened to be there because we had just come back from town. So he got him and I called Fletcher's Neck from the boat house and they came out with the forty-footer and loaded him in that and got him to the hospital.*

It appears that the young man learned very little from this near-death experience. Mrs. Frank continues:

> *Then a while went by and he and another boy came out one day to thank us for saving his life. My husband kind of went up one side of him and down the other because they came out in this old leaky rowboat—out on the ocean—it could have happened all over again.*[172]

Wood Island's rocky shoreline makes it all but impossible to land anywhere but the western end of the island, more than one-half mile from the light station. *Photo by Richard Levy.*

The snow-covered boardwalk leads the way to the light station at sunrise on this winter day. *Photo by Mark Jones, Shutterbugs4charity.org.*

Left: Early morning. A snowy owl watches as Wood Island's light is still flashing its distinctive green and white signal. *Photo by Mark Jones, Shutterbugs4charity.org.*

Below: A spectacular winter sunrise from the north side of the Wood Island Light Station accentuates the Dutch Colonial dwelling restored to its 1906 appearance. *Photo by Mark Jones, Shutterbugs4charity.org.*

The beginning of a winter day at the Wood Island Light Station highlights the light tower. The dwelling with its open porch is the centerpiece of FOWIL's restoration to its 1906 appearance. *Photo by Mark Jones, Shutterbugs4charity.org.*

Looking east along the boardwalk as the winter sun rises over the Gulf of Maine and the Wood Island Lighthouse. *Photo by Mark Jones, Shutterbugs4charity.org.*

Fall brings a distinctive quality to the 5/8-mile boardwalk connecting the boathouse on the west end of the island to the station at the east end. *Photo by Mark Jones, Shutterbugs4charity.org.*

As dusk casts the Wood Island Light Station into silhouette, its enigmatic personality becomes even more evident. *Photo by Sean Murphy.*

Left: Rising from the base of the tower to the top of the stairs requires visitors to ascend sixty steps. The wooden handrails were installed by FOWIL and replaced the original rope railings, which were not considered safe for present-day guests. *Photo by Richard Levy.*

Right: The property's grounds and gardens are maintained weekly throughout the season by volunteers who affectionately refer to themselves as "Woodchucks and Woodchicks." *Photo by Sean Murphy.*

This sign marks the halfway point of the 5/8-mile boardwalk. It was created and installed by volunteer "Woodchucks and Woodchicks." *Photo by Richard Levy.*

Right: In the distance, the sun in the eastern sky rises over the Wood Island Light Station, framing the boats moored in Wood Island Harbor. *Photo by Sean Murphy.*

Below: The path leading from the oil house to the dwelling, restored to its 1906 appearance. The Dutch Colonial–style lighthouse is the only one of its kind still standing in Maine and has been restored to standards established by the State of Maine Historic Preservation Commission. *Photo by Brad Coupe.*

Left: Approaching the light station from the boardwalk, visitors get their first introduction to the unique Dutch Colonial–style dwelling. The A-shaped structure on the right is a solar array—part of the modern power system. *Photo by Bob Trapani.*

Below: The rocky shoreline and protruding rocks are evident in this view of the Wood Island Lighthouse taken from Biddeford Pool. *Photo by Richard Levy.*

Top: The oil house with its slate roof played an important role in FOWIL's restoration effort. The original structure was built in 1903 to hold kerosene and other flammable liquids. *Photo by Richard Levy.*

Middle: A stunningly clear winter night. The Wood Island Lighthouse characteristically flashes green and white, alternating every ten seconds, thus distinguishing itself from other nearby lighthouses. *Photo by Mark Jones, Shutterbugs4charity.org*

Bottom: An iconic view of the lighthouse station. A covered walkway connects the dwelling to a vestibule that then leads into the tower. The small angular structure on the right is the well cover. *Photo by Richard Levy.*

Above: The 1906 station, seen here from the north side. Visitors traveling to the lighthouse aboard *Lightrunner* will travel all the way around the island if conditions permit. *Photo by Sean Murphy.*

Left: Low clouds and fog add a mysterious quality to the light station, further inspiring stories of legends and ghosts. *Photo by Shari Robinson.*

Left: Visitors to the island are invited to climb the sixty steps leading to the top of the light tower. From the top of the tower, Old Orchard Beach is visible on the mainland in the far distance. *Photo by Shari Robinson.*

Below: Seagulls are prolific and nest on the island. The large black back gulls often land on top of the chimney. *Photo by Sean Murphy.*

In July, visitors to the island enjoy the view from the top of the tower. Others participating in the tour gather on the platform below awaiting either their turn to climb the tower or an opportunity to explore the dwelling. The mowed area behind the flagpole provides a landing pad for helicopters. *Photo by Jeremy D'Entremont.*

Looking southwest from the top of the tower. The Flying Santa used the helicopter landing area when he delivered gifts to the keepers and their families. *Photo by Shari Robinson.*

The tour. Vines Landing in Biddeford Pool where visitors embark on the first portion of their journey to the Wood Island Lighthouse. Here, guests await *Lightrunner* as it returns from an earlier tour. Visitors will have the opportunity to explore the dwelling house and grounds and to climb to the top of the tower if they choose. *Photo by Sean Murphy.*

The boathouse. The Coast Guard retains ownership of the station and leases it to the American Lighthouse Foundation. The Friends of Wood Island Lighthouse (FOWIL) is a chapter of ALF and maintains the restored station with financial support from the public. *Photo by Shari Robinson.*

Above: The boat landing. Visitors walk up the boat ramp as they debark from *Lightrunner*. Near the boathouse, notice the remains of the original "slip" in the middle of the ramp. The keepers would often grease these rails to make conveying the boat a little bit easier. *Photo by Shari Robinson.*

Left: The boardwalk. The lighthouse comes into view as visitors complete the half-mile stroll that began at the boathouse. *Photo by Shari Robinson.*

The voyage. *Lightrunner* is circling the island on its return to Biddeford Pool. This specially designed landing craft is ideally suited to its purpose. The front drops down to allow visitors to easily enter and exit the boat. *Photo by Sean Murphy.*

No two days are ever alike in the Gulf of Maine. Clouds begin to gather in the late afternoon and offer a striking view of the light station from the north. *Photo by Kyle Noble.*

Sharp angles and a clear blue sky dominate this unique view of the back side of the station. *Photo by Richard Levy.*

A volunteer work party looking down at their accomplishments from the top of the light tower. *Photo by Sean Murphy.*

The cattails in the near ground show the presence of fresh water. The environment of Wood Island has changed dramatically over the last two hundred years. Today, it is marked by low-lying shrubs, grasses and just a few trees. *Photo by Shari Robinson.*

Reconstruction of the light tower and dwelling began in 2007 and has lasted for more than ten years. Today, visitors to the island experience the station much as it was in 1906. *Photo by Bob Trapani.*

Chapter 14

WOOD ISLAND POETS
1900–2013

"The Dog That Rang the Bell"

Waldo Stillson Verrill was the grandson of Nathaniel Verrill and nephew of Lyman Frank "L.F." Verrill, both of whom had been appointed as keepers of the Wood Island Light Station and served during the years 1853–58. Waldo, like his grandfather, father and uncle, became a successful fisherman but also took great delight in writing poetry. Over the course of his ninety-three years, Waldo Stillson Verrill published his poems in magazines and periodicals and recited them from the lecture platform. As a result, he acquired a significant following and a reputation that earned him the title "Biddeford Pool Poet."[173]

W.S. Verrill and his fellow residents were deeply saddened by the misfortune that ended in tragedy for the *Marshall Perrin* during that November gale in 1906. His poem commemorating the calamity appeared in the *Biddeford Record* on November 21, 1906, and is reproduced in a previous chapter. The lines speak not only to the specific events of that terrible night but also to the vulnerability that all must feel before the powerful and capricious forces of nature.

> *Two widows weep; oh dreadful deep!*
> *How many now are sleeping*
> *In watery graves, beneath the waves,*
> *While loved ones dear are weeping.*[174]

Verrill's poems touched a variety of subjects, but he seemed particularly moved to write in the memory of recently departed friends and loved ones. Titles such as "Faith—The Consolation," "In Memory of Little Ted" and "Her Christian Warfare" suggest the melancholy spirit characteristic of his work. These lines from "The Great Beyond," written as a tribute to his 104-year-old grandmother, are representative:

THE GREAT BEYOND
By W.S. Verrill

Sweet still she lives friend, neighbor
Saint.
Sweetly, calmly without complaint
She bides her time.

Where to the unseen "Great Beyond"
Here kindred souls and friendships
Fond.
Again unite in loyal bond
In Heavenly clime.[175]

Keeper Thomas Orcutt's famous "Lighthouse Dog," Sailor, brought widespread fame to the little Biddeford Pool community and earned its profound affection. The dog's passing in the fall of 1905 was broadly felt and moved W.S. Verrill to write "The Dog That Rang the Bell" in Sailor's memory. His poem is reminiscent of both Verrill's themes and style:

The Dog That Rang the Bell
Waldo S. Verrill

Poor Sailor was a faithful dog
On yonder Isle of Wood
Through many years of rain and fog
Near by his duty stood

And rang the bell when passing boats
Too near the breakers came
Until they heard its warning notes
The dog now known to fame

For he was oft times photographed
As he would ring the bell
By some white winged pleasure craft
Out sailing on the swell

Sailor's salutes were often heard
By fishers passing by
And friends were made and hearts were stirred
But Sailor had to die

But faithful masters noble dog
And none could him excel
For fifteen years in storm and fog
When asked he'd ring the bell

Sailor was glad when strangers came
And seemed to love them well
Kindly disposed to all the same
The dog that rang the bell

No more we'll hear his joyous bark
As he would rush pell-mell
So full of sport and gay's a lark
When he would ring the bell

But this we'll miss a long long while
And oft the story tell
Of the faithful dog on wooded isle
The dog that rang the bell

And when we sail the lighthouse by
And roll on ocean's swell
We'll think of Sailor the noble dog
The dog that rang the bell

With our island friends we sympathize
To whom this loss befell
For Sailor's gone the pet so wise
The dog that rang the bell[176]

Portrait of Sailor, the Lighthouse Dog, whose talents brought international acclaim. *FOWIL Archives.*

"My Dear Sister Mary Was Filled with Delight"

Albert Norwood Jr. was the light keeper at Wood Island a little more than a quarter century prior to Sailor's passing in 1905. Norwood was one of fourteen children born to Abraham and Nancy Norwood, who themselves lived at the Wood Island Light Station between 1833 and 1841. Keeper Albert Norwood's actions between the years 1872 and 1886 reveal his competence, even heroism, in all matters related to his job. Surviving letters from the period also reveal that he was something of a romantic.

Throughout his life, the keeper remained close to his siblings and corresponded with them frequently. One of his sisters, Lucinda, whom he affectionately called Lucindy, hints at Albert's romantic disposition in a letter from the fall of 1877. "Your geranium scented letter was received last night. I also received one last Monday," she writes.[177]

Albert was also close to his brother Abraham Norwood Jr., who appears also to have acquired an impulse for the romantic. Abraham wrote the following letter to Albert's wife, Mary, his sister-in-law. In the letter, Abraham makes reference yet again to his brother Albert's preference for letters scented with "a beautiful, fragrant bouquet." The note, carefully crafted in rhyme, was written in anticipation of Mary's birthday (March 23). Abraham's sister-in-law had earlier received a perfumed letter from her husband, Albert, which she then shared with Abraham. Consequently, at the top, Abraham addresses his message on March 20, 1880, to both Mary and Albert.[178]

The Letter

To Mary Albert; Mar 20, 1880
My dear sister Mary
  Was filled with delight
By a letter received from our Albert to-night,
Containing a beautiful, fragrant boquet [sic],
That was cherished & kissed e'er you sent it away.
It received on arrival as fond an embrace
As though it had been a small part of your face;
And you may be certain in answer to this,
I send you my thanks and will owe you a kiss,
Which could I be there on your coming birth-day,

Stories from the Edge of the Sea

> To Mary Albert; Mar. 20, 1880.
> My Dear Sister Mary, —
> By a letter received *Was filled with delight*
> Containing a beautiful, fragrant boquet
> That was cherished & kissed e'er you sent it away
> It received on arrival as fond an embrace
> As though it had been a small part of your face,
> And you may be certain in answer to this,
> I send you my thanks & will owe you a kiss
> Which, could I be there on your coming birth-day,
> I would with warm interest eagerly pay.
> But as I cannot I thus hastily plan
> To send this short missive as soon as I can
> And hope it will reach you on Tuesday, you see,
> With words of good cheer & affection from me
> And also kind wishes from Parker & Ruth,
> With the Odd Fellows motto, "Love, Friendship & Truth."
> Your years have been many, your duties well done
> And now towards its setting advances your sun;
> May its softest & sweetist & mellowest rays
> Illumine & hallow the rest of your days
> Rejoicing your heart in devotion & praise!
> Accept these few words from the spirit and pen
> Of your ever affectionate Brother,
> A. N.

The original letter written in rhyme by Abraham Norwood in 1880. *FOWIL Archives*.

> *I would with warm interest eagerly pay.*
> *But as I cannot I thus hastily plan*
> *To send this short missive as soon as I can,*
> *And hope it will reach you on Tuesday, you see,*
> *With words of good cheer & affection from me,*
> *And also kind wishes from Parker & Ruth,*

With the Odd Fellows motto "Love, Friendship & Truth."
Your years have been many, your duties well done,
And now towards its setting advances your sun;
May its softest & sweetest & mellowest rays
Illumine & hallow the rest of your days
Rejoicing your heart in devotion & praise![179]
...
A. Jr.

"Oh What Is the Bane of a Lightkeeper's Life"

Wood Island's lighthouse keepers in the early twentieth century were talented and skillful men generally capable of managing the problems with which they were confronted. Occasionally, though, they had to call in an expert tradesman or engineer to deal with more complex issues. Such was the case toward the end of January 1929, when Keeper George E. Woodward reported that the fog bell and lens clock were not working properly. On January 25, he felt the need to telephone the office for new parts and assistance, and on the following day, he wrote in his logbook that "Mr. Morong arrived at 12 pm to fix lens clock." The two men worked together for several days before they were able to find a remedy for the problem, and on January 30, Keeper Woodward reported that "Mr. Morong went ashore at 9 am."[180]

The mention of Morong is noteworthy because of the acclaim that he later received as the "Lighthouse Keeper's Poet Laureate." Frederick Morong Jr. was the machinist for lighthouses in the First District. When local keepers were baffled by issues related to the increasingly complex machinery of the era, he was the engineer called in to assist. Because his work often required more than a few hours to complete, he was frequently asked to remain at the lighthouse for several days. Morong's affable personality made him a welcome overnight guest. The stories he collected from his lighthouse hosts, regularly peppered with complaints about the repetitive nature of their work, inspired the limericks that eventually became his signature poem: "Brasswork: The Light-Keeper's Lament."

Logbook records show that Morong returned to Wood Island many times during the 1920s and 1930s. An entry logged on Thanksgiving Day 1935 suggests that the district machinist's association with the Wood Island Light Station may have been both professional and personal. Keeper Benson

Keeper David Katon (1957–59) proudly displays his polished brasswork in the lantern room. *FOWIL Archives.*

was on leave during the holiday, and the identity of his substitute remains a mystery. In any case, the entry, written by the temporary keeper, reads, "Frances Kreidler arrived for Thanksgiving."[181] In 1935, Frances Kreidler was married to George Morong, the nephew of Frederick Morong Jr. This personal connection of Frederick Morong Jr. to Wood Island, along with his documented frequent visits, qualifies him as a poet of Wood Island. His lines most certainly capture the spirit of the light keeper's experience and are reproduced here:

BRASSWORK: THE LIGHT-KEEPER'S LAMENT
By Frederick Morong Jr.

Oh what is the bane of a lightkeeper's life
That causes him worry, struggle and strife,
That makes him use cuss words and beat on his wife?
It's BRASSWORK

Wood Island Lighthouse

What makes him look ghastly consumptive and thin,
What robs him of health, vigor and vim,
And causes despair and drives him to sin?
It's BRASSWORK...

The devil himself could never invent,
A material causing more world wide lament,
And in Uncle Sam's service about ninety percent
Is BRASSWORK

The lamp in the tower, reflector and shade,
The tools and accessories pass in the parade,
As a matter of fact the whole outfit is made
Of BRASSWORK

The oil containers I polish until
My poor back is broken, aching and still,
Each gallon, each quart, each pint and gill
Is BRASSWORK

I lay down to slumber all weary and sore,
I walk in my sleep, I awake with a snore,
And I'm shining the knob on my bedchamber door
That BRASSWORK

From pillar to post rags and polish I tote,
I'm never without them, for you will please note,
That even the buttons I wear on my coat,
Are BRASSWORK

The machinery, clockwork, and fog signal bell,
The coal hods, the dustpans, the pump in the well,
No I'll leave it to you mates...If this isn't...well,
BRASSWORK

I dig, scrub and polish, and work with a might,
And just when I get it all shining and bright,
In comes the fog like a thief in the night,
Goodbye BRASSWORK

Keeper Edward Frank (1952–56) winding the fog bell—just one of the many tasks listed in poet Morong's "Lament." *FOWIL Archives, photo in* Life *magazine.*

> *I start the next day when noontime draws near,*
> *A boatload of summer visitors appear,*
> *For no other reason than to smooch and besmear,*
> *My BRASSWORK*
>
> *So it goes along all summer, and along in the fall,*
> *Comes the district machinists to overhaul,*
> *and rub dirty paws all over,*
> *My BRASSWORK*
>
> *And again in the spring, if per chance it may be,*
> *An efficiency star is awarded to me,*
> *I open the package and what do I see?*
> *More BRASSWORK*
>
> *Oh, why should the spirit of mortal be proud,*
> *In the short span of life that he is allowed,*

If all the lining in every dark cloud,
Is BRASSWORK

And when I have polished until I am cold,
And I have taken my oath to the Heavenly fold,
Will my harp and my crown be made of pure gold?
No! BRASSWORK[182]

"We Three Are Alone"

Wilbert Freeman Lurvey took charge of the Wood Island Lighthouse on April 1, 1917, and remained there with his family until October 1923.

W.F. Lurvey, born in 1879, was the oldest of nine children raised by Ezra Dodge Lurvey and Abigail Eliza Hunt. He spent his childhood in Southwest Harbor, Maine, looking out over Mount Desert Island and the Gulf of Maine. When his mother died in 1907, Keeper Lurvey's father remarried,

The back side of the Wood Island Light Station with the bell tower, light tower and dwelling visible beside the "billowy ocean." *FOWIL Archives, photo in* Life *magazine.*

making Elmenia Thompson Spurling Preble Lurvey his stepmother. The groom was fifty-five at the time of their marriage; the bride was sixty-eight.

The new Mrs. Lurvey was from Cranberry Isles, a unique town that consists today of several small islands just off the coast of Mount Desert Island and is a refuge for artists and writers, especially poets. Elmenia was among the latter.

Ezra and Elmenia visited their son on Wood Island toward the end of his appointment in 1923. While there, she wrote "Lines from a Lighthouse," at once both a reflection on the many arduous tasks that challenged the keeper of a lighthouse and, at the same time, a reminder of the grateful welcome his efforts received by those he served.

LINES FROM A LIGHTHOUSE
By Elmenia Thompson Spurling Preble Lurvey

I am sitting beside this billowy ocean,
And gazing on naught, but the sea and the sky;
The crystal waves roll with an unceasing motion,
As they rush on the sea shore, in foam breaking high.

We three are alone on this desolate island:
Alone with my husband and Wilbert, his son.
He is lightkeeper here on the Wood Island Light Station,
When daylight is ended his work is undone.

For, when nearly sundown, he ascends the high tower,
He lights the big lantern that gleams through the night;
For the sea-faring sailors, roaming over the ocean,
Who patiently watch for the red beacon light.

When the clock points to midnight, he again mounts the tower,
To wind the machinery revolving the light.
He carefully watches till its beams shine forth brightly,
Then wakefully slumbers through the rest of the night.

At the dawning of sunrise he starts for the tower,
To put out the light, tidy up for the day.
There's enough work to do to keep things running smoothly,
It is work while the day lasts, not much time for play.

More especially now, since the burning of soft coal,
Keeping everything covered with black, smutty dust;
It is useless to growl at the U.S.A. government,
But shovel the coal and in Uncle Sam trust.

Both outside and inside the tower must be painted,
The stairs painted too, winding up to the light;
The dwelling inside must be painted and varnished,
Outside every building is all painted white.

In sea fog and snowstorms he enters the tower,
To mind the big weight so the clock may run well;
For the benefit of seamen approaching the harbor,
Who anxiously listen for the sound of its bell.[183]

"Her Glory Is Reborn"

Russ and Terry Lowell were assigned to Wood Island in 1979 and remained there for two and a half years before Russ was transferred to sea duty. The Lowells returned to southern Maine in time to see their "island home" undergoing restoration by the Friends of the Wood Island Lighthouse, a chapter within the American Lighthouse Foundation formed in 2003.

Asked to recall their experience as lighthouse keepers, Terry was quick to respond: "It was wonderful. It was real tranquility, total serenity." Russ agreed: "I wouldn't call it isolation; I would call it very peaceful….It was great."[184]

Terry's poem expresses the gratitude that she and many others felt for the opportunity to have played a key role caring for the lighthouse during the second half of the twentieth century. She also voices appreciation to those who are currently assuming the role of a new generation of lighthouse keepers dedicated to rehabilitating these important symbols of America's past. In dedicating her poem, Terry Lowell said:

> *Russ and I wish to express our heartfelt appreciation to F.O.W.I.L. for their selfless devotion and passionate affection for this Jewel of Saco Bay. To every docent, volunteer, member and guest, we send our fond gratitude for your time and interest. The best is yet to come!*[185]

Sheri Poftak looks on in admiration as Terry and Russ Lowell present Terry's hand-crafted Lighthouse Quilt to the Friends of the Wood Island Lighthouse in 2013. *FOWIL Archives.*

WOOD ISLAND LIGHTHOUSE
By Terry Lowell, September 2013

Our life on an island lighthouse was wonderful for him and me,
Standing atop the tower, great views far and wide to see.
We were young and foolish, but never were we scared,
Because the adventure before us was wondrous beyond compare.

As we gazed upon the ocean, two pots of morning coffee we did share,
The surf the sea brought to us was so mesmerizing, we just had to stare.
Most days the wind was friendly, other days it was our foe,
The American flag we flew proudly, always indicated direction of the blow.

Our daily chores though mundane, we felt fortunate to be tasked to do them,
Mowing the lawns, painting inside or out, and the weather we did send.
Keeping the light glowing, signaling the path for mariners on their way,
Watching for the ghostly fog that would blanket over us, the fog horn sounds okay.

Wood Island Lighthouse

The Wood Island Light Station in 1980 during the assignment of Keeper Russ Lowell. The front porch has been extended and enclosed as a "sun porch," and the light tower is "headless." *FOWIL Archives.*

We had no concerns for time, and quickly learned it was the tide we must know,
It was wind, rough seas and low tide that determined if we stay or we could go.
Most trips to and from Biddeford Pool were uneventful in our small open boat,
But when you lose all sight of land in the bottom of a deep swell, safe travel you hope.

Every beacon has its own characteristics, this one white then green,
During our tour of duty, the tower was "headless," not much glass to keep clean.
The long history of this island, even before the first stones were stacked, draws you near,
The spirits that roam thru thicket and closet door are anxious to speak, if you are willing to hear.

My best friend and I were a strong team, there was nothing we could not do,
Our talents complimented each other, which always got us thru.
We lovingly call this home "The Rock," there are many reasons to love her so,
From December of '79 to May of '82, we cherish every moment we had, we did not want to go.

In 1986 the final keeper left "The Rock," sad times beset, her struggle was rough,
The wind, the weather, the ocean and the sea gulls too, made the passing years very tough.
But with the growing concern of caring folks onshore, in 2003 a group of Friends was formed,
Now joy and rejuvenation of this sentinel has returned, thanks to them, her glory is reborn.

Chapter 15

MONSTERS, SERPENTS AND THINGS THAT GO BUMP IN THE NIGHT

1905–2006

Keeper Earle Benson was following his usual routine on July 1, 1937, when an unusual disturbance caught his attention, causing him to look out to sea. In the near distance, as the commotion continued, he strained to determine its cause. Baffled at first, he eventually figured it out and thought the event significant enough to remark in his logbook: "Whale and swordfish in death battle off station pm."

Sightings of whales and black snakes in the waters near the light station were certainly mesmerizing occurrences and may have caused some initial confusion, as well as accounts of mysterious creatures spotted offshore. But even the unexplained logbook entry of Keeper George Woodward on December 26, 1932, in which he noted simply, "killing creature," is insufficient to lead us to believe that the keepers at Wood Island ever saw a sea serpent.[186]

And yet, reports of such local sightings persist. Perhaps, as many would argue, these stories are the products of energetic imaginations acting in response to unusual and compelling incidents like the one Benson witnessed. Or maybe there is something out there…

SEA MONSTERS AND STRANGER THINGS

"Major General H.C. Merriam and his sons were sailing to Wood Island Light in 1905, when they spotted a 'monster serpent,' which proceeded to swim circles around their boat." So reports the author in an essay examining

"The Great Sea Serpent of Casco Bay," recently published online in *Emergence Magazine*. The major general offered this description of the creature:

> *Its head was several feet above the surface of the water, and its long body was plainly visible, slowly moving toward our boat by sinuous or snake-like motion....It had no dorsal fin unless it was continuous. The color of its back appeared to be brown and mottled, shading down to a dull yellow on the belly. The head was like that of a snake, and the part shown above the surface—that is the neck—appeared to be about 15 to 18 inches in diameter. If it had any pectoral fins we did not observe them. I estimated its length at 60 feet or more.*[187]

Reports of a "monster" in Casco Bay have existed for more than two centuries—long enough that residents along the southern coast of Maine have provided a name: Cassie. Sightings in the 1870s were so common that researcher and historian Sharon Cummins refers to a "serpent population explosion" during that decade.[188] It was in 1905, however, that monster sightings began to be taken a bit more seriously. General Merriam's account, for example, found its way to the director of the American Museum of Natural History in New York. But it was a report described in the *Biddeford Record* in June, two months before General Merriam's cruise, that increased the heartbeat of the York County community in 1905:

> *For the entire month of June residents flocked to the site at Old Orchard Beach where the skeletal remains of a sea-going monster were on display. A local seafaring man, Captain W.S. Boyden offered up the observation that he has "...heard captains tell about getting a glimpse of sea serpents but not until now did I ever take any stock in their yarns. But if that thing on the beach ain't a serpent I miss my guess."*[189]

Early speculation based on the skeleton maintained that the creature must have been serpentine in shape and seventy to eighty feet long. The body's diameter probably measured about five feet. The huge nine-foot-long skull was reminiscent of an alligator except for a smooth and apparently toothless beak. Some were convinced that the bones were those of an extinct ichthyosaurus, a prehistoric carnivore, which had become encased in ice and later thawed. Still others recalled the recent report of an ocean liner that had struck a large creature—some thought to be a whale—two to three weeks earlier off the Grand Banks.

It was definitely not his runaway imagination that caused Richard Gagne to have the "hell scared out of him" as he pulled up one of his lobster traps near the mouth of the Saco River in August 1967. Entangled in the line just below the surface, Gagne noticed what proved to be the skeletal remains of a large creature, nearly eight feet in length, with a snake-like head, nostrils the size of silver dollars and eye sockets large enough to take in a man's fist.[190]

Members of the community, many having spent the better part of their lives earning a living from the sea, were dumbfounded. "Darned if I know what it is," was typical of the comments uttered as hundreds of residents gathered at the wharf to gawk at the unusual "catch." Newspapers all over New England ran headlines sensationalizing the "thing" from Biddeford Pool. Experts were called, first from the science department of the local high school and, later, biologists from nearby colleges. Many were inclined to agree that the sea monster from Biddeford Pool was, as suggested by the three biologists, the decomposed carcass of a basking or sand shark or perhaps a creature occupying an ancient niche in the evolutionary progression. Nonetheless, skeptics remained unconvinced, confident that Cassie and her offspring continue to swim in the icy waters of the Gulf of Maine.[191]

FREAK OF THE SEA CAST UP.

Monster Of The Deep Left By the Nights Tide at Ocean Park.

It Will Have To Pass For Fabled Sea Serpent.

With Tail Missing It Measures Forty-Two Feet

Serpentine Shape And Not Over 15 Feet In Circumference.

Big Skull Terminates In Beak Nine Feet Long.

Headlines seemingly confirmed the existence of a sea serpent and contributed to the legend of "Cassie, the Sea Monster of Casco Bay." *Biddeford Record*, June 8, 1905.

GHOSTS, GOBLINS AND THINGS THAT GO BUMP IN THE NIGHT

Chroniclers of most lighthouses will eagerly spin yarns about ghosts for anyone willing to listen. So when Catherine Roche, wife of Keeper James

Roche (1969–70), was asked if anything strange happened while they were stationed on Wood Island, her immediate response was, "All lighthouses have ghosts." Without hesitation, she told her interviewer, "I always knew I was never alone in the house even when I was alone with the kids, on any lighthouse I went to. I always felt like I was never alone."[192]

Recalling the couple's first lighthouse assignment in Boothbay Harbor, Catherine went on to reminisce about bringing her newborn daughter home from the hospital. "I would hear this baby crying the minute I put her in her crib. And I would go in and she would be sound asleep, and yet the baby was still crying. After investigating, I found out that there was a baby there that died, a little girl." When their appointment to the Cuckholds Lighthouse ended and they went to their next assignment, Roche said, "I knew Wood Island had a lot of them [ghosts]. They were there and I would just say to them, you know what, I am not hurting you, you don't have to hurt me."[193]

Although lighthouses and ghosts seem to be inseparable, not all of Wood Island's keepers have reported ghostly phenomena. Eloise Frank, for example, told her interviewer, "I never saw anything strange."[194] Nevertheless, in 2005 and 2006, the Wood Island Lighthouse was visited by specialists from the New England Ghost Project, who arrived armed with

This skeleton on the stairway of the light tower adds a bit of supernatural tension as visitors ascend the sixty-five steps to the top. *Photo by Kathleen Larsen (detail).*

investigative equipment that included electromagnetic field meters, heat-sensitive/thermal imaging and 35mm cameras, electronic voice recognition detectors and a human medium. The Ghost Project was joined on its overnight investigation by representatives from the Friends of the Wood Island Lighthouse, who included past lighthouse keepers. Following their inquiry, the report concluded that the investigators "witnessed a parade of unexplainable green lights in the attic. High levels of EMP [electromagnetic phenomenon] readings were recorded in the lighthouse and throughout the keeper's house. Maureen [the medium] contacted two spirits: a woman… and a man. While investigating the island, [the thermal camera] captured a black shadow swooping down…moments before Maureen began to trance channel the spirit of a frightened girl trying to escape."[195]

The results reported by the Ghost Project came as no surprise to Keeper Russ Lowell and his wife, Terry. In the early 1980s, when they resided on Wood Island, they owned a Ouija board that they would occasionally use to pass the time. In an interview conducted in October 2006, a few months after the visit by the New England Ghost Project, Russ and Terry revealed their own mysterious experiences. First, they explained their interaction with the Ouija board. "A lot of people are skeptical of the Ouija board, but Russ and I were doing it and you just barely have your hands on it. We had trouble keeping up with it. It was almost moving without us. And usually you would have to put both hands on it, but out there you could do it with one hand and that thing would shoot out from underneath your fingers if you didn't and they [the spirits] would laugh at you."[196]

Terry Lowell was referring to their encounters with the male spirit contacted by Maureen from the Ghost Project when she commented:

> *I am almost guessing that "Peter" was one of those people. Peter was one of the spirits that we were talking to via the Ouija board. He crewed on a ship captained by Sir Jovo and later stranded. He told us, "We are not allowed to go back to the ship."…I think Peter is really the only one that we spoke to. We didn't get any last name. He just said that he was there with a couple of other crewmen. We really didn't ask [about dates]. I would surmise that it was during the time of masted sailing ships. He said that the captain wouldn't allow us on the boat. We asked him why, and he said because he didn't want us near his gold.*[197]

The Lowells had other strange and unexplainable experiences. The grease pencils that they would use for notes would disappear and then

An unnerving, ghost's-eye view of the spiral stairway leading to the top of the light tower. *Photo by Sean Murphy.*

inexplicably reappear in the corner of the stairwell or other odd locations. "We would open the kitchen cupboards and there would be markings with the grease pencils, or in the stairwell there would be grease pencil markings above arms' reach. The calculator, which was turned on if we didn't put it in the drawer."[198]

Terry found walking through the passageway in order to turn on the foghorn particularly eerie and unnerving. "That was the spooky area for me where I felt someone was over my shoulder." Russ mentioned, "We had dogs and of course we had Kelly, the island dog. Our German shepherd especially would get shaky and nervous. The dogs would stand on the knoll and just bark. We asked Peter on the Ouija board if they were barking at him, and he would respond, 'Oh yeah.'"[199]

Chapter 16

KEEPER BENSON'S WAR

1934–51

WORLD WAR II

At a time when war clouds in Europe and Asia were threatening to envelop the United States, and with the Depression still dogging the country, the years during which Earle Benson served as Wood Island's lighthouse keeper tested the nation at every turn. And yet, when interviewed for *Biddeford-Saco Journal* in 1976, the keeper's wife, Alice, insisted that the years from 1934 to 1951 were spent on her favorite island. She noted that conditions "improved greatly under the Coast Guard."[200] She and her husband felt secure in their quarters with three square meals a day and knowing that the government checks they received during the Depression were the only ones the banks would cash. While living on an island meant that the movies were out of the question, at least there was the television, which the Bensons brought to their dwelling in 1950, just before their reassignment to Portland Head Light. Although the *Lone Ranger* was their favorite program, Keeper Benson noted that they were thrilled to be able to view the World Series game so clearly that he could "see the lines on the ball."[201]

And life was never dull. Alice remembered a time when she and Earle ventured outside during a storm. Without warning, lightning struck their two-way radio, which was right behind the chair where she had just been sitting. Although only her organdy curtains were singed, the phone was blown out, making it necessary to communicate with shore by flashing lights using Morse code.[202]

Keeper Earle Benson, like every citizen, was infuriated by the Japanese attack on Pearl Harbor, exclaiming in his logbook on December 7, 1941:

"Japan the...cowardly bastards attacked without warning our fleet at Pearl Harbor. Let's give them hell." In the same entry, the keeper's unrestrained anger gave way to a more measured reminder that he had "received orders this date to be on lookout for enemy ships and planes."[203]

During World War II, lighthouses presented a special challenge to the maritime community, the coastal population and the authorities charged with overseeing the lights themselves. On the one hand, the movement of goods and services from port to port was essential to both the economy and the war effort. On the other hand, the beacons that lighted the routes through safe channels and into secure harbors were equally visible to friend and enemy alike. A Nazi attack on a lighthouse in Iceland in August 1942 made it clear that lighthouses too easily could become military targets and affirmed the Coast Guard's decision to require that some navigational aids be altered or removed from service. Along the coast, many lights had been extinguished immediately following the attack on Pearl Harbor, and newspapers cautioned all mariners in New England that navigational aids, including lights, fog signals and radio beacons, may be interrupted, suspended or visibility reduced without notice. According to Mrs. Benson, during the war years, the Wood Island Light was lighted with a dimmed "mantel lamp" intended exclusively for fishermen and patrol boats at the Pool.[204]

Portrait of Earle Benson (keeper, 1934–51). Keeper Benson and his wife, Alice, maintained the lighthouse during the tense years of World War II. *FOWIL Archives.*

Mrs. Benson's memory helps to explain Keeper Benson's logbook entry in July 1942, in which he expresses both frustration and understanding of the need to make wartime sacrifices. On July 28, he reports "Installed 4th order wick lamp this date does not look like a lighthouse? [illegible]" In the next few days, his irritation seems to grow deeper: "4th order lamps are no good but this is war so it is necessary....Cannot do anything with 4th order wick lamps. All they do is smoke and make everything a mess. Reported same to Officer in Charge."[205]

The war's impact on the nation's psyche is reflected periodically in Benson's logbook entries. Both as an American and as a veteran, having served honorably in the Coast Artillery Corps during World War I, he joined with others in commemorating Memorial Day in 1942. He wrote:

"Memorial Day once again. Have been to cemetery with flowers. This is a solemn day for the good old United States of America." Later that year, as the first full year of war came to an end, he recognized December 7, 1942: "Remember Pearl Harbor." A few days later that month, when Keeper Benson sat down to make the entry into his logbook on Christmas Day, he wrote: "May there be peace on earth this time next year." New Year's Eve inspired another touching entry: "So ends this year of 1942. With God's will may [fighting?] be over in 1943."[206]

Timothy Harrison, representing the *Lighthouse Digest* in 1993, interviewed Alice Benson and published her recollections of life at Wood Island in the magazine's March edition. During their conversation, Mrs. Benson recounted several intriguing stories relating to World War II. At times, the waters near Wood Island and apparently even Wood Island itself were used for naval training exercises. According to Mrs. Benson, "One time the military called up and said they were going to use Wood Island as a target and dropped flares that nearly set the bell tower on fire. While Earle was doing lookout duty in the tower tracer bullets were whizzing all around him." When Keeper Benson called to report the shells rushing past the bell tower, the military responded at the time that they were not even firing in the direction of Wood Island. Still, bullets have been known to go astray.[207]

Keeper Earle Benson and his wife, Alice, who, at the age of ninety, remembered her years at Wood Island with fondness. *FOWIL Archives.*

The insensitive shelling of targets located near the station created the tipping point for Mrs. Benson, who decided that she had just about enough and declared a silent war of her own—this time against the U.S. military. When a crew came out to Wood Island to give directions to the gun crews firing from East Point, Harrison reported that Alice watched with a sense of revenge as they "headed to this little knoll. And under the bushes was a real jungle of poison ivy. 'I never said anything [and] I don't know how the C.O. made out. But this I do know: He never came out to the station again.'"[208]

Another equally tantalizing tale might even have the feel of a Hollywood movie script. Harrison's article reports that Alice remembers that "an Italian submarine surfaced and sent a rubber raft ashore to Old Orchard Beach.

Stories from the Edge of the Sea

Keeper Benson painting the tower. Alice reported that Benson was in the tower one day during World War II when the navy's shells were whizzing all around him while they were conducting training exercises. *FOWIL Archives.*

The Italians walked around for a while and couldn't find anyone. Finally, when a U.S. Patrol boat arrived at Wood Island, the Italians were ready to surrender. It seems that's what they wanted to do at Old Orchard Beach but couldn't find anyone to surrender to. They wanted to change sides and join the U.S. Navy."[209]

There is an account of a German U-boat surrendering in Maine toward the end of World War II. Perhaps Mrs. Benson remembered the story that appeared in the *Portland Press Herald* titled "U-Boat Surrenders off Cape Elizabeth."[210] However, there are no available records of attempts by Italian submarine crews to surrender to the U.S. Navy anywhere in Maine during the Second World War. Nevertheless, when Italy signed an armistice with the Allied forces in September 1943, several submarines (which had been built according to German U-boat specifications), along with their Italian crews, were brought to Portland, Maine. There, the Italians worked with U.S. Navy personnel to develop effective tactics to use against the Germans. It seems more likely that the Italians Mrs. Benson remembered were by this time already friendly and no longer in need of surrender. In fact, at least ten members of the Italian crew serving on the submarine *Vortice* fell in love with local Portland girls and were married—all on the same date. Some of their descendants live in the Portland area to this day.[211]

Evidently, during the war the military had an impact on the island in another significant way as well. Nearly seventy-five years after a series of violent storms stripped Wood Island of its majestic trees, another assault on the island's vegetation occurred. A single, terse logbook entry on April 17, 1942, reports the "Army burning over the island." Benson's comment more or less concurs with information reported by Alan Casavant—that the island was stripped bare when "the army decided to cut all the remaining trees for defensive purposes."[212]

In 1951, Earle Benson left Wood Island and the following year assumed his position as the fourth Coast Guard keeper of the lighthouse at Portland Head. In 1954, Keeper Earle Benson and Alice retired to their home at 545 Pool Road in Biddeford. For the next fifteen years, they enjoyed the company of family and friends and lived within sight of Wood Island and the lighthouse that Alice considered her favorite. On August 5, 1969, at age seventy-one, Earle Benson passed away. Today, his final resting place is marked by a stone in the Woodlawn Cemetery in Biddeford, Maine.

Earle Benson was the last keeper of the Wood Island Lighthouse whose period of service lasted more than three years. The average length of time for Coast Guard keepers during the period 1952–86 was less than two years. For

Stories from the Edge of the Sea

The stone marking Benson's grave in the Woodlawn Cemetery in Biddeford. *Photo by Billion Graves.*

many, their assignment consisted of only a single year or less. Nevertheless, the careful attention given to maintaining the buildings and grounds as well as the tradition of springing into quick action during times of emergency continued until the light station became fully automated in 1986 and the last keeper left the island.

Chapter 17

WRECKS AND RESCUES, PART II

1917–86

Wilbert Freeman Lurvey took charge of the Wood Island Light Station on April 1, 1917. Up to that point, the United States had managed to avoid the full force of the overseas conflict involving the European powers, which had been grinding on for two and one-half years. But recent headlines announcing the interception of the Zimmerman Telegram in January 1917, proposing an alliance between Mexico and Germany, followed by the resumption of submarine warfare by Germany the next month, made America's involvement in the Great War all but inevitable. The day after Keeper Lurvey moved on to the island with his wife, Celia, and two young children, President Wilson went before Congress to request a declaration of war. Four days later, on April 6, the nation was at war with the Central Powers. In his logbook, Keeper Lurvey is silent on the conflict's beginning, mentioning only that on April 5, 1917, the previous keeper and his wife left the station in his charge.

R.P. TIBBETTS

On June 8, 1917, approximately two months after assuming his new role as keeper, Wilbert Freeman Lurvey remarks that a vessel burned at 10:00 a.m. about two miles from the station. The accident likely involved the gas-powered fishing vessel named the *R.P. Tibbetts*.

The captain of the fourteen-ton "seiner" and his brother-in-law narrowly escaped being burned when they launched their dory just in time. About three miles from the shore of Biddeford Pool, the men noticed their "engine commenced to backfire and it seemed no time before the between deck was a regular blaze." By the time they were able to pull away from their boat, it was fully engulfed in flames.[213]

Captain Staples and members of the lifesaving crew at Fletcher's Neck spotted the fishing boat on fire and quickly responded but were helpless to do anything but stand by and watch for the forty-three minutes it took the *Tibbetts* to burn to the waterline and eventually sink. Captain Sennott carried no insurance on the boat and unfortunately suffered a very big financial loss but managed to avoid any physical injuries.

ROGER DRURY

On January 14, 1918, the headline in the *Biddeford Weekly Journal* read:

Roger Drury
M'Ginty-Like
Goes Down

Plenty of Coal Free To
Any Who Will Go for It[214]

On January 12, 1918, Keeper W.F. Lurvey's logbook comments that a vessel went ashore on the Saco River Bar. The first notices claimed that the three-master had come through the storm "all right." Soon, however, it became clear that the situation was not nearly as benign as was hoped. The vessel to which the keeper referred was the *Roger Drury*, a three-masted schooner loaded with five hundred tons of hard and soft coal. The crew was saved by the "surf-men" of the Biddeford Pool Life Saving Station, but the *Drury* was left behind near Basket Island under the assumption that following a shift in the wind's direction, it was in a safe position. Later the following day, however, substantial gusts combined with a heavy sea to send the schooner and its cargo to the river bottom.

During this time of serious shortages caused by the war, the value of the *Drury*'s shipment was not lost on the reporter at the *Biddeford Daily Journal*, who wrote, "In this critical time, when coal is scarce and costly, this is an opportunity to get coal for nothing which should not be neglected. It is absolutely free to all who will take the trouble to get it and take it away....

Go early and avoid the rush."²¹⁵ The following week, unrelated to the *Drury* incident, President Garfield confirmed the shortages and the impending emergency by announcing an "order suspending industry throughout the United States in order to end the fuel famine."²¹⁶

Perhaps it speaks to the importance of the nation's lighthouses, and in particular to the Wood Island Light Station, that Lurvey mentioned no disruptions of fuel deliveries in his logbooks during the war years. In fact, throughout the months of the war and after, deliveries of oil and coal were made and recorded on a regular basis. To illustrate, during the years 1917–19, which of course included the war years, tenders landed coal and oil specifically in June 1917, August 1917, August 1918, November 1918, August 1919 and September 1919. The delivery of "supplies" (which may have included fuel) was noted in December 1917, April 1918, February 1919 and April 1919.

Motorboat Ashore

Even when the lighthouse keeper carefully performed his duties, unpredictable weather and an angry sea would still take its toll. On May 5, 1919, Keeper Lurvey recorded one of his most extensive notations: "Bell going 6 hours for fog. A motor boat with three young men in it ran ashore at the north end of Wood Island. The Coast Guard No. 11 by the use of a anchor haul the boat of not much damaged the owner of the boat was given dry clothes and food and lodging at the light time 12:30 owner of boat Emile Dueurl."²¹⁷

Anahuac

Seasonal residents along the beachfront at Fletcher's Neck and Biddeford Pool were warned of impending trouble on April 16, 1923, when a blaring siren interrupted their late Sunday evening contemplations. Many hastened to the scene of the disturbance to discover the seventeen-man crew swiftly abandoning the freighter *Anahuac*, which had struck the rocks along the treacherous shore of Fortune's Rocks. Keeper Lurvey made note of the disaster the following day: "Standard Oil Tanker went in on the ledges at Fortunes Rocks about 10 PM night of the 15ᵗʰ and was taken off by rescue cutter and the Portland tugboat with the *Prince* standing by."²¹⁸

The Standard Oil tanker was on a return trip to East Braintree, Massachusetts, and luckily was not carrying any cargo when a faulty compass in the heavy snowstorm caused Captain Stewart to lose his bearings. He told the *Biddeford Weekly Journal* that his first "intimation of his proximity to the shore was when the vessel grounded on the rocks." Little actual assistance was required from the good citizens who hurried to the site Sunday evening, as all seventeen crew members made it to safety, and, as Lurvey reported, the freighter was taken off the rocks at high tide and towed to Portland for repairs.[219]

Coast Guard Heroes

In the years following the end of World War II, the lighthouse keepers of Wood Island shared a good deal more than their Coast Guard affiliation with the surf men of the nearby Fletcher's Neck Lifesaving Station. From its inception in a small wood-frame boathouse in 1874, the men from Fletcher's Neck worked collaboratively with the lighthouse keeper to maintain safety along what was described as one of the four most dangerous points on the Maine coast. That relationship was especially evident when Joseph Staples, the officer in charge of the lifesaving station, served at the same time that his son, Clifford Blanchard Staples, was the keeper at Wood Island (1914–17).

After 1939, when the administration of the lighthouses came under the control of the Coast Guard, the men who operated the light at Wood Island, as well as their substitutes, were often drawn from the crews at Fletcher's Neck. And not infrequently, after leaving the lighthouse, the keepers returned to a career of distinguished service with the Coast Guard's lifesaving service.

Such was the case of David Katon (keeper, 1957–59), who was assigned to Fletcher's Neck following his lighthouse duty and in less than ten years became the officer in charge of the nine-man lifesaving station. He was in command when President Lyndon Johnson recognized the Coast Guard branch of the military service on its 175th anniversary. The honor seemed especially appropriate, as earlier that same year, Officer in Charge Katon had provided an account of a Coast Guard undertaking on June 19, 1965, that resulted in the towing of a disabled lobster boat to safety at Cape Porpoise. A few days before, the same Fletcher's Neck crew had come to the aid of five vessels in distress during one weekend alone.[220]

Jack Netherwood (keeper, 1962–63) may have been involved in one of the most unusual search-and-rescue efforts involving the Wood Island

Keeper David Katon firing up the coal-burning furnace at Wood Island. He later would become the officer in charge at the Fletcher's Neck Lifesaving Station. *FOWIL Archives.*

Lighthouse. Late in the afternoon of August 29, 1962, two eighteen-year-old summer residents of Hills Beach left for a ride in their seventeen-foot outboard. A thick fog enveloped the area that evening, and when the two young people had not arrived by 9:30 p.m., the alert that went out to the Coast Guard created a search effort that included most of the residents of Hills Beach. An estimated 150 citizens lined the shore with flashlights pointed out to sea. They were joined by automobiles whose owners had switched on their headlights with the hope that the light would provide guidance for the lost voyagers. The *Biddeford Saco Journal* reported that although the light on Wood Island was obscured by the fog, "the lighthouse keeper stood outside most of the night and beat a noisy drum, the sound of which one member of the search party said she would 'never forget.'" The adventure of cousins Nancy Labelle and David Hart came to a happy ending when they were found at 2:30 a.m. by a local lobsterman.[221]

David Bichrest (keeper, 1964–67) came to his position on Wood Island following heroic actions as a crew member aboard the U.S. Coast Guard cutter *Coos Bay*. In February 1964, the *Coos Bay* received an emergency call to come to the assistance of a British merchant ship, *Ambassador*, sinking in forty- to fifty-foot seas in the mid-Atlantic. According to his commanding officer, Bosuns Mate Bichrest "went over the side with a knife but without a life line to save the life of one of the [British sailors]." When Bichrest returned to Portland, the hero was welcomed with the news that he had become a father while at sea. Perhaps it was as a reward for his service, combined with the fact of his changed family status, that the twenty-two-year-old new father and his bride were appointed to keep the light at Wood Island.[222]

A portrait of Keeper Jack Netherwood (1962–63), who joined in an unusual rescue of two young mariners who had become disoriented on a foggy August night in 1962. *FOWIL Archives.*

Catherine Roche, like so many wives of Wood Island Light keepers, loved the view from her kitchen window. At around 7:45 p.m. on the evening of Saturday, July 19, 1969, while doing the dishes, she gazed outside, expecting on this calm, clear evening to once again be mesmerized by the spectacular view across the islands in Saco Bay. In the distance, a summer crowd swelled by weekend merrymakers had flocked to Old Orchard Beach to take advantage of the popular strand and the entertainment provided by its famous amusement park, which featured rides, music, dancing and other pleasures.

What the keeper's wife spotted on this night, though, was anything but what she expected. In the far distance, billowing smoke caused her to call to her husband, "Jim, do you want to come out here? Something looks really bad over at the park." Hastily grabbing their binoculars, they were able to confirm that the "White Way" and the famous pier at Old Orchard Beach were ablaze. The fire, which rapidly spread from an overheated fuse box, took only about twenty minutes to engulf the pier and nearby amusements.

Even at a distance of nearly five miles, Jim and Catherine Roach were able to observe individuals jumping from the pier to avoid the flames. Without hesitation, Keeper Roche (1969–70) called the Coast Guard, started the motor on his peapod and left the island, intending to provide aid if needed. When he was close to the affected area, he noticed thousands of onlookers crowding the beach and dozens of cars cluttering the roadways. While the sheet of flames and billowing smoke created a nightmare scenario, happily, no one was in immediate danger. When the smoke cleared on Sunday

The "massive blaze" resulted in over half a million dollars in damage, but thankfully, no lives were lost. *Biddeford-Saco Journal*, July 21, 1969.

morning, it was evident that the two-block area along the "White Way" was a total loss. Damage to concessions and rides including the world-famous merry-go-round totaled half a million dollars. Although several firefighters were taken to the hospital, there were no serious injuries and no deaths. And apparently, there were no calls for Jim Roche to save anyone who had jumped from the pier into the chilly Atlantic Ocean.[223]

Laurier A. Burnham (keeper, 1959–62) and his two-year-old daughter were at the center of one of the most celebrated stories recounting the heroism and courage of the men and women of the Coast Guard. This further serves to establish the close connection between the Wood Island Lighthouse and the Fletcher's Neck Lifesaving Station.

The date was November 29, 1960. In the early afternoon, Keeper Burnham and his wife, Lily, realized that their two-and-a-half-year-old daughter, Tammy, had become ill and was running a dangerously high fever. Over the phone, the doctor instructed the parents to make arrangements to transport their daughter to the hospital in Biddeford. An angry sea conspired with a combination of fog and rain to make the passage to the mainland particularly treacherous, and Keeper Burnham was ordered to remain on the island and contact the lifesaving station to come for the child.

Stories from the Edge of the Sea

Because the thirty-foot lifeboat dispatched by the lifesaving station at Fletcher's Neck was too large to land at the boat slip on Wood Island, a smaller skiff was lowered and sent with two men, Ed Syvinski and Raymond Bill, to meet Burnham and his daughter at the foot of the ramp at the westernmost tip of the island. The two sailors, in constant battle with the fog-shrouded, restless sea, nevertheless managed to reach their objective. There, they were met by the distraught father, who gently handed them his ill daughter and wished them well as they struggled back out into the choppy sea, eventually disappearing as the fog gradually enveloped them.

Now, out of sight of the lifeboat and with the fog obscuring the land, a sudden and unexpectedly large swell swamped the little skiff, tossing all three occupants into the frigid waters of Saco Bay. Summoning every survival instinct and skill available to them, the two seamen determined that Bill would swim in what was thought to be the direction of the thirty-footer while Syvinski, remaining behind, clung to the child and the sinking skiff. Within minutes, as their swamped boat sank beneath them, Syvinski found himself treading water with one hand while holding on to Tammy with the other. Enshrouded in fog, seaman Syvinski began to stroke, hoping to head in the direction of one of the bay's several islands or shallow reefs.

When Keeper Burnham received word that the lifesaving skiff had not yet made it back to the thirty-footer, he launched his fifteen-foot peapod and went in search of his daughter. Meanwhile, Raymond Bill managed to make his way back to the thirty-footer and promptly informed his commander of the impending tragedy. Now, both Burnham and Commander Kennedy were searching for two lost souls battling for their lives.

Fighting against the cold, waves and fog, Syvinski struggled to keep little Tammy's head above water while staying afloat himself. Exhaustion and hypothermia were taking their toll, and more than once the child's rescuer was forced under the water and compelled to thrust himself off the rocky bottom. Incredibly, the two survivors found themselves in the shallows of Negro Island, where the guardsman scrambled ashore, desperately hugging Tammy. They sought shelter behind a boulder, hoping that help would reach them before it was too late.

Good fortune accompanied Keeper Burnham after he launched his own boat in search of his daughter. He headed first toward the ledges of Negro Island and miraculously discovered the two survivors. With local residents banging on fifty-gallon drums to indicate the direction to shore, Tammy, now unconscious, was hastily carried first to the thirty-footer and then transferred to the boat of a local lobsterman, Preston Alley, who transported her to an

The three Coast Guard heroes in the Tammy Burnham rescue. *From left*: Keeper Laurier Burnham, Ed Syvinski and Raymond Bill. *FOWIL Archives.*

awaiting ambulance at Biddeford Pool. From there, she was conveyed to a nearby hospital, where she eventually fully recovered. Seaman Apprentice Edward Syvinski returned to the Coast Guard station at Fletcher's Neck, where, in spite of his recent adventure, he was ordered to take his turn on watch for the remainder of the night.

Thirty-three years later, in 1993, Ed Syvinski, Preston Alley and Laurier Burnham were recognized for their heroism during this heart-stopping incident and awarded the Gold Lifesaving Medal, the highest award presented by the commandant of the United States Coast Guard. The medal recognizes men and women whose selfless actions are "made at the risk to one's own life and show extreme heroic daring."[224]

Chapter 18

ANIMAL KINGDOM
1939–86

Though not all dogs were as sensitive to the paranormal as the Lowells' German shepherd or as talented as Sailor, Thomas Orcutt's "Lighthouse Dog," most of the lighthouse keepers during the Coast Guard years and their children had pets, and many of them were dogs. The Burnham family remembered their little beagle, Squeaky, who jumped into the water one day, unbeknownst to Keeper Laurier Burnham, and swam behind the peapod all the way to Biddeford Pool. The disoriented dog became lost on the mainland, and when Burnham returned to Wood Island, he inadvertently left Squeaky behind. Luckily, one of the local residents noticed the poor dog running all around the village in a frenzy. He notified the Burnham family, and Squeaky was eventually returned to her home.[225]

Edward and Eloise Frank took charge of the lighthouse in January 1952 and remained there for the next four years. During their tenure, they were often conveyed back and forth to the mainland by a Coast Guard vessel under the control of David Hoff, who eventually became a friend of the keeper. Hoff, some fifty years later, remembered that the Franks had a St. Bernard dog that would travel with Mrs. Frank when she made excursions to shore. "When it was low tide, the keeper's wife and I would struggle to get that pup up the ladder on Dr. Oddy's wharf."[226]

In addition to their St. Bernard, Eloise Frank remembered that they also had an English springer spaniel named Chrissey, as well as two cats, a bunch of hens and a rooster. A wire enclosure was intended to protect the chickens from the hungry fox and owls, but one day, Eloise recalls, "we lost all the chickens [and] couldn't find them." As a last resort, they enlisted Chrissey,

Left: Tammy Burnham with her beagle, Squeaky, circa 1960. *FOWIL Archives*.

Right: Steve Frank is the same size as Henry, his St. Bernard (circa 1955). *FOWIL Archives*.

hoping that the dog's "retriever" instincts would respond to their command to "find the chickens—find the chickens!" Well, Chrissey would go into the rocks and put his nose right on those chickens, and Eloise and her daughter Michel managed to pick them all up from their little hiding places among the rocky shoreline.[227]

Jim Roche, reflecting back on the days when his father was the lighthouse keeper on Wood Island, recalls a sad story involving Brownie, one of his three dogs. Brownie was killed by a seal bomb, a small explosive device intended to keep mammals away from fishermen's nets. Jim tells it this way:

> *Supposedly some fisherman put a seal bomb in a fish and threw it overboard. Brownie, who was quite the fishing dog spotted an opportunity and went fishing as usual. My dad remembering how much Brownie loved to chase after fish, saw what was about to happen and yelled out to him—and then there was a boom; Brownie was gone. At the end of his story my Dad said that a similar incident happened to another dog on the Island. However, I don't remember a name.*[228]

Most of the animals on Wood Island would not qualify as pets, although in some cases they began to behave as if they were indeed members of the lighthouse family. Keeper Russ Lowell recalled heading down to the boathouse one morning on his way to get the mail. His dogs Kelly, Boo Boo and Yogi followed him as usual.

> *I get to the boathouse and the dogs would run around to the front side to the ramp and they would be at the door when I opened up the side door. Well, the end door was cracked a bit and sunlight is coming in underneath it and I can see that something is laying up against the door. I am thinking that one of the dogs ran around there and I am going to open the door and scare her. So I grabbed the door and I threw the door open and went "Hurrah!" This poor seal had been laying there sunning itself. It turned around and looked at me and went* argh argh argh!!! *Eyes about the size of dinner plates. I am falling back and the dogs are behind me going "what's that?" The poor seal is now trying to find its way down into the water. I am thinking "that poor thing." They would show up all the time.*[229]

A snowy owl was an annual winter visitor on the island during the 1950s and early 1960s. Eloise Frank would enjoy grabbing the binoculars and watching the majestic creature when it landed on the flagpole in the latter part of the day. Apparently, the abundance of rabbits that inhabited the island made attractive substitutes for the arctic lemmings that normally sustained the owls in their more northern summer habitat.[230]

In 1967, nearly ten years following the owl's sightings during the Franks' residency, Keeper A.J. Savageau also reported the presence of a snowy owl. The owl, which unfortunately dove at his wife while she was hanging clothes out to dry, went just a bit too far for the keeper. Savageau, incensed that the winged predator was already slaying the rabbits on the island, some of whom he kept in hutches near the dwelling, sought revenge for the bird's latest indiscretion and shot it—something that his son, in 2011, remembered as an unfortunate mistake.[231]

Less welcome and by far more numerous were the many seagulls that inhabited Wood Island. These gregarious and all too frequently irksome birds often made their presence known to the light keeper and his family. In the summer, Cliff Trebilcock would trade in his winter snowshoes for his bicycle as his preferred method of commuting from the dwelling to the boathouse. On one occasion, he was knocked off his bike by one of these aggressive, diving gulls. His cat was equally at risk. The kitty, which was in the habit of following the keeper, could not go more than ten feet before the gulls would dive at him.[232]

When a seagull attacked a much less tolerant Keeper David Winchester on the top of his head, he required butterfly bandages to close the severe wound that the belligerent bird had caused. The furious keeper went on a tirade following the incident and got his revenge by marching across the island and stomping on every seagull nest he could find.[233]

An important feature of life at the Wood Island Lighthouse for the Roche family children centered on caring for the local wildlife. Catherine Roche recalled that following a particularly severe storm that stranded her keeper husband on the mainland, her son created what she termed their "veterinary school." Four-year-old Jim Roche Jr. brought injured ducks, seagulls and baby rabbits in for treatment. One recovering duck spent a week in their bathtub, and a seagull with a broken wing apparently wouldn't eat anything but pork chops.[234]

For Kelly, the resident Wood Island Lighthouse dog, the seagulls presented a different kind of diversion. According to Susan Murray, the wife of Keeper Jerry Murray, the peripatetic pup came home one day with a little bloody spot on her upper lip where she "probably got dug by a seagull claw." Upon closer inspection, the human residents found that in her mouth was a seagull egg. Evidently, Kelly had been on a little hunting foray.[235]

On occasion, a deer could be spotted on the island. One day, Keeper Andrew Pruneau was about to leave the boat slip on his way to Biddeford Pool when he saw a deer climbing out of the water and just beginning to make its way up the rocks and dry land. When interviewed in 2003 by the history group of the Friends of the Wood Island Lighthouse, he was upset to learn that a herd of deer, which had become established on the island, was hunted periodically by local sportsmen. "That is a shame," he commented. "Wrong, wrong, that's wrong."[236]

Perhaps the most captivating animal story during this Coast Guard era involved Keeper James and Catherine Roche (1969–70), their son Jim and a dog that wasn't a dog. Here's how Mrs. Roche remembered it:

> *Well, I had two dogs, four-legged dogs. He [Jim] kept saying to me, "Oh Mom, hurry up breakfast, hurry up, hurry up, we have to go play with the black doggie!" "Jim, we don't have a black dog. We have two brown dogs." He would say, "No no no, we have a black dog and it swims here every day and plays with us." I said, "Where does it play with you?" He says, "Oh, over there, by the bell." And I said, "Jim, we do not have a black dog." He says, "Yes we do Mom, yes we do." Well, my husband came home one day. It was cold, and he said, "I am going to go take a bath." I said,*

Stories from the Edge of the Sea

"All right." Jim had snuck the seal in the house and put it in the bathtub. When my husband went in there, there was the seal. Jim domesticated this seal so much that they had to take the seal to the Boston Aquarium to give it a home....It took a couple of weeks before I got to see it myself. But they played every day. I couldn't understand why the dogs were so worn out. They would come in after an hour and just collapse. Dogs thought of the seal as just another dog that swam up out of the water.[237]

Although there is no way to know for sure, the seal that Keeper Roche shared his bathtub with was probably the same creature remembered by Rick Savageau, son of Keeper Alfred "Fred" Savageau (1967–68), who had been assigned to Wood Island just the previous year. Rick reported that he was four years old when his father left the island to go grocery shopping in Biddeford Pool. As he was preparing to return in the peapod, a small seal jumped into the boat. Although he searched in the waters nearby for the seal's mother, the keeper was unable to locate any likely prospect and so brought the seal back to Wood Island. For the next several years, the seal swam nearby, coming ashore when the opportunity presented itself to play with Rick and, later perhaps, with Jim Roche and his brown dogs.[238]

When Susan Murray's mother-in-law came to visit during the summer, she would occasionally bring her pet parrot and a rooster along. The parrot got so used to hearing Murray's daughter cry that "eventually she would cry just like Jessica did." The rooster, named Gregory Peck, wandered around the yard for a time but then inexplicably flew away.

The Murrays hoped that their goat, Nanny, would find that the lawn was so delicious that they would no longer have to mow it. Instead, Nanny found that Susan's flower garden was much more enticing and became such a nuisance that she had to be driven away with a slingshot. Today, Nanny lies in an unmarked grave somewhere within the boundary of the lighthouse property.[239]

Russ Lowell had two cats, Smokey and Tibet, in addition to caring for his several dogs, Boo Boo, Yogi, Maggie-Mae and Kelly. Paul Sodano (1982–83) and his wife replaced the Lowells on Wood Island and also remembered the island's resident Border Collie named Kelly, who by 1982 was twelve years old. Kelly had been a fixture on Wood Island for a number of years, having been brought to the lighthouse as a six-month-

Rick Savageau, the keeper's son, with his mother and the playful seal that seems to have adopted lighthouse families in the late 1960s. *FOWIL Archives.*

Above: Keeper Jerry Murray; his wife, Susan; and their daughter, Jessica. The island dog, Kelly, and the Murrays' goat, Nanny, are in the background, circa 1975. *FOWIL Archives.*

Left: Two of Keeper Lowell's dogs, Boo Boo and Maggie-Mae, circa 1980. *FOWIL Archives.*

old puppy. Kelly absolutely refused to board a boat and so remained on Wood Island her entire life. She greeted and then adopted the families of the keepers who came and went, offering them an immediate welcome and providing an early warning when any visitors arrived.

All agreed that Kelly was a good dog, and according to Sherry and Paul Sodano, she was not only very undemanding but wouldn't even come in the house unless the weather was "wild and raging outside."[240] Susan Murray was equally fond of their adopted dog. Kelly was healthy, seemed happy and was always good with their daughter, Jessica. Because she would not

Kelly, the "salty dog," remained on the island throughout her life. *FOWIL Archives.*

leave the island, when Keeper Jerry Murray would go to the mainland on an errand, Kelly would sit down at the boathouse and wait until he returned. When the Murrays left for another assignment, like the keeper before them, they left Kelly behind to welcome the next lighthouse family. Says Susan, "She was quite a dog—the original salty dog."[241]

Chapter 19

COAST GUARD WIVES
1939–86

On June 30, 1934, just a few months after arriving on Wood Island, Keeper Earle Benson wrote in his logbook: "Wife and I whitewashed tower in the P.M. Looks nice." An entry early the following year, on February 23, 1935, reads, "Helping wife clean pantry." When taken together, these two comments demonstrate the partnership that a husband-and-wife lighthouse team formed when they agreed to their assignment as lighthouse keepers during the Coast Guard period.[242]

Women have played important roles throughout lighthouse history. However, most often, wives and daughters were relegated to the background, where they were recognized only for supporting their husbands as they performed their official duties. As the public's interest in lighthouses intensified during the latter half of the twentieth century, journalists, in examining the daily lives of America's lighthouse keepers, also cast a sharper light on the day-to-day participation of lighthouse women, thus bringing their role into clearer definition.

In an interview with Terry Lowell, the wife of Russ Lowell, who served as keeper at Wood Island from 1979 to 1982, the keeper's spouse outlined her "job description": "I would turn the light on and off, the fog horn on and off and send the weather." Terry's weather report, generally sent five times a day, included the sky conditions, wind speed and direction, temperature, barometer and the height and period between waves. When pressed regarding how she determined the wind speed, her response was that after a while "we would just look at the flag. If it was just kind of blowing, that would be five kilometers per hour, flapping harder, that would be ten kilometers per hour, if it was really flapping, that would be twenty kilometers per hour and if the

Keeper Russ Lowell and his wife, Terry, circa 1980. *FOWIL Archives.*

pole was bending a bit we would grab the handheld [anemometer] and go to the top of the tower. We got pretty good at guestimating it."²⁴³

The Lowells revealed that there were lighthearted moments as well. One evening between 10:30 p.m. and 12:30 a.m., long after retiring, they received a call from a new person at the Portsmouth Light Station requesting their weather report. Only partly annoyed but full of mischief, Russ Lowell responded to the call: "Portsmouth Harbor this is Wood Island Light are you ready to copy?" When the other end called back and answered, "Send it," Lowell was sure to wait a few seconds before delivering his tongue-in-cheek report: "Dark out." Laughter rang all the way from Portsmouth to Portland, commented Terry Lowell, because they all listen on the same communication channel.²⁴⁴

Pat Winchester, the wife of Keeper Dave Winchester (1963–64), told her interviewer in March 2010, "When we were there, **we** painted the house, **we** painted the house [emphasizing **we**] inside and out….Whatever he did, I had to learn just in case he became ill."²⁴⁵

A reporter from the *Hartford Courant* interviewed the family of Jerry Murray, who served as lighthouse keeper from 1973 to 1976. Referring to his wife, Susan (whom he affectionately called "Sam"), he said, "She is half the team out here….Sam is my bookkeeper, the answering service…and she knows how to fire up the light if I happen to be on a rescue mission." Susan herself remembered:

> *There were always things from the Coast Guard, different pages to be slipped into the manuals and substituted for other pages, little paper work things that had to be done. When we got inspected, they would take the manuals and notebooks and check to make sure that he had put in all the changes. Most of that was my work actually.*

Keeper Murray, who found himself ashore more often than his wife, was the one who managed the family shopping, a task that he refers to as "switching roles."²⁴⁶

This sense that lighthouse keeping was a collaboration is further confirmed by Catherine Roche, who commented in an interview with the Friends of the Wood Island Lighthouse that "it was understood that us wives were part of the working team, no ifs, ands or buts about it. You were at the

Pat "P. Jaye" Winchester, the wife of Keeper Dave Winchester, showing off her skating skills to son Ricky during the winter of 1963–64. *FOWIL Archives.*

Jessica Murray admiring the typewriter often used by her mother, Susan, in her role as "bookkeeper," circa 1975. *FOWIL Archives.*

lighthouse, and it was as much your responsibility as it was your husband's." That responsibility became a reality on one occasion when a freak storm with howling sixty-mile-per-hour winds broke the underwater cable and left Catherine and her three children stranded on the island. Her husband, Keeper James Roche, had gone ashore and was not able to return, leaving Mrs. Roche without electricity. She not only had to care for her family but also attend to the business of the lighthouse for three unnerving days.[247]

On any return trip from the mainland in their peapod, some serious acrobatics were usually required when landing at the island, even in the best of weather. Clifford Trebilcock, the keeper in the early 1970s, remembered in an interview conducted in 2006 how the waves near the boat slip would occasionally reach fifteen to twenty feet. The landing procedure was generally more successful when the arrival was accomplished as a team effort.[248] Even then, Jerry Murray remembered that you would "almost always get a soaking."[249] When Nebraskan Patsy McQuade first arrived on the island with her husband, Keeper Michael McQuade (1976–78), she recalled being a bit afraid to go ashore for almost a year because she would find herself drenched up to her waist whenever they brought the boat back in.[250]

Russ Lowell (1979–82) recalls an incident when he asked for his wife's assistance with landing the peapod while he battled the unpredictable waves after returning from a shopping trip to Biddeford. When they had departed earlier that morning, the sea was smooth as glass. But when they returned, shifting winds had created fearsome seas that threatened their little boat. His wife, Terry, successfully made the leap to the landing and gathered up the line used to winch the peapod onto the boat slip. But as she was returning, Russ

Winds and heavy seas all too often posed a serious challenge when landing the peapod. *FOWIL Archives.*

noticed an obvious limp and became concerned that she had injured herself in her effort to make it ashore. He was relieved when it became evident that as she jumped, she had vaulted right out of one of her shoes, which caused her to favor one foot as she proceeded down the slippery boat slip.[251]

Lily Burnham, in an article published in the *Lighthouse Digest* (1992), is equally unrestrained about telling stories involving the landing of the peapod following an excursion ashore. The ordeal would begin when Keeper Burnham

> *would carefully circle the waters near the boat slip waiting and watching the surf and timing his approach to the slip. Upon landing, he would quickly jump out and attach a line to the boat and hand operate the small winch located in the boat house. In bad weather, landing was so tricky and treacherous that upon landing, large waves would roll in lifting our boat off from the slip before we had time to attach it to the winch; and over and out we would all go into the rocks and seaweed and surf with our two small daughters, Tammy & Holly, plus all the groceries and any equipment we were taking back to the island....In the winter, crossing the "choppy" harbor from the gut at Biddeford Pool involved my sitting on the keel with a baby under each arm covered with canvas while my husband weathered the wind and salt spray which, by the time we reached the boathouse, had frozen to his face so that the children thought he looked like Santa Claus, with his frozen beard, eyebrows and eyelashes....*
>
> *And then there was still the 7/8-mile walk to the dwelling before anyone could begin warming themselves.*[252]

Apparently, any venture involving the peapod could be a risky one. In 1963, Keeper Netherwood and his family were transferred to Cape May following their assignment at Wood Island. They packed their goods into boxes, loaded them into the peapod and made their way out to the Coast Guard thirty-footer, where they would hand their belongings off for transport to shore and a waiting moving van. In the process, the keeper's daughter, Jackie Netherwood Kennedy, remembered that the sea claimed two of the boxes, which, in the scramble to transfer them, were lost overboard and never recovered.[253]

For many of the Coast Guard wives, life at the lighthouse was an "amazing adventure." Looking back on their experience, some described it as a quiet, peaceful, utopia, "something everyone should experience." For Susan Murray, who celebrated her birthday just weeks after moving onto the island, "it was kind of like the whole island was a birthday present for me."[254] For others, it was a struggle. For Paul Sodano's (1982–83) wife, Sherry, it was both. At Christmastime in 1982, the keeper couple was interviewed for an article that appeared in their hometown newspaper, the *Springfield Daily News*. Sherry, who was trying to manage her conflicted feelings of being alone and secluded during the holidays, described life on Wood Island this way: "Sometimes it's so beautiful you almost can't stand it, like when the sea smoke makes the ocean look on fire....Other times, when the fog doesn't lift for seven, eight days, you think you'll go out of your mind."[255] Nebraskans Patsy McQuade and her husband, Keeper Michael McQuade, contained their enthusiasm as well. They preferred the word "satisfied" to describe their secluded life on Wood Island. It took some time for Patsy to adjust, she says, to the inconveniences, the responsibility and the worry that all came with their appointment. She recalled that one keeper left after nine months—"his wife couldn't stand living out here."[256]

Something as routine as a trip to the post office required at least an hour—and that was with no time taken to talk to friends along the way. And organizing a shopping trip represented a major undertaking. The Sodanos

Keeper Paul Sodano and his wife, Sherry, pose in front of the "headless" light tower, circa 1982–83. *FOWIL Archives*.

Keeper Edward Frank maneuvers their tractor-cart along the boardwalk. The walkway, constructed in the summer of 1952, was a considerable improvement over the primitive pathway that previously required a three-quarter-mile trek and was covered with poison ivy. *FOWIL Archives.*

generally made a trip to the grocery store every two weeks. Their journey would begin with a ride in their small tractor three-quarters of a mile down the boardwalk to the boathouse; then, a boat trip to Biddeford Pool, where they kept their parked truck; and then on to Biddeford, where they normally would purchase enough food to fill twenty bags. "You have to handle each bag six times," says Sherry. "From the cart to the truck. From the truck to the boat. From the boat to the boathouse. From the boathouse to the tractor. From the tractor to the garage. From the garage to the house."[257]

While there was a powerful sense of collaboration between husband and wife lighthouse keepers during the Coast Guard era, the expectation held that housekeeping and childcare remained within the sphere of the wife. When questioned about what it was like cooking, Eloise Frank responded simply that when she was first there in the early 1950s, "It was awful." The coal-burning stove, which also heated the hot water, had to be kept going all the time and created miserable conditions in the summer, when she was "plastered" with poison ivy. Fortunately, during a visit from the district commander, she requested that the old stove be replaced, and sure enough, her wish was granted. On another occasion, she expressed her unhappiness with the unreliability of the kerosene refrigerator. That concern was acknowledged as well, and by the time the Franks left the lighthouse, they had a new propane refrigerator, complete with a freezer section.[258]

Michael McQuade (1976–79) was equally direct but did not hesitate to employ a bit of guile as well. He was exhausted after spending nearly thirty days removing fourteen to sixteen inches of snow from the boardwalk after a particularly severe storm. After finishing with the snow, he attacked the three to four inches of solid ice, "taking a sledgehammer, raising that and bringing it down on every board between the house and the boathouse." A month or so later, Group Portland arrived on the island for an inspection. Following their review, they casually asked the keeper if there was anything he wanted or needed on the island. Recalling his recent snow-removal experience, and knowing that the Coast Guard was a bit tight with their funds, he responded, "I said I would like a snow blower because I really feel guilty sending my pregnant wife out to shovel snow so I can get down to the boathouse." His request was heard, and "two days later, I had a snow blower."[259]

When Lily and Laurier Burnham took over the lighthouse in 1959, the station remained without shore electric power. A generator, intended primarily for the light in the tower, was available to the family four to six hours a day. Viewing their small black-and-white television provided a special treat on occasion, but if the generator was required for the light, the television went dark and kerosene lamps and flashlights were needed to get around. Both the stove and the small refrigerator continued to run on gas. "With two babies in cloth diapers and no washer," Lily recalled, "we certainly used the old-fashioned scrub board for many hours on a daily basis."[260]

The family of Keeper Laurier Burnham includes his wife, Lily, and daughters Tammy and Holly. *FOWIL Archives.*

Chapter 20

CHILDREN OF THE LIGHT

1939–86

The new breed of lighthouse keeper that arrived during the Coast Guard era usually brought along families of one or more children who lived with them in the dwelling on Wood Island. Of the roughly twenty families that filled the post during those years, only a few experienced the birth of a child while stationed at the lighthouse. In every case, children who were born while their parents were assigned to Wood Island as lighthouse keepers were delivered in hospitals on the mainland.

When James Roche (1969–70) came to Wood Island with his two small children, his wife, Catherine, was pregnant with their third child. Jim Roche, the older son of the former keeper, tells the story of his brother's birth this way:

> *When Mom went into labor on the island, Dad called Fletcher's Neck for a 40-footer. He loaded her up in the tractor, down the mile-long board walk to the boat, launched and away they went. The 40-footer arrived and commenced escort, because Dad, who was heading for the station, was not slowing down. Then Dad ran over a lobster pot buoy, fouling the small boat prop. This just escalated the situation and then Dad yelled to the forty-footer wanting a knife. At the time, the Coast Guard required advanced First Aid training for the boat crews, and all were required to carry a knife, with a knife also required on board all lighthouse boats. At this point there was no transferring my mother so, I'm sure at this point panic is spreading on the 40-footer. Why would he want a knife? Finally, a small pocket knife was*

located on the boat. The line was cut out of the propeller and the race began again. They reached the beach and Dad ran the boat up on the beach boat ramp, Mom was transferred to the ambulance, off to the hospital and here comes baby brother, Michael Patrick Roche.[261]

That incident, according to Catherine Roche, who was interviewed by the history group of the Friends of the Wood Island Lighthouse in 2009, brought a policy change to the Coast Guard. From that moment on, "they gave all the guys training on how to deliver a baby," she said.[262]

Judy Pruneau, the wife of Andrew Pruneau (1972–73), left the island in mid-November, nearly four weeks before their baby was due. The sea was especially rough the day she was scheduled to make her way to the mainland, and so Andrew enlisted the help of lobsterman Marshall Alexander to take her to shore. Following the birth of Scott Andrew on Christmas Day, Alexander was recruited once again, this time to bring the new mother and her newborn son back. Keeper Pruneau waited anxiously and joyfully met them at the boat slip when they arrived.[263]

The experience of Russ and Terry Lowell marked another policy change with the Coast Guard. When Terry returned from the hospital with their two-week-old newborn, she was asked about her lack of concern about bringing an infant of that age to their island home. She commented, "We have always been pretty mellow. We just waited for a calm day…and we bundled him up." Russ's mom came out and assisted for a few days. While they were still assigned as lighthouse keepers, the Coast Guard determined that it was not safe to have toddlers on Wood Island. Consequently, the Lowells were the last keeper family to have children living with them at the lighthouse; they were transferred off in 1982.[264]

Any young mother knows the importance of periodically paying a visit to the pediatrician. So, when Keeper Pruneau took his wife and child to visit Dr. O'Sullivan, he was required by the Coast Guard to leave the light and foghorn on in the event that the weather suddenly changed while he was away. Apparently, this was an annoyance for the baby doctor, according to Judy Pruneau: "He'd be in there with his cigar, never smoked a cigar but chewed on it. He would say, 'Why don't you tell that husband of yours to shut that damned foghorn off in the middle of the day, sun's shining.'"[265]

Illness and emergencies are always a concern for young parents, but for mothers removed from the benefits of nearby medical assistance, the responsibility must have felt even weightier. For expectant parents, the apprehension would be multiplied. In the case of Michael and Patsy

Keeper Lowell takes a break with son Zachary. Shortly after Zachary was born, the Coast Guard altered its policy and no longer permitted keepers to bring children to their Wood Island assignment. *FOWIL Archives.*

McQuade, stationed at the lighthouse from 1976 to 1979, a November snowstorm washed away most of the boat slip, virtually stranding the couple. Another blizzard resulted in much of the island being under water "while waves crashed at the doorstep [with] the raging sea leaving thousands of rocks covering the ground." Weather events like these were undoubtedly an important consideration leading the McQuades to make the decision to move into temporary living quarters in the area around Biddeford Pool, where the couple could peacefully await the arrival of their first child. Damien arrived in a timely fashion in early May, and a year later, on May 2, 1979, they all celebrated his first birthday on Wood Island with a red-and-white cake shaped in the form of the lighthouse.[266]

David Bichrest was himself only twenty-two when he brought his bride of one year and their infant child, Cynthia, to Wood Island in 1964. His predecessor, David Winchester, and his wife, Pat, had two children: Robyn, who was one year old, and Rickie, who was four at the time they lived at the lighthouse. When asked what it was like raising kids on the island, Pat said modestly, "Actually, my oldest son raised himself....He followed his father around like a puppy."[267]

Stories from the Edge of the Sea

Top: Keeper Michael McQuade at the top of the light tower with son Damien, circa 1977. *FOWIL Archives.*

Bottom: Damien McQuade celebrates his first birthday with a lighthouse cake, circa 1977. *FOWIL Archives.*

David Katon's father (also named David) was lighthouse keeper from 1957 to 1959 before going on to become the officer in charge of the Fletcher's Neck Lifesaving Station and later a city planner for the Town of Biddeford. David Jr. recalled that as he grew older, he enjoyed accompanying his father to the South Portland Coast Guard Station. There, during training exercises, he and occasionally some friends would play the role of victim as the Coast Guard trainees would go through their rescue procedures. Taking advantage of the pool table at the station afterward was his well-earned reward.[268]

For the children of the lighthouse keepers, life on a relatively isolated island would seem to have all the qualities necessary for a true child's fantasy. The thrill revealed in the smile displayed by Jim Roche Jr. following a day of fishing with his father requires no commentary. In an interview conducted with the *Biddeford-Saco Journal* in June 1969, James and Catherine Roche reported that there was plenty of time for their two children to play.

Above: Keeper David Katon with his wife, Claire, tuning their vintage TV, circa 1958. *FOWIL Archives.*

Left: Jim Roche and his son, Jim, proudly display the catch that resulted from their angling skills. *FOWIL Archives.*

Following a winter storm, one of the three dogs was "hitched to a sled and proudly pulled the children to and fro."[269]

For Jackie Netherwood, the daughter of Jack Netherwood (1962–63), her fondest memories of Wood Island were during the summer, when she, her two brothers and their visiting cousins would sit and watch the fireworks at Old Orchard Beach every Saturday night. But the winters were great too. "At five years old," she says, "snow is like any kid's dream…what any kid dreams of." In a photograph taken during the winter of 1962–63, Jackie and her brothers are peeking out from their homemade igloo following one of Maine's winter storms.[270]

Jackie Netherwood and her brothers peer out from their snow shelter, winter 196–63. *FOWIL Archives.*

Susan Murray thought that raising a child on Wood Island was, well…*interesting*. However, for her daughter Jessica, riding a tricycle alone along the boardwalk may have gotten old after a while. As an only child, Jessica was likely to have felt the isolation more than some children. When she celebrated her fourth birthday on July 4 with a traditional birthday cake decorated with four candles, her mother felt some regret that "she doesn't know what a real big-time birthday party is, with lots of games." After some thought though, Mrs. Murray predicted, "Maybe next year when we're transferred."[271]

Happy Holidays

Children of all ages take special pleasure in celebrating the holidays, and thanks to one of the legends of lighthouse lore, Christmas on Wood Island was made into a very special time. In 1929, William "Bill" Wincapaw, in gratitude for the lighthouse keepers who had provided him with a lighted safe passage when piloting his floatplane along the Maine coast, made the initial flight that led to the tradition of the "Flying Santa." In 1936, Wincapaw was superseded by his teacher and author of more than three dozen books, Edward Rowe Snow. For the remainder of the twentieth century, the Snows' ritual of delivering Christmas packages containing dolls, games, books, coffee and razors to the families of lighthouse keepers along the Atlantic coast continued. The first mention of this practice in the story of the Wood Island Lighthouse is found in the logbook of Earle Benson, who wrote on December 23, 1934, "Capt. Bill dropped Xmas bundle." And again, the following day, on December 24, "Capt. Bill dropped another Xmas package." On Christmas Day 1936, Benson was especially thankful: "Christmas ideal day. Capt. Bill dropped annual Xmas package. God bless him!"[272]

Earle and Alice Benson's gregarious personalities ensured that their out-of-the-way station would be made more jovial by gathering friends and family together whenever possible. Alice later remembered that Christmas was an especially festive time. The visits from the "Flying Santa" were only a part of the tradition that they followed during their seventeen years on Wood Island. They would "always build a fresh fire and put the turkey in and then go to shore and look at Christmas Trees. When they [returned] the turkey would be done and ready for Christmas dinner."[273]

Laurier and Lily Burnham and their children had equally fond memories of Christmas on Wood Island and always looked forward to the visits of Flying Santa. Lily recalled that the famous author Edward Rowe Snow, in his role as Santa, "would fly low waving to us as he made a few passes to alert us."[274]

Apparently though, on some occasions, even the best of intentions did not always pan out as hoped. In her interview with Tim Harrison for the *Lighthouse Digest* in 1992, Lily Burnham reported that one year, the family watched as Santa's package missed the island and floated out to sea. Another year, the package was hopelessly buried in the snow and not recovered until the spring. By then, "the razor blades were rusty and the 'old Nick' candy bars were soggy. We were however, able to salvage his books which he usually enclosed in his Christmas package—his very interesting books on lighthouses and New England shipwrecks."[275]

Dave Winchester with his wife, Pat, and two children, Robyn and Rickie, remembered going ashore and then transporting their Christmas tree to the dwelling on Wood Island. Following the one-mile trip to the mainland, the Winchester family still had to wrestle the tree into the cart of their small tractor and haul it another half mile from the boathouse to their home. Although Rickiee, age four at the time, was expecting Santa to come in a helicopter, Edward Snow's "Flying Santa" did not switch to a helicopter until 1978, when regulations governing airspace over lighthouses became more restrictive.[276]

Russ and Terry Lowell preferred to celebrate the holidays by themselves. Sitting outside with a prime rib or rib-eye steak or lobster or both, and

Keeper Dave Winchester celebrates the Christmas holidays in 1963 with his daughter Robyn. *FOWIL Archives.*

perhaps a peck of clams, the couple would enjoy the tranquility and "total serenity" of their island assignment. And, of course, they couldn't help but gleefully anticipate the arrival of the Flying Santa, who now made his entrance in his helicopter.[277]

For Andrew Pruneau (1972) and his wife, Judith, the birth of their son, Scott Andrew Pruneau, on December 25, 1972, made a visit from the "Flying Santa" totally unnecessary.

Chapter 21

LIVING AT THE EDGE OF THE SEA

1939–86

MANAGING LONELINESS AND ISOLATION

Observers of lighthouse history have periodically commented on the burden imposed by living an isolated existence. Keepers and their wives, overwhelmed by loneliness, boredom or monotony, occasionally are reported to suffer from illness and mental strain. Such psychological disorders may sometimes result in aggressive behavior and even attempted suicide.

Keeper Clifford B. Staples and his bride hardly had time to settle in to their new assignment in 1914 when Elsie began to experience intense pain. The logbook on November 10 and 11 reports that Staples left the station in charge of a substitute, Wallace Mullen, because his wife was suffering from appendicitis and had to have an operation. While the keeper returned from Biddeford at 4:45 p.m. on November 12, it would not be until mid-December that his wife had recuperated sufficiently for him to write: "Left station at 11:45 am returned 3 pm brought wife back to station."[278]

Elsie Staples's struggles with illness did not end with her attack of appendicitis in November 1914. She again became ill in April 1915 and is reported to have left the island to spend time recuperating at her sister's home. Finally, it appears that two and a half years of a secluded and lonely existence took its toll on the lighthouse keeper's wife. On March 2, 1917, this note appeared in the *Biddeford Weekly Journal*:

> *Mrs. Clifford Staples of Wood Island and, Biddeford Pool, is in the city, visiting at the home of Mr. and Mrs. George W. Carter, Elm Street, and*

with other friends. She is recovering from an attack of nervous prostration and is under the physician's care. Light Keeper and Mrs. Staples having given up his position, and they will locate in Massachusetts.[279]

In his logbook on that same March 2, Staples wrote, "Left station at 11:30 AM returned 1 PM went ashore with *special letter* [italics added]." We'll probably never know the contents of the "special letter," but we do know that by the end of the month, Staples's successor, Mr. W.F. Lurvey, had arrived to take charge of the station.[280]

When Clifford Blanchard Staples and his wife, Elsie, returned to gather their furniture and other belongings during the first two weeks in April, their visit and ultimate departure would mark the end of their employment as lighthouse keepers.

The weighty responsibility that Keeper George E. Woodward (1926–34) carried on behalf of his family, when added to the demanding duties of his official assignment, created a tension and mental strain and perhaps even a susceptibility to illness that could sometimes overpower his ability to carry out the chores demanded by his position. In nearly eight years of service at Wood Island, Keeper Woodward records no fewer than sixty days when injury or illness made it necessary for him to ease off from his normal routines, writing for the record that the minimal "general duties" have been attended to. Keeper Woodward was especially vulnerable to flu-like symptoms. At the end of December and into early January 1926, for example, he tells us that he was "sick with grippe." Again, for five days in March 1927, five days in April and four days in December 1928, six days in January 1931 and then nearly ten days in March of that same year, he reports suffering from grippe and a "bad cold."[281]

During one of these bouts, his condition became quite serious. On April 15, 1928, Woodward records that he performed "General duties. Sick with cold." On the following days, the cold turned into "grip," tonsillitis, "brancitis" (bronchitis) and asthma, eventually requiring hospitalization for seven days. The following year, on June 14, 1929, he returned to the hospital to finally have his tonsils removed.[282]

Curiously, one of Keeper Woodward's most serious medical conditions receives no mention in his logbook. On May 30, 1930, a headline in the *Biddeford Weekly Journal* announced, "LIGHTKEEPER AT WOOD ISLAND STRICKEN." When an effort to get a doctor to go to Wood Island to attend to George Woodward failed, according to the *Journal*, a trained nurse from the Trull Hospital in Biddeford was sent to attend to the keeper. The paper went on to report that Keeper Woodward was suffering from a "nervous breakdown."[283] Woodward's logbooks, though silent on his illness, do hint that something unusual was occurring. His customary descriptive entries increasingly were replaced with the comment, "General duties." And, beginning on May 23, all writing is replaced by ditto marks; this trend continued during the following month of June, but gradually, especially when workmen arrived on the island, there is a return to a more typically informative account.[284]

Keeper Woodward's determination to somehow match the requirements of his job with the demands of his family did come at a cost. Even before his breakdown in May 1930, the keeper signals that managing his family's affairs was taking a toll on his emotional health. On more than one occasion, he expressed his need to go ashore in search of relief. "Went ashore after mail and peace" (December 20, 1926); "General duties. After mail and peace" (February 5, 1927); "Went ashore after mail and peace" (February 23, 1927).[285]

Lifestyle Sacrifices and Accommodations

When compared to life on the mainland, inhabiting a small, unoccupied island required lifestyle accommodations that many would consider inconvenient indeed. Nevertheless, over the course of nearly fifty years, keepers during the Coast Guard era reported increasing accessibility of various modern services and a gradual movement toward a more contemporary standard of living.

Eloise Frank, who lived on the island from 1952 to 1956, offers an insight into what residing on Wood Island entailed at that time: "When we first went there the refrigerator that we had ran on kerosene. So you were down on your belly pulling the thing out and looking at the light, making sure the thing wouldn't go out. It wasn't really that dependable. If you put something frozen in the freezer well it didn't stay frozen. So we switched into canned food because at least it was edible." Mrs. Frank made it clear to the inspectors that she was not pleased. "I said I would like to get rid of this refrigerator.... So they said that that wasn't unreasonable—you have to feed a family you don't want everything to go down the drain and throwing it out. So, they sent through a gas refrigerator that worked on propane gas. Well that was just like being in heaven—glorious you know."[286]

Keeper Sodano and his wife, Sherry, pass a winter day playing a board game while waiting for Santa to arrive, circa 1982. *FOWIL Archives.*

It would take several more years before an underwater cable brought electricity out to Wood Island. Before 1963, a generator provided the power to run the light during the night and pump water into the cisterns in the basement during the day. The Burnham family reported that they were permitted four to six hours of electricity each day to use for their tiny black-and-white television. Kerosene lamps were required to chase away the darkness in the residence when the generator was required for its primary function each evening and on days when gray skies obscured the daylight.[287]

For Keeper McQuade, it was disappointment over the absence of the little indulgences in life that brought regret:

> *There were a few things that we would do without. One was any frozen product such as ice cream, ice cream bars, popsicles or something like that. By the time you brought them back to the island, it was all mush and they would never refreeze right. So that was something that would end up being a treat when we went to town. Usually we would stop at Friendly's Ice Cream. You would get your chocolate shake or cone and just kind of savor it because you knew that was the last time you were going to get one until you showed up in town again.*[288]

Wood Island Lighthouse

Water and Electricity

When asked about the water, Mrs. Frank had this to say:

> *The Coast Guard decided prior to our coming there that they were going to put artesian wells on the islands. As I understood it, Wood Island was one of the first ones that they attempted, and they went down 550 feet before they struck good water. They hooked up the toilet and so forth to the good water and the kitchen sink and the sink in the bathroom and so forth. There was runoff from the roof into the cisterns. We didn't use the cisterns because we had the artesian well. It was a lovely well. We would send in samples a couple times a year and we would get the report back, and I was always amused because it would say that it had a high saline content. Well, it figures. I always thought that the water had something to do with Steven having such good teeth because his formula was made up of that water from the time that he was ten days old. Up until the time that he was twenty-one or twenty-two, he never had a cavity.*[289]

In the original contract signed on June 15, 1807, Benjamin Beal and Duncan Thaxter agreed to include "a well to be sunk and walled with stone at a convenient distance and furnished with the necessary apparatus for drawing water."[290] A survey taken in the late nineteenth century shows the original well to have been located on the south side of the dwelling and approximately seventy-five feet away. Over the course of the nineteenth century, very little is mentioned regarding the well, but it has been assumed that the water supply depended to a large extent on a cistern that was supplied primarily by rainwater.

Sometime during the latter half of the 1930s, while Earle Benson served as keeper, the decision was made to dig a new well. A photograph taken during the construction indicates that the new well was built sometime after the completion of the sun porch in 1937.

Some years later, in 1992, Lily Burnham provided a description of the well when she was interviewed for the article in the *Lighthouse Digest*. "The source of our water supply was a very deep well [approximately more than five hundred feet] which was then pumped into a 1,500-gallon cistern in a walled area of the cellar under the main house." The brackish water had to be boiled in order to make it safe to drink, but that process did little to improve the taste. The solution for the Burnham family was to add Kool-

Aid. However, she maintained, "the coffee made with Wood Island water left something to be desired."[291]

Pat Winchester had a different perspective on the condition of the water; she thought "it tasted like any water." However, she went on to explain that whenever they needed fresh water, the buoy tenders would bring it out to the island. It was an occasion to look forward to and required the entire day. The Winchester family would pack a lunch and sit out there to watch the entire operation. The tender would come to the "backside" of the lighthouse and shoot a weighted line to Keeper Winchester. He would then haul the line, which was attached to a larger hose, and then put it in the cisterns. "That was the children's outing for the day."[292]

Keeper Andrew Ralph "A.R." Pruneau was in charge of the station in 1972 and explained how drinking water was obtained and tested:

> *You had a deep well pump, and you had to pump water into your basement. There was a reservoir in there. And you had to let the water sit and you had to take samples and stuff. Yeah, that was the drinking water and well. Actually, you had two basins in there....You had a big cement wall like a swimming pool; it was divided in half. One was drinking water, the other side was for water so you could do laundry and stuff.*

Keeper Pruneau mentioned that the authorities were not sure how potable the water was, and so it was allowed to settle for a while and periodically tested. He concluded by boasting, "Probably why we are so healthy now."[293]

By the mid-1970s, Keeper Michael McQuade could report that "electricity was provided by a submarine cable coming across water and then power poles coming from the boat house on up to the dwelling. Water was provided by a deep, fresh-water well, which pumped the water into the cistern, and then from the cistern the house pump brought it through the kitchen faucet and bathroom faucet."[294] Eventually, the system could be electrically operated from a switch that first brought water from the well to the cisterns, and then another switch would pump the water into the house. Russ Lowell, keeper from 1980 to 1982, reported, "We always had water."[295]

Garbage and Sanitation

And what about refuse? In an era when the general culture was not as sensitive to the impact of human activities on the environment, the methods used to dispose of trash strikes us as somewhat scandalous. When a new refrigerator was delivered to Keeper Earle Benson in August 1951, he informs us in his logbook that he simply removed the old refrigerator and threw it over the bank. Mrs. Frank recalled that when she and her husband took over from the Bensons in 1952, there was a trash dump out near the oil house. "There used to be kind of a trash place there," she said. "Of course, with the tide coming in it would pretty much take it all away....It wasn't exactly the ideal recycling, but it was the best that you could do at the time."[296]

A few years later, Catherine Roche told her interviewers that they no longer put the garbage in the "dump site" between the oil house and the dwelling. "We burned it. Cans and bottles we took to the mainland....All the burnable stuff was burned in a fifty-five-gallon drum; whatever couldn't be burned was taken to the mainland and put in the dumpster at the Coast Guard base."[297]

Happily, with time and greater awareness, the Coast Guard put more effective systems in place. By 1980, Terry and Russ Lowell mentioned, "Mostly when you went ashore you took the trash. We had a trash compactor in the kitchen, and we had a couple of bags a week." John Oddy, who owned the dock and parking space where they kept their car, would inform the keeper that the trash pickup would be on such and such a day, and "if you can get in here the day before or the morning of, bring it up and set it out here, it will be picked up and taken care of."[298]

Susan "Sam" Murray was delighted by the "pleasure of living on her own island, surrounded on three sides with a view of open sea and the most glorious sunrises you can imagine." Still, when pressed, she commented that there was an inconvenience or two. "I guess the electric toilet would top the list. It is temperamental and has to be emptied every day or so." She recalled one time in particular when an admiral came to inspect the station. "He didn't realize that the electric toilet wasn't working, and he used it and flushed it and kind of got his shoes wet....I'm sure he remembered that trip."[299]

Keeper Jerry Murray, circa 1975. *FOWIL Archives.*

Damien McQuade is fascinated by their family's new flush toilet—a significant improvement over the incinalet it replaced. *FOWIL Archives.*

McQuade also remembered the electric toilet with something less than fondness:

> *When we originally reported to the island, we initially had what was known as an incinalet. It operated on 220 volts. When we had power, it operated fine. The only problem we had with it was you had to get rid of the ash every couple of days, and you had to make sure that you kept the back of your legs away from the toilet or you would burn them. So once we got that flush toilet in, we looked at it as entering the twentieth century.*[300]

Keeping Warm and Dry

During the early twentieth century, coal gradually replaced wood as the fuel used to heat the dwelling. Mrs. Frank remembered what an undertaking it was to land the coal on the island in the early 1950s. The lighthouse tender *Cowslip* would come in as close at it could off the east end of Wood Island. "There wasn't much of any path or anything. Then they would launch a small boat and they would fill it up with coal bags and they would be about fifty pounds apiece.…Then they landed on the rocks. Well, then they had to manually climb up the rocks with this on their backs to the edge of the grass and then walk over and throw it in the coal bin." At the time, the coal bin was a fenced-in area located just to the right of where the stone oil house is today. At first, they would use the wheelbarrow to bring the coal along a boardwalk from the coal bin to the house, where they would slide it down the cellar window. Later, "when we had the tractor, we could put a lot of bags on

Wood Island Lighthouse

Above: Unloading coal from the lighthouse tender *Cowslip*, circa 1955. *FOWIL Archives.*

Left: The tender *Cowslip* preparing to deliver fuel to the station, circa 1970. *FOWIL Archives.*

it and bring it up and drive it right by and dump it in. It took a long time to put fifteen tons of coal in."[301]

Twenty-five years later, "the heat on the island was provided by an oil furnace," recalled Keeper McQuade. "We received oil from one of the Coast Guard's buoy tenders out of Boston. We had three two-thousand-gallon fuel tanks. They would show up about every four years to fill it. I would have to say that we probably used a little less than two thousand gallons a year, depending on how the winter was."[302]

Keeper Russ Lowell described the delivery process in an interview conducted in 2006:

> *The buoy tender would show up; they would usually schedule it in advance. We had fair warning that they were coming. They would anchor at the point off the light. They would have a line-throwing gun, and from the line-throwing gun they would shoot basically a projectile to the island. We would grab hold of it. Had to climb down onto the rocks usually...and pull the light line, what they called the shot line and pull it in. They hook the heavier line to it, and you get the heavier line and bring that in; that's a working line, which is a little bigger and more manageable, and you grab onto that and you have the fuel line....They would send a couple of crew members over to give me a hand on the island to haul it in, as we had to haul it all the way up to the tanks. It took three or four hours to fill the tanks depending on how much fuel we needed.*[303]

THE END OF AN ERA

The last of the Coast Guard light keepers at Wood Island Lighthouse closed the door and walked away from their position in October 1986, 180 years following the light's formal authorization by the Ninth Congress of the United States. During those last months of their tour at Wood Island, the keepers, Merton Perry and Warren Rowell, alternated working two days on and two days off. Perry's wife, whose job commitment required that she remain on the mainland, visited the island only on the weekends when her husband was on duty. In an interview conducted with a reporter from the local paper just prior to locking up the station for the last time, Perry remarked, "There's plenty to do out here, plenty of things that need fixing....And the grass has to be mowed at least twice a week." But now, with automation inevitably pointing the way to the future, the character of the lighthouse seems to have changed. Wood Island was no longer a family station. And with the caretaking tasks having become routine and repetitive, the role of lighthouse keeper apparently had lost its attraction. In concluding his interview, Perry remarked about his keeper role, "I won't miss it."[304]

EPILOGUE

BY BRAD COUPE, PAST CHAIRMAN AND CO-FOUNDER OF THE FRIENDS OF THE WOOD ISLAND LIGHTHOUSE

On August 1, 1986, Keeper Philip Brothwell's 3-year tour as the last official keeper of Wood Island Lighthouse ended, and he handed the keys over to Bosun's Mate First Class Merton Perry and departed. Brothwell's departure closed out 178 years of human occupancy at the light station.

Perry and another Coast Guardsman, Warren Rowell, worked as interim caretakers over the next two months, sharing alternating two-day shifts maintaining the light station and preparing for its full automation. On August 27, a Coast Guard helicopter arrived and gently set a replica lantern room back on the top of the "headless" tower, so named when the original lantern room had been removed fourteen years earlier to accommodate an oversized rotating aero beacon.

By October 1, Perry and Rowell were gone and the new light was fully automated and operating without human presence. The elements continued their relentless work, unimpeded, to wear the buildings down.

Then, as now, Coast Guard teams made periodic visits to ensure the continued operation of the navigational aids, but regular maintenance of the decaying and less-needed lighthouse was minimal. This scene was repeated at lighthouses throughout the country, and these now-uninhabited icons fell into serious decline.

In the decade of the 1980s, the Coast Guard took steps under the National Historic Preservation Act to transfer responsibilities for maintenance and preservation of these endangered lighthouses to other federal or state agencies, qualified nonprofit groups or even individuals. This was done by

Epilogue

short-term licenses or outright transfer of the properties with conditions ensuring that the structures would be saved under the secretary of the interior's rigorous preservation standards applicable to buildings in the National Register of Historic Places. By these devices, the Coast Guard was able to offload some of the significant costs that were now ancillary to its military mission.

In 1994, the Coast Guard made some important repairs at Wood Island. The roof and siding of the keeper's house were replaced, as was the half-mile boardwalk across the island to the boathouse. The rails or "ways" for the now-departed keeper's peapod to slip down from the boathouse to the water were removed and replaced by a wide ramp to provide more space for visitors on foot and access by smaller boats. The undersea electrical supply cable from the Biddeford Pool shore to the light station was also repaired.

Perhaps these extensive repairs to an uninhabited lighthouse were designed to entice a group to sign up to restore and maintain the lighthouse. An appeal actually was made around that time to persuade eligible local groups to step forward, but there were no takers.

Then, in 2002, the Coast Guard made another attempt. On October 22, 2002, Commander Thomas W. Jones, commanding officer of the Coast Guard's Construction Engineering Unit in Warwick, Rhode Island, wrote a letter to the city manager of Biddeford, Maine, inviting the city to propose a plan by which the city might receive a short-term license "to rehabilitate and maintain the lighthouse property in accordance with historic preservation standards." The letter also encouraged submitters to "afford an opportunity for public involvement and enjoyment" of the restored premises.

The city forwarded the letter to its seaside village of Biddeford Pool for its possible interest. Biddeford Pool has a civic organization that is very active in the community affairs called the Biddeford Pool Improvement Association (BPIA), which has a land trust arm as well. Both entities, the BPIA and the land trust, authorized two members to write to express their interest and explore the opportunity. And so, on December 2, 2002, Brad and Anita Coupe responded to Commander Jones, expressing interest.

The Coast Guard immediately responded and reported that the American Lighthouse Foundation (ALF), an already-qualified nonprofit with experience in this kind of licensing arrangement, was also making a proposal. He suggested that the Coupes contact ALF to collaborate. Brad contacted the president of ALF, Tim Harrison, and a meeting was set up to talk about creating a chapter of ALF to become ALF's local operation to take on the license obligations.

Epilogue

It happened that at about the same time, Sean Murphy, a Massachusetts state trooper with a summer home in Hills Beach, also connected with Harrison expressing his interest in becoming involved. And, so in February, Coupe, Murphy and Harrison met in Biddeford Pool and planned an organizational meeting to invite interested community members to join in and form an ALF chapter. That meeting took place on April 5, 2003, at the local fire barn. The chapter was formed and named the Friends of Wood Island Lighthouse (FOWIL). A chair and vice chair of the chapter's executive committee to be formed were elected, with Brad as chair and Sean as vice chair. The chapter quickly adopted a comprehensive mission statement addressing restoration, historic research, the protection of the island's natural habitat and fostering community involvement through public access and education. And so began the next era of this fortunate lighthouse's saga.

In the eighteen years since, FOWIL has largely completed the repair, restoration and furnishing of this landmark light station. Under the interior secretary's National Historic Preservation Standards, the party for the property can choose one of four permissible methods or "treatments" to govern the restoration process. One of these treatments allows the party to restore the building to a particular "period of significance." Under that choice, the restorer can remove later modifications and thereby regain an earlier appearance. FOWIL chose 1906 as its ideal period, the year when the current configuration of the house was originally built. Doing so allowed FOWIL to remove an unsightly closed-in porch, built in 1939, and re-create the attractive open porch with columns on stone pillars and restore other original details. The restored interior of the house was furnished with period-appropriate furniture and appliances of the day.

Likewise, significant progress has been made on all of FOWIL's mission objectives. Those objectives will remain guideposts for the chapter into the foreseeable future. Unlike the original function of lighthouses, FOWIL's mission will never become obsolete as long as we and our heirs—keepers of the future—remain dedicated to telling the lighthouse story and passing on its valuable history to future generations.

This book recounts the lives and times of Wood Island Lighthouse and its keepers over 178 years of vital and constant service to the nation and the needs of mariners. This service ended 35 years ago. The need for this kind of account becomes more acute as we lose the remaining actors who performed on that stage and rendered those services. The technology of navigation has become more exact and no longer dependent on a human operator for visual identification of landmarks or in need of the now-obsolete flashing

Epilogue

Keeper Cliff Trebilcock, waves from the porch of the fully restored dwelling of the Wood Island Lighthouse attired in a replica of his lighthouse uniform. He was married on Wood Island in August 2007. *FOWIL Archives, photo by Sheri Poftak.*

light signals to warn mariners of hazards or to bring vessels traveling to our shores into port. This book has captured the essence of that Wood Island era and has preserved it for all to enjoy.

FOWIL's preservation focus is increasingly shifting away from saving the physical buildings to upkeep and promoting the memory and detail of this vital period. What is being done today to keep the buildings maintained and involve the public in learning about the past will be the continuing work of literally dozens of inspired and dedicated FOWIL volunteers. The events of the last eighteen years are themselves interesting and inspirational. The volunteers' work and their accomplishments deserve to be memorialized and celebrated in a future written account of this lighthouse's continuing relevance and importance.

NOTES

Introduction

1. "Wood Island Light Station Added to Doomsday List," *Lighthouse Digest*, June 1992.
2. Folsom, *History of Saco and Biddeford.*
3. "Miscellany," *Newburyport Herald*, March 30, 1821, 1.
4. Petition to Congress, Journal of the House of Representatives of the United States, December 28, 1825, 98.
5. Samuel Knight, petition to Congress, March 25, 1846, Twenty-Ninth Congress, First Session, 253.
6. "The house on stage island...," *Saco Union and Journal*, April 4, 1879.
7. De Champlain, *Voyages of Samuel de Champlain.*
8. Ibid.
9. Jordan to Pendleton and Spencer (1658), Spencer to Pendleton (1658), Bryan Pendleton to Pendleton Fletcher (1671), York County Registry of Deeds, 45 Kennebunk Road, Alfred, ME.
10. Fletcher to Pepperell (1734), York County Deeds, Part I, Fol. 76 (original spelling and language retained), York County Registry of Deeds.
11. Albert Gallatin, secretary of the treasury, to Benjamin Lincoln, superintendent of lighthouses for Massachusetts, March 27, 1806, NARA, Record Group 26, Series: Letters Concerning Lighthouses, 1789–1819, File Unit: Wood Island Light, Fletcher's Neck, Biddeford, Maine, 1805–1819 (Arc Identifiers 81128636_12, 13, 14).

Chapter 1

12. Jeremiah Hill, collector of customs, Biddeford, to Benjamin Lincoln, collector of customs, Boston, May 4, 1807, NARA (Arc Identifier 81128636_30).
13. Judge George Thatcher to Benjamin Lincoln, collector of customs, August 22, 1807, NARA (Arc Identifier 81128636_40).
14. Jeremiah Hill, collector of customs, to Benjamin Lincoln, collector of customs, August 26, 1807, NARA (Arc Identifier 81128636_37).
15. Albert Gallatin, secretary of the treasury, to Benjamin Lincoln, superintendent of lighthouses in Massachusetts, July 30, 1807, NARA (Arc Identifier 81128636_34).
16. Jeremiah Hill, collector of customs, Biddeford, to Benjamin Lincoln, collector of customs, Boston, October 10, 1807, NARA (Arc Identifier 81128636_43).
17. "Loss of the Schooner *Charles*," *Portland Gazette*, July 14, 1807.
18. Benjamin Cole, keeper, Wood Island Lighthouse, to Benjamin Lincoln, collector of customs, Boston, November 9, 1807, NARA (Arc Identifier 81128636_61).
19. Benjamin Cole, keeper, to Benjamin Lincoln, collector of customs, Boston, April 23, 1808, NARA (Arc Identifier 81128636_47).
20. Benjamin Cole, keeper, to Benjamin Lincoln, collector of customs, Boston, June 6, 1808, NARA (Arc Identifier 81128636_45).
21. Benjamin Cole, keeper, to Benjamin Lincoln, collector of customs, Boston, August 11, 1808, NARA (Arc Identifier 81128636_51).
22. Benjamin Cole, keeper, to Benjamin Lincoln, collector of customs, Boston, September 9, 1808, NARA (Arc Identifier 81128636_53).
23. Merchants of Biddeford and Saco to Albert Gallatin, secretary of the treasury, October 12, 1808, Archives of the FOWIL (reproduced at the NARA).
24. Merrill, "Samuel Merrill Diaries."
25. Richard Cutts, shipmaster, to Albert Gallatin, secretary of the treasury, January 7, 1809, Archives of the FOWIL (reproduced at the NARA).
26. Albert Gallatin, secretary of the treasury, to Henry Dearborn, superintendent of lighthouses, April 12, 1809, NARA (Arc Identifier 81128636_57).

Chapter 2

27. "Gallatin Report," June 1, 1809, NARA, Record Group 26, Series: Letters Concerning Lighthouses, 1789–1819, File Unit: Wood Island Light, Fletcher's Neck, Biddeford, Maine, 1805–1819 (Arc Identifier 81128636_59).
28. "Gallatin Report," June 1, 1810, NARA (Arc Identifier 81128636_63).
29. "Gallatin Report," June 1, 1812, NARA (Arc Identifier 81128636_76).
30. Merrill, "Samuel Merrill Diaries."
31. Daniel Granger, collector of Saco, to Henry Dearborn, superintendent of the public lights, September 13, 1814 (Arc Identifier 81128636_82).
32. Philip Goldthwait, keeper, to Henry Dearborn, superintendent of lighthouses in Massachusetts, October 1, 1814 (Arc Identifier 81128636_80).
33. Merrill, "Samuel Merrill Diaries."
34. Winslow Lewis to Henry Dearborn, superintendent of lighthouses, 1816 (undated) (Arc Identifiers 81128636_84, 85, 86).
35. Daniel Granger to Henry Dearborn, superintendent of lighthouses in Massachusetts, August 10, 1816 (Arc Identifier 81128636_87).
36. Winslow Lewis to Henry Dearborn, superintendent of lighthouses (undated) (Arc Identifier 81128636_85).

Chapter 3

37. Reports of Committees: Sixteenth Congress, First Session–Forty-Ninth Congress...Vol. 4, April 8, 1842, books.google.com/books?id=zqcFAAAAQAAJ&pg=RA15-PA97&lpg=RA15-PA97&dq=%22rule+of+ignorant+and+incompetent+men%22&source=bl&ots=2SKsFweFu0&sig=ACfU3U0puBhX2OzgLM4wGIctS9uPcTq5UQ&hl=en&sa=X&ved=2ahUKEwjov7Cd75HvAhXtYd8KHU1OAwg4ChDoATABegQICxAD#v=onepage&q=%22robert%20winthrop%22&f=false.
38. "Compilation of Public Documents and Extracts from Reports and Papers Relating to Light-Houses, Light-Vessels, and Illuminating Apparatus, and to Beacons, Buoys and Fog Signals," 1789–1871, U.S. Light-House Establishment, Washington, D.C.: Government Printing Office, 1871, 99. See also Dolin, *Brilliant Beacons*, 105.
39. Reports of Committees.
40. "Heads Off," *Daily Eastern Argus*, July 21, 1841.

41. "Grumbling," *Daily Eastern Argus*, July 21, 1841.
42. "Statement of John Adams, Keeper of Wood Island Revolving Light, August 15, 1842," Examination—Light-House Establishment, Twenty-Seventh Congress, Third Session, Document No. 183.
43. Nathan Cummings, Superintendent of Light-houses in Maine, "Report to Congress on the Condition of Lighthouses on the East Coast," March 2, 1843, Archives of the FOWIL.
44. "Statement of John Adams."
45. Dolin, *Brilliant Beacons*, 117.
46. *Saco Union*, June 6, 1845, 3.
47. I.W.P. Lewis Report, Examination—Light-House Establishment, "Letter from the Secretary of the Treasury," February 25, 1843, Twenty-Seventh Congress, Third Session, Document No. 183.
48. "Gross Carelessness," *Saco Union*, July 1, 1846. See also "Outrageous Carelessness in Keeping a Light House," *Middletown Constitution*, July 22, 1846.
49. "Treasury Department Fifth Auditor's Office," June 7, 1851, *Report of the Officers Constituting the Light-House Board to Inquire into the Condition of the Light-House Establishment of the United States, Under the Act of March 3, 1851*, Senate Thirty-Second Congress, First Session.
50. "Light House Commission," *Maine Democrat*, May 6, 1951.
51. "At One Fell Swoop," *Maine Democrat*, September 21, 1852.
52. "Appointments," *Saco Union*, May 4, 1853, 2.
53. "Appropriations and Expenditures for 1808–1858," Wood Island Light Station, Archives of the FOWIL (reproduced at the NARA).

Chapter 4

54. "The storm of last week…," *Maine Democrat*, November 13, 1849.
55. "Minot Light House in the Late Storm," *Saco Union*, April 18, 1851.
56. "Minot Ledge Light," *Saco Union*, April 25, 1851.
57. "Disaster," *Maine Democrat*, April 22, 1851.
58. *Boston Journal*, April 17, 1851.
59. "The Last Words from Minot's Ledge," *Maine Democrat*, June 17, 1851.
60. Hanson, "Biddeford Pool Poet." The author includes a clipping reproduced from the *Portland Sunday Telegram*, October 14, 1928, Archives of the FOWIL.
61. Casavant, "Wood Island Light Station."

62. Alfred, Eldon, *Lewiston Journal*, February 15, 1936; *Biddeford Daily Journal*, February 22, 1936.
63. Quoted in Casavant, "Wood Island Light Station."
64. "The storm of Monday and Tuesday…," *Union and Journal*, November 22, 1866.
65. "The Great Gale," *York County Independent*, September 14, 1869.
66. "The Great Gale," *Maine Democrat*, September 16, 1869.
67. "Isle of Shoals," *Union and Journal*, October 8, 1869.
68. "The storm that set in about midnight Tuesday…," *Union and Journal*, November 17, 1871.
69. "A Heavy Shock at the Pool," *Biddeford Record*, October 21, 1906.
70. "Bridge Broken by Earthquake," *Boston Globe*, October 21, 1906.

Chapter 5

71. "Cast His Last Vote," *Biddeford Weekly Journal*, March 12, 1897.
72. "Sad Disaster," *Union and Journal*, February 26, 1864. The *Bohemian* tragedy is commemorated by a celebrated painting in the South Portland Post Office. The circumstances surrounding the wreck are described in Batchelder, *Shipwrecks and Maritime Disasters Along the Maine Coast*, ch. 3.
73. "We have learned some additional particulars…," *Union and Journal*, March 31, 1865. An account of Emerson's heroic rescue can be found in an unpublished monograph written by his descendant Iona Desmond and published by the History Group of the FOWIL.
74. "The nice present awarded…," *Union and Journal*, June 16, 1865.
75. Letter in the Archival Collection of the FOWIL.
76. "Uncle Eben Emerson wears a brand new hat today…," *Biddeford Daily Journal*, December 4, 1896.
77. "Cast His Last Vote," *Biddeford Weekly Journal*, March 12, 1897.

Chapter 6

78. Wood Island, Description of Station, 1875 Report (RG 26 E9), NARA.
79. Ibid.
80. *Biddeford Evening Times*, August 4, 1873.
81. *Biddeford Daily Times*, December 26, 1872.
82. Ibid., December 27, 1872.

83. *Daily Times*, December 28, 1872.
84. Ibid., December 30, 1872.
85. Ibid.
86. W.K. Mayo, lighthouse inspector, First District, to Professor Joseph Henry, chairman, Light House Board, NARA Archives of the FOWIL.
87. "Boat Capsized," *Daily Times*, September 6, 1877.
88. "The Body of Maloney Found," *Daily Times*, September 12, 1877.
89. "Jottings," *Daily Times*, October 9, 1877.
90. *Union and Journal*, April 11, 1879.
91. *Biddeford Daily Journal*, May 13, 1886.

Chapter 7

92. Letter from Minnie Orcutt to Miss Whitney, 1889, from the Archives of the Wood Island Light Station, courtesy of the FOWIL.
93. Bassett, "Thomas Henry Orcutt."
94. Cummins, "Sailor, the Wood Island Light Fog Dog."
95. "Was a Loyal Dog. Sailor Is Missed at the Wood Island Lighthouse," *Biddeford Weekly Journal*, September 22, 1905, 6.
96. "Very Intelligent Dog," *Weekly Standard*, June 1, 1894.
97. "Clever Canine Employed at Wood Island Lighthouse," *Stevens Point Journal*, July 10, 1896.
98. "A Sailor Collie," *Atlanta Constitution*, September 9, 1900.
99. "A Knowing Dog," *Strand Illustrated Magazine*, May 1900, 597.
100. "Was a Loyal Dog," *Biddeford Weekly Journal*.
101. "New England Lighthouses: A Virtual Guide. The History of Wood Island Lighthouse, Biddeford Pool, Maine," www.newenglandlighthouses.net/wood-island-light-history.html.
102. "T.H. Orcutt Drops Dead," *Biddeford Record*, March 12, 1906.
103. "Baby Book of Henry Albert Jeffers."

Chapter 8

104. The image "The Murder House on Wood Island, Biddeford, 1921," was made available courtesy of the McArthur Public Library, Biddeford, Maine. It can be viewed online mcarthur.pastperfectonline.com/photo/D09DB792-755B-4C94-BC4E-363592195578.

105. "Suicide Follows Murder," *Evening Record*, June 2, 1896.
106. Ibid.
107. Ibid.
108. Ibid.
109. Ibid.
110. "Wood Island Hospitality," September 16, 1910.
111. Ibid.
112. *Biddeford Daily Journal*, August 21, 1911.
113. Chapter 12 revisits the "scrapbook" and its relevance to the keeper's family on Wood Island and the incident described here.
114. "Home Personals," *Biddeford Weekly Journal*, October 9, 1914.
115. "Wood Island Fire," *Biddeford Weekly Journal*, May 12, 1916.
116. Clifford B. Staples, *Logbook*, May 7, 1916, NARA, Record Group 26, Series: Logbooks of Lighthouses, 1872–1944, Arc Identifier 559753 (Wood Island, Box 495).
117. Wood and Kolek, *Ghost Chronicles*. See episode 17 for a full accounting of the Wood Island investigation. See also Roxie J. Zwicker, *Haunted York County: Mystery and Lore from Maine's Oldest Towns* (Charleston, SC: The History Press, 2010), "Ghostly Yarns from the Sea," "The Ghosts of Wood Island Lighthouse."
118. "Is Anyone There? Local Ghostbusters Investigate the Supernatural on a Lonely, Windswept Maine Isle," *Boston Globe*, October 23, 2005.

Chapter 9

119. John Chandler, collector and superintendent of lighthouses in Maine, to Stephen Pleasonton, fifth auditor of the treasury, January 8, 1833, NARA, RG 26 E 17C.
120. "Statement of John Adams."
121. "Jottings," *Daily Times*, August 17, 1878.
122. "During a heavy thunder shower…," *Biddeford Weekly Journal*, September 26, 1884.
123. Wood Island, Description of Station, 1875 Report, NARA, Record Group 26, E9.
124. "Mr. A. Norwood, the keeper…," *Union and Journal*, February 17, 1882.
125. "Summary of Reports and Repairs to the Wood Island Light Station," NARA copy located in Archives of the FOWIL.

126. NARA, Record Group 26, Series: Logbooks of Lighthouses, 1872–1944, Arc Identifier: 559753 (Wood Island, Box 495). Keepers Lurvey, Albert Staples and Woodward all report farming-related activities.
127. George E. Woodward, Logbook, NARA, Record Group 26, Series: Logbooks of Lighthouses, 1872–1944, Arc Identifier: 559753 (Wood Island, Box 495). See entries January 1933 and August 1933.

Chapter 10

128. "Coast Strewn with Wrecks," *Eastern Argus*, November 29, 1898. Coverage in local newspapers lasted for several days. See also *Eastern Argus*, November 27, 28, 1898.
129. "Stuck on Beach," *Biddeford Daily Journal*, June 20, 1898.
130. "End of Old Orchard Pier Gone," *Biddeford Daily Journal*, December 5, 1898.
131. "Worst in Years," *Biddeford Daily Journal*, November 28, 1898.
132. "*Thomas B. Reed* a Wreck," *Biddeford Record*, December 5, 1900.
133. "The Crew All Saved," *Biddeford Daily Journal*, December 6, 1900.
134. "Lime Schooner Goes on to the Liedge and May Go to Pieces," *Biddeford Record*, April 13, 1905.
135. "Harbor Was Aglow," *Biddeford Daily Journal*, April 14, 1905.
136. "The Wreck of the *Marshall Perrin*," *Biddeford Record*, November 21, 1906.
137. Charles A. Burke, Logbook, NARA, Record Group 26, Series: Logbooks of Lighthouses, 1872–1944, Arc Identifier: 559753, see entries February 7, 1907, and February 8, 1907.
138. "British Schooner *Maple Leaf* Towed into Port Disabled," *Daily Eastern Argus*, February 9, 1907.
139. Burke, Logbook, see entry October 28, 1909.
140. "Abandoned Schooner Boarded by Pool Men," *Biddeford Record*, October 29, 1909.
141. Burke, Logbook, see entries July 17, 1908, and July 27, 28, 1910.
142. Cummins, "Presidential Summer Visits from 100 Years."
143. "Two Girls Drowned, Launch *Item* Capsized," *Biddeford Record*, July 31, 1909.
144. Ibid.
145. "*Sylph* Sailor Tells of Rescue," *Biddeford Record*, August 3, 1809.
146. "Two Girls Drowned, Launch *Item* Capsized."
147. "Is Found Floating with Face Downwards," *Biddeford Record*, August 13, 1909.
148. "Verdict Condemns *Item* as Being Unsafe," *Biddeford Record*, August 5, 1909.

Chapter 11

149. Keeper Albert Norwood to sister Lucinda, November 30, 1873, Archives of the FOWIL.
150. "Albert Norwood, resident on Wood Island…," *Union and Journal*, May 17, 1878.
151. Orcutt's salary increased from $500 per year in 1886 to $540 per year in 1888. NARA microfilm publication M1373 (Roll 1), *Registers of Lighthouse Keepers, 1845–1912*, National Archives at Boston.
152. Letter from Minnie Orcutt, lighthouse keeper's daughter, to Miss Whitney, 1889, Archives of the FOWIL.
153. William Freeman Lurvey, Logbook, NARA, Record Group 26, Series: Logbooks of Lighthouses, 1872–1944, Arc Identifier: 559753, February–August 1919.
154. Ibid. See entries March and June 1920, October 1921.
155. Woodward, Logbook. See various entries: 1928, 1929.
156. Ibid.
157. Jackie Netherwood Kennedy, interview with Sheri Poftak (FOWIL), August 1, 2009.

Chapter 12

158. All images and direct quotations in this chapter are to be found in the Logbook turned Scrapbook (Collections of the Maine Historical Society, Coll. 2025) located in Portland, Maine. The archivists and librarians at the MHS have been most generous in allowing the use of the images found on the pages of this chapter.

Chapter 13

159. "Biddeford and Saco People May Get a Good View of Eclipse of the Sun," *Biddeford Weekly Journal*, January 16, 1925.
160. Albert Staples, Logbook, NARA, Record Group 26, Series: Logbooks of Lighthouses, 1872–1944, Arc Identifier: 559753, see January 24, 1925.
161. "The eclipse was wonderful…," *Biddeford Weekly Journal*, February 6, 1925.
162. Staples, Logbook, see July 3 and 4, 1925.

163. "Large Number Get Fine View of *Shenandoah*," *Biddeford Weekly Journal*, July 10, 1925.
164. Woodward, Logbook, August 31, 1932.
165. "Science Makes Discoveries through Eclipse. Animals and Birds Deceived by Two Nights in One Day," *Biddeford Daily Journal*, September 1, 1932.
166. Russ Lowell and Terry Lowell, interview with Judy MacGillivray and Sheri Poftak (FOWIL), October 21, 2006.
167. Ibid.
168. Mike McQuade, interview with Sheri Poftak (FOWIL), September 3, 2010.
169. "Alone. Home Is Private Place for McQuades," *Maine Sunday Telegram*, April 23, 1978.
170. "Waterboro Man Feared Drowned at Pool," *Biddeford Saco Journal*, July 26, 1976.
171. Lily Burnham and Holly Burnham, interview with Judy MacGillivray and Sheri Poftak (FOWIL), December 29, 2003.
172. Eloise Frank, Steve Frank and Michele Blake (daughter), interview with Judy MacGillivray and Sheri Poftak (FOWIL), November 21, 2006.

Chapter 14

173. Hanson, "Biddeford Pool Poet."
174. Ibid., 45.
175. Ibid., 56.
176. Bassett, "Thomas Henry Orcutt."
177. Personal letter, Lucinda Norwood to Albert Norwood, September 18, 1877, FOWIL Archives.
178. Personal letter, Abraham Norwood Jr. to Mary and Albert Norwood, March 20, 1880, FOWIL Archives.
179. Ibid.
180. Woodward, Logbook, January 26 and 30, 1929.
181. Earle Benson, Logbook, NARA, Record Group 26, Series: Logbooks of Lighthouses, 1872–1944, Arc Identifier: 559753, see November 27, 1935.
182. Fred Morong Jr., "Brasswork or, The Light Keeper's Lament," uslhs. org/sites/default/files/attached-files/Poem-%20Brasswork%20or%20 the%20Lighthouse%20Keeper%27s%20Lament.pdf.

183. The poem appeared in the *Bar Harbor Times* on February 14, 1923, and was reprinted on the website of the American Lighthouse Foundation on September 27, 2017 (www.lighthousefoundation.org/2017/09/wood-island-lighthouse-poem-by-a-keepers-wife). The poem has been mistakenly attributed to the keeper's wife, but the poet was, in fact, his stepmother.
184. Lowell and Lowell, interview.
185. Terry's comments and her unpublished poem are reproduced from the Archives of the FOWIL.

Chapter 15

186. Woodward, Logbook, December 26, 1932.
187. Steinauer-Scudder, "Great Sea Serpent of Casco Bay," 1.
188. Cummins, "Old News. Sea Serpents."
189. "Freak of the Sea Cast Up," *Biddeford Record*, June 8, 1905.
190. Dietz, *Tales from the Sea*, ch. 2, "Of Monsters and Men."
191. "Skeleton Found in the Atlantic Puzzles Marine Biologists," *Bennington (VT) Banner*, August 9, 1967.
192. Catherine Roche, phone interview with Sheri Poftak (FOWIL), June 22, 2009.
193. Ibid.
194. Frank, Frank and Blake, interview.
195. Wood and Kolek, *Ghost Chronicles*, episode 17, "The Wood Island Lighthouse."
196. Lowell and Lowell, interview.
197. Ibid.
198. Ibid.
199. Ibid.

Chapter 16

200. Kathleen O'Connell, "Nothing Dull about Living in a Lighthouse," *Biddeford-Saco Journal*, June 1, 1976.
201. Jeremy D'Entremont, "History of Wood Island Lighthouse, Biddeford Pool, Maine," www.newenglandlighthouses.net/wood-island-light-history.html.

202. O'Connell, "Nothing Dull about Living in a Lighthouse."
203. Benson, Logbook, December 7, 1941.
204. O'Connell, "Nothing Dull about Living in a Lighthouse."
205. Benson, Logbook, July 28–31, 1942.
206. Ibid., May 31, 1942; December 7, 1942; December 31, 1942.
207. Timothy Harrison, "Recollections and Reflections," *Lighthouse Digest*, March 1993.
208. O'Connell, "Nothing Dull about Living in a Lighthouse."
209. Harrison, "Recollections and Reflections."
210. "U-Boat Surrenders off Cape Elizabeth," *Portland Press Herald*, May 16, 1945.
211. Rutledge, "Italian Submarines," 72–78. See also Sargent, "Romance of the Italian U-Boat," 27.
212. Benson, Logbook, April 17, 1942. See also Casavant, "Wood Island Light Station."

Chapter 17

213. *Biddeford Weekly Journal*, June 15, 1917.
214. *Biddeford Daily Journal*, January 14, 1918.
215. Ibid., January 12, 1918.
216. *Weekly Record*, January 18, 1918.
217. Lurvey, Logbook, May 5, 1919. The actual name of the boat's owner is unclear from the handwriting of Keeper Lurvey. The incident is included here because of the lengthy entry. No record of this event is to be found in the local newspapers, and Lurvey's note is likely the only evidence that documents this accident and the generosity of the keeper.
218. Lurvey, Logbook, April 16, 1923.
219. *Biddeford Weekly Journal*, April 20, 1923.
220. *Biddeford Saco Journal*, June 14, 1965. See also June 19, 1965; August 4, 1965.
221. Ibid., August 29, 1962.
222. Ibid., February 24, 1964.
223. Catherine Roche, interview. See also *Biddeford-Saco Journal*, July 21 and 22, 1969.
224. The account represented here is based primarily on the interview conducted by the FOWIL with Lily Burnham and her younger daughter Holly in December 2003. The rescue was covered extensively by local newspapers at the time. See, for example, *Portland Press Herald*, November

30, 1960; *Biddeford-Saco Journal*, November 30, 1960. In addition, see Alley, *Rogue Wave*; *Lighthouse Digest*, "Heroic Rescue Brought to Light," Holiday Issue 1992; *Lighthouse Digest*, "Medals Awarded for Amazing Bravery," June 1993. The FOWIL has collected an extensive archive documenting the rescue and the official actions that followed.

Chapter 18

225. Burnham and Burnham, interview.
226. David Hoff, letters to FOWIL, April 27, 2011; May 10, 2011.
227. Frank, Frank and Blake, interview.
228. Jim Roche, son of Keeper James Roche, in email correspondence with the author, 2019.
229. Lowell and Lowell, interview.
230. Frank, Frank and Blake, interview.
231. Rick Savageau, phone interview with Sheri Poftak (FOWIL), February 5, 2011.
232. Clifford Trebilcock, interview with Sheri Poftak (FOWIL), August 29, 2003.
233. Pat "P. Jaye" Winchester, interview with Sheri Poftak (FOWIL), March 3, 2010.
234. Catherine Roche, interview.
235. Susan Murray, interview with Sheri Poftak (FOWIL), February 6, 2012.
236. Andrew Ralph Pruneau, phone interview with Judy MacGillivray (FOWIL), November 21, 2003.
237. Catherine Roche, interview.
238. Savageau, interview.
239. Murray, interview.
240. "Couple Prepares for a Lighthouse Christmas," *Springfield Daily News*, December 24, 1982.
241. Murray, interview.

Chapter 19

242. Benson, Logbook, June 30, 1934; February 23, 1935.
243. Lowell and Lowell, interview.
244. Ibid.
245. Winchester, interview.

246. Murray, interview.
247. Catherine Roche, interview.
248. Trebilcock, interview.
249. Chip Maury, "Lighthouse Life Has Advantages and Drawbacks" (undated and unknown newspaper article).
250. "Alone. Home Is Private Place for McQuades."
251. Lowell and Lowell, interview.
252. Burnham and Burnham, interview.
253. Kennedy, interview.
254. Murray, interview.
255. "Couple Prepares for a Lighthouse Christmas."
256. "Alone. Home Is Private Place for McQuades."
257. "Couple Prepares for a Lighthouse Christmas."
258. Frank, Frank and Blake, interview.
259. McQuade, interview.
260. Burnham and Burnham, interview.

Chapter 20

261. Jim Roche, email.
262. Catherine Roche, interview.
263. Pruneau, interview.
264. Lowell and Lowell, interview.
265. Pruneau, interview.
266. Unpublished letter, Michael McQuade to Roberta S. Blanchard, June 17, 1979, response to request for information about Wood Island Lighthouse for a proposed magazine article.
267. Winchester, interview.
268. David Katon Jr., son of Keeper David Katon, phone interview with author, 2019.
269. "There's Something about Lighthouse Living," *Biddeford-Saco Journal*, June 16, 1969.
270. Kennedy, interview.
271. "Family Enjoys Lighthouse Life," *Hartford Courant*, July 4, 1977, 26.
272. Benson, Logbook, December 23, 24, 1934; December 25, 1936.
273. Harrison, "Recollections and Reflections."
274. Timothy Harrison, "Heroic Rescue Brought to Light," *Lighthouse Digest*, Holiday Issue 1992.

275. Ibid.
276. Winchester, interview.
277. Lowell and Lowell, interview.

Chapter 21

278. Staples, Logbook.
279. "Mrs. Clifford Staples of Wood Island...," *Biddeford Weekly Journal*, March 2, 1917.
280. Staples, Logbook, March 2, 1917.
281. Woodward, Logbook.
282. Ibid.
283. "Lightkeeper at Wood Island Is Stricken," *Biddeford Weekly Journal*, May 30, 1930.
284. Woodward, Logbook.
285. Ibid.
286. Frank, Frank and Blake, interview.
287. Burnham and Burnham, interview.
288. McQuade, interview.
289. Frank, Frank and Blake, interview.
290. "Articles of Agreement" between Benjamin Beal, Duncan Thaxter and Benjamin Lincoln, NARA (Waltham), June 15, 1807.
291. Harrison, "Heroic Rescue Brought to Light."
292. Winchester, interview.
293. Pruneau, interview.
294. McQuade, interview.
295. Lowell and Lowell, interview.
296. Frank, Frank and Blake, interview.
297. Catherine Roche, interview.
298. Lowell and Lowell, interview.
299. Murray, interview.
300. McQuade, interview.
301. Frank, Frank and Blake, interview.
302. McQuade, interview.
303. Lowell and Lowell, interview.
304. "Coast Guard Snuffs Out Chapter in Coast's History," *Journal Tribune*, August 28, 1986.

BIBLIOGRAPHY

Alley, Margo. *Rogue Wave*. N.p.: Instant Publisher, 2011.
"Baby Book of Henry Albert Jeffers; As Recorded by His Mother Matilda Orcutt Jeffers." Jeffers/Orcutt Family Album. Unpublished.
Bassett, Carol Orcutt. "Thomas Henry Orcutt, Keeper of the Light. Wood Island Light 1886–1905." Unpublished and undated brochure. Archives of the Wood Island Light Station.
Batchelder, Peter Dow. *Shipwrecks and Maritime Disasters of the Maine Coast*. Portland, ME: Provincial Press, 1997.
Casavant, Alan. "Wood Island Light Station. Keepers of the Light." Unpublished. May 6, 2003.
Collections of the Library of Congress. Bain News Service, Publisher. "SYLPH, U.S., ca. 1910." Photograph. www.loc.gov/item/2014693362.
Cummins, Sharon. "Old News: Sea Serpents Sighted off the Coast." Seacoastonline.com. www.seacoastonline.com/article/20090108/LIFE/901080384.
———. "Presidential Summer Visits from 100 Years." Seacoastonline.com. www.seacoastonline.com/article/20091210/LIFE/912100350.
———. "Sailor, the Wood Island Light Fog Dog." Seacoastonline.com. www.seacoastonline.com/article/20090416/LIFE/904160386.
de Champlain, Samuel. *Voyages of Samuel de Champlain, 1604–1618*. archive.org/stream/voyagessam00chamrich/voyagessam00chamrich_djvu.txt.
D'Entremont, Jeremy. *The Lighthouses of Maine*. N.p.: Commonwealth, 2009.
Dietz, Tim. *Tales from the Sea*. Portland, ME: Guy Gannett Publishing, 1983.

Bibliography

Dolin, Eric Jay. *Brilliant Beacons: A History of the American Lighthouse*. New York: Liverwright Publishing Corporation, 2016.

Fairfield, Roy P. *Sands, Spindles and Steeples*. Portland, ME: House of Falmouth, 1956.

Folsom, George. *History of Saco and Biddeford with Notices of Other Early Settlements, and of the Proprietary Governments, in Maine, Including the Provinces of New Somersetshire and Lygonia*. Saco, ME: A.C. Putnam, 1830. archive.org/details/historyofsacobid00fols/page/94/mode/2up?q=+William+Phillips.

Friends of the Wood Island Lighthouse. woodislandlighthouse.org/about/history/archive.

Hanson, Harold L. "The Biddeford Pool Poet: Waldo Stillson Verrill, 1858–1951." Unpublished family biography, 2007.

In the Senate of the United States. First Session of the Twenty-Ninth Congress. Washington, D.C.: U.S. Government Printing Office, 1846. Google Books: books.google.com/books?id=g3xHAQAAIAAJ&pg=RA12-PP1&lpg=RA12-PP1&dq=%22The+petitioner+alleges+that+while+at+work+on+a+monument,+erected+on+Stage+Island,+in+Maine,+in+the+year+1825%22&source=bl&ots=BB7HzUBZKH&sig=ACfU3U3Yjm984wLllKc6cYBoes4jXwtGtA&hl=en&sa=X&ved=2ahUKEwjvucjW8uzwAhW8STABHUN5AaMQ6AEwAHoECAIQAw#v=onepage&q=%22The%20petitioner%20alleges%20that%20while%20at%20work%20on%20a%20monument%2C%20erected%20on%20Stage%20Island%2C%20in%20Maine%2C%20in%20the%20year%201825%22&f=false.

Lighthouse Digest Magazine: The Lighthouse News and History Magazine. www.lhdigest.com/digest/ArchivePage.cfm.

Merrill, Samuel. "Samuel Merrill Diaries, 1799–1845." Biddeford History Collections, McArthur Public Library, Biddeford, Maine (1845).

National Archives and Records Administration. Record Group 26: Records of the U.S. Coast Guard, 1785–2005. Series: Letters Concerning Lighthouses, 1789–1819. File Unit: Wood Island Light, Fletcher's Neck, Biddeford, Maine, 1805–1819. Arc Identifier 81128636.

———. Record Group 26: Records of the U.S. Coast Guard, 1785–2005. Series: Logbooks of Lighthouses, 1872–1944. Arc Identifier 559753.

Rutledge, Jack. "Italian Submarines Under the Stars and Stripes." *Sea Classics*, August 1944.

Sargent, Colin. "Romance of the Italian U-Boat." *Portland Magazine*, October 1995.

Bibliography

Smith, Joseph Warren. *Gleanings from the Sea: Showing the Pleasures, Pains and Penalties of Life Afloat, with Contingencies Ashore*. Wells, ME: Harding Publishing Company, 1987. (A facsimile of the 1887 book.)

Snow, Edward Rowe. *Great Storms and Famous Shipwrecks of New England*. Boston: Yankee Publishing Company, 1943.

Steinauer-Scudder, Chelsea. "The Great Sea Serpent of Casco Bay." *Emergence Magazine*, June 16, 2018. emergencemagazine.org/essay/great-sea-serpent.

Sterling, Robert Thayer. *Lighthouses of the Maine Coast and the Men Who Keep Them*. Brattleboro, VT: Stephen Daye Press, 1935.

United States House of Representatives. *Journal of the House of Representatives of the United States*. Washington, D.C.: U.S. Government Printing Office, 1825. www.google.com/books/edition/Journal_of_the_House_of_Representatives/WQpFAQAAMAAJ?hl=en&gbpv=1&dq=ensation+for+a+loss+sustained+by+them+in+the+fall+of+a+monument+erected+by+them,+under+ contract+with+the+Government,+on+Stage+Island,+near+Winter+Harbor."&pg=PA98&printsec=frontcover.

Wood, Maureen, and Ron Kolek. *The Ghost Chronicles: A Medium and a Paranormal Scientist Investigate 17 True Hauntings*. Naperville, IL: Sourcebooks, Inc., 2009.

Libraries, Archives and Museums

Dyer Library and Saco Museum
   371 Main Street, Saco, Maine
Friends of the Wood Island Lighthouse
   P.O. Box 26, Biddeford Pool, Maine
Maine Historical Society
   489 Congress Street, Portland, Maine
McArthur Library
   270 Main Street, Biddeford, Maine
National Archives and Records Administration
   Washington, D.C.
National Archives at Boston
   380 Trapelo Road, Waltham, Massachusetts
Portland Public Library
   5 Monument Square, Portland, Maine

Bibliography

York County Deeds
York County Registry of Deeds
  45 Kennebunk Road, Alfred, Maine

Newspapers

Atlanta Constitution
Biddeford Daily Journal (1884–1959)
Biddeford Evening Times
Biddeford-Saco Journal (1959–1977)
Biddeford Weekly Journal (1888–1930)
Biddeford Weekly Record (1895–19--?)
Boston Globe
Boston Journal
Daily Eastern Argus
Daily Times
Eastern Argus
Evening Record
Hartford Courant
Journal Tribune (1977–current) (followed *Biddeford-Saco Journal*)
Lewiston Journal
Maine Democrat
Newburyport Herald
Portland Gazette
Saco Union
Saco Union and Journal (1858–1882)
Stevens Point Journal
Strand Illustrated Magazine
Union and Eastern Journal (1854–1858)
Weekly Standard
York County Independent

ABOUT THE AUTHOR

Richard Parsons taught history and English for thirty years in public schools before joining the staff of the Institute for Learning Technologies at Columbia University. There, he worked with others to digitize resources held by the Franklin and Eleanor Roosevelt Institute and the Library of Congress, among others, to make them available to scholars and educators. Later, as a member of the Center for Technology and School Change at Columbia University Teachers College, he worked with pre-service and in-service teachers to bring more effective uses of technology into the public school classroom. Today, Richard Parsons resides on the coast in southern Maine, where he gazes across the bay at the Wood Island Lighthouse nearly every day. He has joined with others who have devoted their energies to the restoration of America's historic treasures and serves as historian and member of the executive board of the Friends of the Wood Island Lighthouse. He lives in Saco with his wife, Shari Robinson, and his dog, Donner.

Visit us at
www.historypress.com